CLARENDON LATER ~~~~~~~~ ~~~~~~~~~~~

*Series editors: Jonathan Barnes, Balliol College, Oxford
and A. A. Long, University of California, Berkeley*

ALCINOUS

THE HANDBOOK OF PLATONISM

1 − 3   9−10

12 − 16
25 − 29

ALCINOUS

THE HANDBOOK OF
PLATONISM

Translated with an Introduction
and Commentary by
JOHN DILLON

CLARENDON PRESS · OXFORD

Oxford University Press, Walton Street, Oxford OX2 6DP

Oxford New York
Athens Auckland Bangkok Bombay
Calcutta Cape Town Dar es Salaam Delhi
Florence Hong Kong Istanbul Karachi
Kuala Lumpur Madras Madrid Melbourne
Mexico City Nairobi Paris Singapore
Taipei Tokyo Toronto
and associated companies in
Berlin Ibadan

Oxford is a trade mark of Oxford University Press

Published in the United States
by Oxford University Press Inc., New York

British Library Cataloguing in Publication Data
Data available

Library of Congress Cataloging in Publication Data
Alcinous.
[Didaskalikos. English]
The handbook of Platonism / Alcinous; translated with
an introduction and commentary by John Dillon.
(Clarendon later ancient philosophers)
Includes bibliographical references and index.
1. Plato. 2. Neoplatonism—Early works to 1800.
I. Dillon, John M. II. Title. III. Series.
B535.A43D5313 1993 184—dc20 93-4410
ISBN 0-19-824472-X
ISBN 0-19-823607-7 (Pbk)

Printed in Great Britain
on acid-free paper by
Bookcraft (Bath) Ltd
Midsomer Norton, Avon

PREFACE

THE *Didaskalikos*, or *Handbook of Platonism*, by Alcinous has had mixed fortunes since its initial publication, whatever form that may have taken. Ignored, to all appearances, in late antiquity (though it may in fact have been extensively used for the purpose for which it was probably intended, without meriting a reference from any established philosopher), it seems to surface first in the library of Bishop Arethas of Caesarea, in the tenth century AD (from which derives one of the two chief manuscripts of the work, *Vindobonensis philosophicus graecus* 314). Thereafter its popularity both in the Byzantine period and in the Renaissance is attested by the numerous manuscripts and editions emanating from the period of the fourteenth to the sixteenth centuries AD. The *Didaskalikos* is actually the first Greek work to find its way into the new mode of print, albeit in translation (in 1469, as an appendix to the collected works of Apuleius).

However, after a more critical approach to the doctrine of Plato's dialogues became prevalent with the researches of Schleiermacher at the beginning of the nineteenth century, the *Didaskalikos* abruptly lost its status as an accepted introduction to Platonism. It was condemned as 'eclectic', contaminated with much doctrine of Peripatetic and Stoic provenance, and hence thoroughly unreliable as a guide to Plato's thought.

These charges are, of course, largely justified, but it is only in recent times that this fact has come to be seen as irrelevant to the true merit of the work, which is its status as a document of (at least one school of) Platonism in the second century AD. I hope that this translation and commentary will help to bring home to a larger audience than hitherto the importance of this admittedly modest work for an understanding of the development of the Platonist tradition, particularly in the so-called 'Middle-Platonic' period of the first two centuries AD.

I am much indebted both to the editors of this series, Jonathan Barnes and A. A. Long, for much help and useful criticism on knotty points of interpretation, and even more to the unstinting assistance of John Whittaker, who very kindly lent me the text of his splendid Budé edition prior to publication, and even contrived an invitation to

St John's, Newfoundland, where I was able to discuss many aspects of the work with him. My indebtedness to his copious notes will be evident to anyone who peruses both works. It is he who has finally convinced me, contrary to my previous assumptions, that there is no good reason, palaeographical or otherwise, for identifying Alcinous with the otherwise known Middle-Platonist philosopher Albinus.

I dedicate this work to my daughter Ruth, who took a lively interest in it since its inception, not least because its composition kept her from doing more important things on the Apple Macintosh.

J.D.

For Ruth

CONTENTS

LIST OF ABBREVIATIONS

CP	*Classical Philology*
DG	*Doxographi Graeci*
DL	Diogenes Laertius, *Lives of the Philosophers*
IP	Isnardi Parente (ed.), *Senocrate–Hermodoro: Frammenti*
LS	Long and Sedley (eds.), *The Hellenistic Philosophers*
LSJ	Liddell, Scott, and Jones, *Greek–English Lexicon*
N	A. Nauck (ed.), *Tragicorum Graecorum Fragmenta*
PP	Pseudo-Plutarch, *On Fate*, ed. E. Valgiglio, Rome, 1964
SVF	H. von Arnim (ed.), *Stoicorum Veterum Fragmenta*
TAPA	*Transactions of the American Philological Association*

Manuscripts

A, A²	Parisinus graecus 1807
D	Parisinus graecus 1838
F	Vindobonensis 55, Suppl. phil. gr. 39
P	Parisinus graecus 1962
Par. gr. 1309	Parisinus graecus 1309
V	Vindobonensis philosophicus graecus 314
Vat. gr. 1390	Vaticanus graecus 1390
Vat. gr. 1144	Vaticanus graecus 1144
Y	Vindobonensis 21

INTRODUCTION

1. The Author

On this subject one cannot now, I think, even produce the few scraps of biography which it has been customary to produce over the last hundred years, during which period there has been a virtual consensus that the author, though named in the manuscripts as 'Alkinoos', is in fact to be identified with the Middle-Platonist philosopher Albinus, pupil of the philosopher Gaius, and teacher of Galen in the middle years of the second century AD.

The reason for this identification, and for its eventual rejection, is a story worth telling. In 1879, the German scholar J. Freudenthal, in his monograph 'Der Platoniker Albinos und der falsche Alkinoos',[1] advanced the theory that the 'Alkinoos' of the manuscript ascriptions was simply a scribal error resulting from the similarity of *beta* and *kappa* during the period of minuscule script. This was an ingenious suggestion, but it runs into two problems, one awkward, the other, I think, insuperable. The first is that Freudenthal (1879: 300) felt the need to postulate *two* erring scribes, the first to misread the *beta* as a *kappa*, the second (an 'intelligent' one) to emend the unheard-of name 'Alkinou' (the author's name being in the genitive) into the improbable, but at least Homeric, 'Alkinoou' (although it seems to me that Freudenthal's two scribes *could* actually be conflated into one, if the original man, being convinced that he was faced with 'Alkinou', concluded that this must be a slight misprint for 'Alkinoou', and emended accordingly).

The second problem, however, as set out by John Whittaker, the chief modern authority on the *Didaskalikos*, seems decisive. Whittaker points out, very reasonably, that, in the minuscule or any other period, the author's name in the title or the subscription would actually be written in uncials or semi-uncials, where no such easy confusion of *beta* and *kappa* occurs. Whittaker has therefore argued, in a series of articles beginning in 1974, and finally in his Budé edition of

[1] *Hellenistische Studien*, 3, Berlin.

the *Didaskalikos*, that there is no palaeographical justification for Freudenthal's conjecture.

Is there, however, any doctrinal justification for connecting the contents of the *Didaskalikos* with what we know, or think we know, of the distinctive philosophical positions of Albinus (either as appearing in his one attested work, the *Introduction [Prologos] to the Works of Plato*, or in the few testimonia that we have as to his doctrine)? Or, conversely, is there anything which seems to tell against such an identification? Freudenthal naturally thought that he could discern significant connections and no contradictions, and he devotes much space in his monograph to this question. The Italian scholar, M. Giusta, in 1961, in a long article, was the first to challenge Freudenthal's position by pointing to the various ways in which the indirect evidence for Albinus' views, from Tertullian, *de Anima* (28. 1; 29. 4), Iamblichus, *de Anima* (*ap.* Stobaeus, *Anth.* 1. 375. 10 ff. Wachsmuth–Hense), and Proclus' *in Platonis Timaeum Commentarii* (1. 219. 2 ff. Diehl),[2] does not concord with what we have in the *Didaskalikos*. One might quibble with some of Giusta's efforts to prove absolute inconsistency (these authorities, after all, would not in any case be quoting from such a work as *Didaskalikos*, but rather from either commentaries by Albinus on such dialogues as the *Phaedo* or the *Timaeus*, or versions by him of comments by his teacher Gaius, such as we know him to have compiled),[3] but it is undeniable that, on such a question as that of the various possible meanings of *genētos*, and thus of the various possible ways in which the world may be spoken of as 'created' (cf. ch. 14. 3, and commentary), the answer of

---

[2] Tertullian accuses Albinus of trying to defend his master Plato's argument in the *Phaedo* (71b–d) that the living come to be from the dead, even as the dead come to be from the living. No such defence is made in the *Didaskalikos* (though there is a brief reference to the argument from opposites in ch. 25 (177. 36 ff.), but Tertullian would not be referring to such a work as the *Did.* in any case. As for the evidence of Iamblichus, his testimony concerns the reasons for the descent of souls. Albinus is said to have attributed incarnation to 'the erring judgement of a free will', A., also in ch. 25 (178. 36–9), gives various alternatives, none of which is precisely this, though 'intemperance' (*akolasia*) is not far from it. Finally, Proclus makes a reference to two modes in which, according to Gaius and Albinus, Plato presents his doctrines, either 'scientifically' (*epistēmonikōs*) or 'on the basis of likelihood' (*eikotologikōs*), which resembles a distinction made by A. in ch. 4 (154. 25 ff.), though in a different context, between *epistēmonikos* and *doxastikos logos* (see comm. ad loc.). This is, I think, an interesting point of comparison between the Albinus testimonia and the present text, but it is still less than conclusive as to identity of authorship.

[3] It is listed in the table of contents (*pinax*) of the manuscript *Parisinus graecus* 1962, along with 'Alkinoos, *Didaskalikos*', but has unfortunately been lost, when the manuscript was split up in the Middle Ages.

Albinus, as reported by Proclus, is different from either of the two
proposed by Alcinous, and on the question of the reason for the
descent of souls (cf. ch. 25. 6, and commentary), the reasons presented in the *Didaskalikos* do not accord very well with (though they
do not contradict) that attributed to Albinus by Iamblichus in his *de
Anima*.

I am therefore (contrary to my position in 1977 in *The Middle
Platonists*, when I had not fully absorbed the force of Whittaker's
arguments, in particular) prepared to accept that Freudenthal's ingenious conjecture is, at the very least, not proven, and that the work
cannot be confidently attributed to Albinus. Already in *The Middle
Platonists* (ch. 6) I had taken steps to demonstrate that the main pillar
of a further conjecture building on that of Freudenthal, this time by
the Polish scholar Tadeusz Sinko (1905), that a comparison of the
Didaskalikos with the *de Platone et eius dogmate* of the second-century
AD Roman rhetorician Apuleius of Madaura could reveal to us a
coherent strain of Platonism which could then be identified with the
teaching of Albinus' teacher Gaius, is without much foundation (by
reason of the many differences of detail between the two works), so
that one substantial reason for maintaining Albinus' authorship is
removed. In fact the two works agree no more than might be
expected for any two elementary handbooks of Platonism that might
be produced at any time in the first two centuries AD (their agree-
ments and disagreements will be duly noted in the commentary, and a
detailed analysis may be found in *The Middle Platonists*, ch. 6).

We are left, then, after all, with 'Alcinous' (whom I will generally
refer to hereafter simply as 'A.'). Is 'Alcinous' a credible name for
anyone to bear in the first few centuries AD and do we know anyone
plausible of that name? The answer to the first question is in the
affirmative. Both from literary sources and from inscriptions we can
gather a small haul of bearers of this name—enough, certainly, to dispose of the suggestion that no one could have borne it.[4] It is, after all,

---

[4] Apart from the individual discussed just below, one finds an Alcinous, plainly a
Platonist, mentioned by Photius (*Bibl.* cod. 48) as being refuted by one Josephus, in a
treatise *On the Cause of the Universe*. It is possible, despite a reference to *anastasis*, 're-
surrection' (by which reincarnation may in fact be meant), that it is the *Didaskalikos*
that is being referred to. There are in addition a scattering of occurrences of the name
in inscriptions of the 2nd and 3rd cents. AD, e.g. *SEG* XXXI 1032 (from Lydia, AD
190–1), where a young man, Alcinous, son of Apollonius, is being honoured by his
symbiōsis (club-mates?) on his 24th birthday. One may note here the stimulating, but
ultimately, I think, unpersuasive attempt of Harold Tarrant ('Alcinous, Albinus,
Nigrinus', *Antichthon* 19 (1985), 85–95) to argue that 'Alcinous' is simply a *nom de*

no more peculiar, in its Homeric overtones, than that of that noted compiler of philosophical biographies, Diogenes Laertius—the 'god-sprung son of Laertes'.

As for the second question, Giusta (1961: 186 ff.) offered as a candidate a certain 'Alcinous the Stoic', mentioned by Philostratus in his *Lives of the Sophists* (1. 24), as being credited by some with an oration generally attributed to the sophist Marcus of Byzantium. There is really very little to commend this identification, though Whittaker, after initial scepticism (1974: 453), is prepared to entertain it in the introduction to his edition (pp. ix–xi). It is true that certain sophists affected a 'philosophical' stance. Maximus of Tyre and Apuleius wished to be known as Platonists, and indeed, especially in Apuleius' case, did something to deserve that appellation. It is also true that we know of at least one philosopher of this period (early third century), a certain Tryphon, mentioned by Porphyry in his *Life of Plotinus* (17. 3), who is described as 'the Stoic and Platonist'. But we would then be obliged to assume that the *Didaskalikos* is a piece of hack-work (largely copied, or adapted, in Giusta's view, from the work of Arius Didymus—also officially a Stoic—*On the Doctrines of Plato*) composed by a sophist (necessarily, I think; otherwise he is hardly a plausible candidate to bě the author of an epideictic speech) who had Stoic sympathies, but who suppressed them sufficiently to compose a thoroughly sympathetic (Peripateticizing, if anything) account of Platonic philosophy. Admittedly, Apuleius did just that, but he proclaims himself a Platonist, so he is not relaying the tenets of an alien philosophical system. A. may not be a very distinguished philosophical mind, but his book does read, as I think will be agreed by anyone who goes through it carefully, like the work of a committed and well-informed Platonist. I think, then, that we are obliged to admit that, if A. is not Albinus, we do not know who he is.

But if we now do not know who he is, have we any means of deciding, even approximately, when he wrote? There are, after all, no chronological indications whatever (apart from a verbatim borrowing of Arius Didymus in chapter 12), on which we can base a conclusion. A. makes no mention of any philosopher later than Plato, so nothing is to be derived from that quarter. We can at least assert that there is no trace of anything specifically 'Neoplatonist' in A.'s exposition of Platonic doctrine (even the quasi-hypostatic system presented in

plume taken on by the philosopher Albinus (who would also be Lucian's 'Nigrinus', in consequence of some sort of 'conversion' to the philosophic life.

chapter 10, as we shall see, is reconcilable with other Middle-Platonic data), but, as John Whittaker points out in his Introduction to *Didaskalikos* (p. xii), at the level of elementary handbooks, doctrine developed slowly, so that a date in the middle or late third century could not be ruled out. However, it remains true, I think, that A. fits most comfortably into a period bounded by the writings of Plutarch on the one hand, and Galen and Alexander of Aphrodisias on the other, with Apuleius, Albinus, Atticus, Numenius, the Peripatetic Aspasius, and the Platonizing sophist Maximus of Tyre as approximate contemporaries. It is these authors, along with the earlier Antiochus of Ascalon (*ap*. Cicero) and Philo of Alexandria, that will be found most often drawn on, in the commentary, as sources of terminology and concepts analogous to those of our author.

2. The Work

We may direct our attention first of all to the title, as this, correctly interpreted, throws some light upon the nature of the work. As explained at the beginning of the Commentary, there is actually some slight confusion as to what the title was, but the balance of probability is in favour of *Didaskalikos tōn Platōnos dogmatōn*, a title which is picked up in the first sentence of the work itself, *tōn kyriōtatōn Platōnos dogmatōn toiautē tis an didaskalia genoito*. I have chosen to render *didaskalia* simply by 'presentation', but 'teaching' or 'instruction' would be a more literal translation. A *didaskalikos* (*logos*), therefore, is an 'instructional account' or 'instructor's manual'. The other candidate for the title, *Epitomē ton Platōnos dogmatōn*, 'a summary of the doctrines of Plato', also gives an accurate description of the contents, but is not quite so informative about the purpose of the work. As Whittaker well shows (Intro. pp. xiv–xv),[5] the term *didaskalikos* was firmly established in the second century as a technical term for a manual of instruction, as distinct from, say, a *protreptikos* ('hortatory') or *elengtikos* ('refutatory') *logos*, so there is nothing strange about the title, though it (or a Latin equivalent) is not employed by the only other such manual that we have from antiquity, the *Liber de Platone et eius dogmate* of Apuleius, which otherwise, as I have said, proceeds along closely parallel lines to the work of A.

[5] He quotes, *inter alia*, Epictetus, *Diss.* 2. 21. 19, and 3. 23. 33; Galen, *Script. min.* 2. 73. 3–6 Müller; and Clement of Alexandria, *Paed.* 1. 1. 2. 1, and 3. 8. 3.

The *Didaskalikos*, then, is a manual of instruction in Platonism. But for whom is it intended? The most obvious reply might seem 'beginning students', but there are certain considerations which militate against that. As will become plain even from a superficial perusal of the work, A. presupposes in his reader not only a proficiency in the technical terminology of logic, ethics, and physics, but also a fairly comprehensive acquaintance with the dialogues of Plato. It is not a work, one would think, to put into the hands of a philosophical tiro. And yet at the end of the book A. describes it as an 'introduction (*eisagōgē*) to the teachings of Plato', such as 'will give one the capability to examine and discover in sequence all the remainder of his doctrines'.

It is of course possible that A. was not thinking very clearly about the capacities of his audience when he composed the work, but the alternative suggests itself that the *Didaskalikos* is actually intended rather as a manual for *teachers*, or at least amateurs, of Platonism than as a textbook for beginners. We must bear in mind that instruction in philosophy, as in most other disciplines, in ancient times was primarily oral. One learned one's Platonism, for instance, at the feet of a master, and only secondarily, and under his guidance, turned to a study of Plato's works. It is only thus, I think, that one can explain the remarkable developments that had occurred by A.'s time in what was taken to be Plato's doctrine. The process of transmission is rather like the old parlour game of 'passing on the news' all round the room; the story is very different by the time it gets back to its original author. At various stages in the tradition, however, the 'story' in its current state is captured and recorded by some author, not usually himself a major figure in the tradition, but either an eclectic assembler of philosophical opinions (such as I would take Augustus' court philosopher, Arius Didymus, to be) or a former student who wants to preserve a record of what he learned, and to show off that learning (for so I would see the case of the rhetorician Apuleius of Madaura). One cannot be sure if A. fits either of these descriptions, but in any case I would see his handbook as being intended to serve rather as a reminder for those who have sat through their lectures (and possibly are intending to give some themselves), than as an introduction for anyone coming to Platonism for the first time. The question of the exact purpose of the work is perhaps not of great importance, and is in any case not susceptible of certain decision, but, if my suggestion were found plausible, it might explain the presence of certain features that would seem oddities in a work intended as a self-standing text-book for beginners.

Having at least raised, if not disposed of, this small problem, let us turn to a brief survey of the work itself, and the most interesting aspects of the doctrine it presents.

Despite his (possibly disingenuous) apology at the end of the book (ch. 36), A. has arranged his material in a reasonably orderly manner. After three introductory chapters, concerned respectively with the definition of philosophy and laying down of requirements for the successful philosopher, the distinction of the life of contemplation, or 'research' (*theōria*), from that of action (*praxis*), and an enumeration of the 'parts' of philosophy, denominated by A. here the 'theoretical', the 'practical', and the 'dialectical', but more commonly (and loosely) known as physics, ethics, and logic, he proceeds to take these three topics in order, beginning with logic (chs. 4–6), then turning to 'physics' (chs. 7–26)—comprising both an account of first principles (chs. 7–11), and of the physical world (chs. 12–26)—and finally to ethics (chs. 27–34). He ends with a short disquisition on the difference between the philosopher and the sophist (ch. 35), and a brief conclusion (ch. 36).

2.1 Logic

In choosing to discuss logic first, A. is following the normal Stoic order of topics, but also the order followed by Andronicus in his edition of Aristotle's 'esoteric' works. His calling it 'dialectic', however, seems to be a piece of Platonist 'one-upmanship'. He prefaces the exposition of logic proper with a discussion of the *kritērion*, or basis for making judgements (ch. 4), a topic which by Hellenistic times had become accepted as the first subject to be discussed under logic, and indeed as one of the basic issues of philosophy. A.'s doctrine here fits in interestingly to the spectrum of views represented by Sextus Empiricus, Ptolemy, and others. The distinguishing of three elements, the judging faculty, the object of the judgement, and the judging process itself, finds echoes in these other authors, as does the use of prepositional formulae to express these relationships. Characteristic of A. is the distinction between primary and secondary objects of intellection and of perception, though the attempt at a parallelism between the various stages of intellection and sense-perception seems to break down, as I argue in the Commentary.

In the sphere of logic proper (chs. 5 and 6), A.'s approach is to attribute to Plato without reservation the whole system of Peripatetic logic as worked out by Aristotle, and further elaborated by Theophrastus and Eudemus, finding in the dialogues examples illustrative not only of categorical syllogisms, but also of 'pure' (i.e. Theophrastean) and 'mixed' (i.e. Stoic) hypotheticals. What we have here, then, is a most useful exposition of later Peripatetic logic, presented in such a way as to make it seem essential Platonism.

He begins, in chapter 5, with a number of definitions and general principles, all of which, indeed, are reasonably Platonic. The basic principle of dialectic is to examine the substance of each thing and then its accidents. In all, we get five types of dialectic reasoning, division, definition, analysis, induction, and syllogistic, the first three concerned with substances, the last two with accidents. He then proceeds to illustrate these various methods from the dialogues of Plato.

He ends the chapter with a comment on induction which manages to combine wonderfully in one short sentence three terms, one of which we would take as characteristically Aristotelian, the next Platonic, and the third Stoic. It may be quoted as a neat example of the composite tradition within which A. is working (158. 3–4): 'Induction is particularly useful for stirring up the innate concepts'. The overall inspiration here is certainly Platonic, in particular *Meno* 85c ff., from which comes the term 'stir up' (*anakinein*, 85c9), but the name given to the process is Aristotle's, *epagōgē*, while the term used for the forms is ultimately Stoic, *physikai ennoiai*. In all this, of course, A. himself would not be conscious of any mixture of terminology.

In chapter 6, as mentioned above, we find the theory of the syllogism, the whole of which is claimed for Plato. Here the chief aspect of interest is the treatment of hypotheticals, and I trust that, with the patient help of Jonathan Barnes, I have given an adequate account of the complexities involved. It still seems to me quite obscure how much of Stoic theory, or at least *formulation*, had been anticipated by the Peripatos under Theophrastus and Eudemus, and how later scholars, such as Ariston or Boethus, or indeed Galen and Alexander of Aphrodisias, saw the difference between the two systems. A. himself does not seem to have any consciousness of a distinction between a logic of terms and a logic of propositions.

He appends in sections 10–11 some remarks on etymology and the theory of language, largely derived from the *Cratylus*, particularly 385–90, though overlaid by Stoic theorizing.

2.2 Physics

He turns next, in chapters 7–11, to a survey of first principles, beginning with a chapter on mathematics, heavily dependent on *Republic* 7. 524d–533d, and not exhibiting any great degree of interest or sophistication in the subject. He emphasizes the propaedeutic value of mathematics, as one would expect in the circumstances. He goes through the divisions of mathematics, as set out in *Republic* 7; arithmetic, geometry, stereometry, astronomy, and music. Music does the same for the faculty of hearing as astronomy does for the faculty of sight, that is, it leads the mind through the exercise of that faculty to a knowledge of the intelligible. There is nothing here that goes beyond Plato, except perhaps for an unwillingness to disparage regular, 'vulgar' astronomy as much as Plato did.

In chapter 8 there begins the discussion of Platonist first principles, beginning with the 'lowest', Matter. Here A. basically propounds Plato's doctrine in the *Timaeus*, 49a–52d, with no non-Platonic features except the actual use of the word *hylē* for 'matter', and a formulation which is Aristotelian rather than Platonic, according to which matter is described as 'neither body nor incorporeal, but *potentially* body' (163. 7-8). This formula, which is to be found also in Apuleius and in Calcidius' *Timaeus Commentary* (see Commentary ad loc.), is traceable to Aristotle, *de Generatione et Corruptione* 2. 1. 329ᵃ32–3.

In chapter 9, we pass to the 'paradigmatic' first principle, Form. Here A.'s evidence is important, both as to the definition of form, and what there are forms of, and as to the doctrine of forms as the thoughts of God. A feature of the chapter (sects. 2–3) is a series of syllogistic proofs of the necessity for the existence of forms, couched in the form of Stoic hypotheticals.

In chapter 10, perhaps the best-known section of the whole work, we come to the third *archē*, namely God. Here we find three entities set out in ascending order of importance, a world soul, an intellect of the world soul, and a primal god, who is probably still an intellect of some sort, but said to be 'nobler' than and 'superior' to the intellect of the world soul. The nature of the theology of this chapter has been much discussed, and the problems are given extended treatment in the commentary. Suffice it to say here that I do not see the necessity of supposing that anything here is so incompatible with Middle Platonism as to require the postulation of later interpolation. Apart from the presentation of this system of three levels of being in section 2, notable features of the chapter are the sequence of epithets of God in section 3, and the account of the three methods of describing God, later known as the *via negationis*, the *via analogiae*, and the *via eminentiae*, in sections 5–6.

The section on first principles ends with a short chapter (11) proving, by a series of syllogisms, that qualities (*poiotētes*) are immaterial. Since no Platonist after Antiochus of Ascalon would have disputed this, this might seem superfluous to establish, but in fact the chapter serves as a sort of bridge-passage to the discussion of the material world in the succeeding chapters. A strong contrast is made between the characteristics of the immaterial and the material, in the process of which it becomes clear that *poiotēs* is being connected with *poiein*, 'to make, to create' (166. 27–9).

We turn now, in chapters 12 to 22, to the subject-matter of physics proper, for which A.'s source is the *Timaeus*, or rather, perhaps, a previous epitome based on the *Timaeus*. The beginning of chapter 12 is lifted, with minimal alteration, from Arius Didymus, and a reasonable presumption is thereby created, it seems to me, that Arius' handbook is the basis for this whole section, if not for the whole work. There is a considerable range of opinion on this question, however, which is discussed in the Commentary ad loc.

I will merely select points of interest or possible originality from what is in general a bald summary of Plato's doctrine. First, we have in chapter 13, in connection with the description of the basic geometrical figures in *Timaeus* 54b ff., a detailed treatment of the fifth figure, the dodecahedron, which is merely alluded to by Plato. A. connects the dodecahedron with the twelve signs of the zodiac, the 360 subdivisions of the zodiacal circle corresponding to the 360 triangles in the dodecahedron. We cannot say who first propounded this scholastic elaboration on Plato, but a possible candidate is the obscure figure of Theodorus of Soli, a contemporary of the Old Academy (see discussion in Commentary ad loc.).

In connection with the dodecahedron arises the question as to whether A. accepted the ether as a fifth element. In chapter 13 he is following the *Timaeus* closely, and makes explicit mention of only the Platonic four elements, but since he interprets Plato's vague phrase 'the universe' in *Timaeus* 55c as meaning 'the heavens', it seems likely that he did in fact postulate a fifth element. This impression is confirmed by chapter 15, where, in his discussion of daemons, he mentions them as inhabiting all the elements except earth—*aithēr*, fire, air, and water. At the end of the chapter, admittedly, he confuses things somewhat by referring to ether as the outermost element. 'divided into the sphere of the fixed stars and that of the planets', to which he adds: 'following on these [sc. two spheres] is a region of air, and in the middle is the earth, with its wet element'. In a thorough-going five-element universe there should be a sphere of fire between ether and air, in and around the moon. Perhaps after all A. only means by 'ether' pure fire, in the Stoic manner. But the complexities of the problem are discussed at more length in the Commentary.

Another question on which A. might seem to vacillate, but in fact does not, is whether or not the world is subject to a temporal creation. When he is following the *Timaeus* closely, as is the case in chapters 12 and 13, he gives the impression—as does Plato, after all—that the Demiurge fashioned the world out of chaos, but in chapter 14 he is careful to set things right, and in the process makes an interesting contribution (sect. 3) to the Platonist position on the various possible meanings of *genētos*, worked out most elaborately by Calvenus Taurus in his *Commentary on the Timaeus* (*ap.* John Philoponus). For the details, see the Commentary ad loc.

This is followed by an interesting description of God's ordering of an apparently previous dormant world soul (sects. 3–4), which has some connection with certain doctrines propounded by Plutarch. A. then turns, for the rest of chapter 14 (sects. 5–7), to an account of the heavens and the creation of time, in the course of which he produces a rather odd definition of eternity as 'the measure of the stability of the eternal world' (170. 26)—a formulation concocted on the basis of the Stoicized definition of time he presents, but really devoid of much meaning.

Following on his exposition of the planetary gods, A. turns in chapter 15 to deal with daemons, a section which contains a certain amount of interest, particularly the notion that they are present in all the elements, which is derived, presumably from an interpretation of *Timaeus* 40a (which is actually referring, not to daemons, but to birds and fish) in the light of *Epinomis* 984d ff., which does postulate daemons in all the elements.

We next turn to the creation of man and other living beings (ch. 16), which leads to a series of chapters (17–22) closely based on the latter part of the *Timaeus*. There is nothing much here that is of any doctrinal originality, though there is interesting evidence of scholastic editing and splicing, which is noted in the commentary. He deals in turn with the construction of the human body (17), sight (18), the remaining senses of hearing, smell, taste, and touch (19), then a note on heaviness and lightness (20), then breathing (21), and finally the diseases of men and their causes.

Chapters 23 to 25 concern the soul, its relation to the body (23), its parts (24), and the question of immortality (25). As one would expect, A. combines a formal acceptance of the Platonic tripartition of the soul (23) with an actual division of it (24) into rational and irrational, or 'affective' (*pathētikon*), as he terms it (176. 39). A. seems to take literally the spatial distinction of the parts of the soul as described in the *Timaeus*, in contrast to such authorities as Posidonius and Plutarch (see Commentary).

Chapter 23 is a description of the fashioning of the mortal parts of the soul by the 'young gods' which follows closely *Timaeus* 44d–e and especially 69c–72d. In chapter 24 he turns to a defence of the distinction between the rational and irrational parts. Such an argument is directed ultimately against the Old Stoa and in particular Chrysippus. A. is simply giving a summary of what by his time must have been the standard Platonist position that contraries cannot exist simultaneously in the same place, and the parts of the soul may often be observed to be at variance with one another.

Proofs of the immortality of the soul take up most of chapter 25. The proofs are mainly taken from the *Phaedo*, along with the 'self-motion' argument from *Phaedrus* 245e. It is interesting to observe, in view of later disputes among the Neoplatonists, that A. has no doubt that all the proofs in the *Phaedo*, including the Argument from Opposites and Argument from Recollection, are full proofs of immortality. His description of the process of recollection (*anamnēsis*) is rather fuller than one finds in Plato, and reflects the centuries of theorizing on the subject that had gone on in the interval, particularly in relation to the Stoic theory of general concepts.

That the rational soul is immortal A. establishes as Platonic doctrine. But what of irrational souls? This he regards as a disputed question (sects. 5. 178. 25 ff.), but he himself holds them to be mortal, since they have no share in mind. Following on this, A. discusses the occasion and the reasons for the soul's descent into bodies (s. 6). The soul enters the body at the moment of the formation of the embryo. This is a contradiction of the Stoic position that it enters at the moment of birth, and was obviously a matter of active school controversy. A. next asserts that the soul passes through many incarnations, in both human and non-human bodies, thus committing himself to the literal interpretation of Plato's remarks about incarnation into animal bodies, an interpretation which was rejected by the Neoplatonists, from Porphyry on.

He then runs through a series of four suggestions as to the reasons for the soul's descent, the details of which are discussed in the Commentary, which correspond between them to most of the reasons which we find offered elsewhere in the Platonist tradition. The four reasons given, (1) the maintenance of a constant number of souls, (2) the will of the Gods, (3) wantonness, and (4) love of the body, are not necessarily mutually exclusive, but A. might be suspected of favouring the last, if only because he amplifies it by an illustration.

The chapter ends with a most interesting account of the structure of the divine and the disembodied soul, perhaps the result of exegesis of the myth of the *Phaedrus*, where the souls of gods too are portrayed as charioteers and pairs (though each horse of the pair is of equally noble birth). From this, however, one might derive the theory that in divine souls there must be archetypal equivalents of the spirited and libidinous parts of the human soul. A. here gives the details of these. The divine soul has three aspects, the critical or cognitive (*gnōstikon*), corresponding to our rational part, the appetitive or 'dispositional' (*parastatikon*), corresponding to our spirited, and the 'appropriative' (*oikeiōtikon*), corresponding to our libidinous. This is also the case with souls before they have descended into bodies. On embodiment, they undergo change into the parts which we possess. This is a theory with interesting implications for psychology, some of which are discussed in the Commentary.

A. turns next (ch. 26) to the subject of fate, providence, and free will, a topic which might seem to us more closely connected with ethical speculation, but which counted in ancient philosophical systems as part of 'physics'. It does, however, in A.'s scheme, form a kind of bridge to the ethical section of the treatise, even as, perhaps, the chapter on Quality formed a bridge to the discussion of the physical world.

What we have is a sketch of what seems to have been the 'basic' Middle-Platonic doctrine on fate and free will, without the distinctive elaborations exhibited in a nest of texts, Pseudo-Plutarch's *de Fato*, Calcidius, *in Timaeum* 142–90, and Nemesius of Emesa, *On the Nature of Man* chapter 38 (discussed in the commentary). It is none the worse for that, in fact. What A. does do is to try to preserve a place for free will (*to eph' hēmin*) by propounding the theory that fate 'has the status of a (general) law', and that it operates hypothetically. It is concerned with what will happen if such-and-such a course of action is taken, but it does not necessitate that we will take a particular course of action. This is less than satisfactory, admittedly: how is one to decide when one is at the *beginning* of a chain of consequences, as opposed to making already-conditioned choices when in the middle of such a chain? At what stage, for instance, could Oedipus have stood back and taken a free decision not to pursue a certain course of action?

But A.'s effort is an honest one, as good as anyone else's in the Platonist–Aristotelian tradition. He also provides a useful discussion of the concepts of possibility and potentiality (179. 20–32), the point of the distinction being that the potential is already 'programmed' in some direction—it is fated to be actualized—whereas the possible remains purely undetermined, and is thus the proper domain of *to eph' hēmin*.

2.3 *Ethics*

We now come to the final section of the work (chs. 27–34), the exposition of Platonist ethical theory. Chapter 27 deals with the highest good and happiness; 28, with the 'end of goods' (*telos agathōn*), or supreme purpose of human life; 29, with virtue and the individual virtues; 30, with the 'good natural dispositions' (*euphyiai*), and the (distinctively Stoic) theory of 'moral progress' (*prokopē*); 31 contains a discussion of the doctrine that no one does wrong voluntarily; 32 surveys the emotions; and 33 discusses friendship. Let us examine these topics briefly in turn.

The good for man, says A. (179. 39 ff.) consists in 'the knowledge and contemplation of the primal good, which one may term God and the primal Intellect'. Every other good is good by participation in this. A., as would any Platonist, equates the Good of *Republic* 6 with the supreme God, who is for him, of course, an intellect.

The question next arises as to what status is to be accorded to the two lower classes of good, the bodily and the external. Here we find A., rather unexpectedly, in agreement with the more Stoicizing (and Pythagoreanizing) wing of Platonism, as represented by Eudorus of Alexandria, and his approximate contemporary Atticus, in declaring that happiness is to be found in the goods of the soul alone; that is to say, A. upholds the principle of the self-sufficiency of virtue. Apart from virtue, the human or 'mortal' goods are simply 'matter', which may be used for good or evil. In ethics, then, A. is not 'Peripatetic' in sympathy, in contrast to such figures as Plutarch and Calvenus Taurus. Indeed, he comes out with a number of distinctively Stoic slogans in the course of chapter 27, such as 'Only the noble is good' and 'Virtue is sufficient for happiness'.

In the formulation of the *telos*, also, A. is at one with Eudorus, but on this topic following the 'Pythagorean' rather than the Stoic tradition. The purpose of life is 'likeness to God', *Theaetetus* 176b being appealed to as the prime authority for this. The alternative, Stoic–Antiochian *telos* of 'conformity to nature' is implicitly rejected. A. does, however, introduce a significant qualification into the 'likeness to God' formula. After giving a number of other Platonic references in support of it, he adds (181. 43 ff.): 'By "God" we mean, obviously, the god *in* the heavens (*epouranios*), not, of course, the god above the heavens (*hyperouranios*), who does not possess virtue, being superior to this.' This has the appearance of a reservation entered by A. himself to what he must have regarded as an insufficiently exact traditional formulation. The 'god in the heavens' is necessarily the Demiurge or 'intellect of the whole heaven', A.'s second god in the scheme presented in chapter 10. To bring the supreme deity of chapter 10 into a relationship of 'likeness' to man would be to compromise his transcendence, presumably, apart from the absurdity of imputing to him virtues in any ordinary meaning of the word. This difficulty had not, it seemed, occurred to earlier Platonists; at any rate we find no trace of such a refinement in Apuleius, *de Platone* 2. 23. It anticipates to some extent Plotinus' position in *Enneads* 1. 2.

Chapter 28 ends with, first (182. 3 ff.), a formulation of the methods by which likeness to God may be attained, utilizing the triad 'natural aptitude' (*physis*), 'training' (*askēsis*), and 'teaching' (*didaskalia*), which is much the same as that presented by Philo of Alexandria (*Abr.* 52–4) early in the first century AD, and is thus likely to be the basic Middle-Platonic doctrine. A. then continues (181. 8 ff.) with another image much beloved of Philo, but also favoured by such writers as 'Heraclitus', author of *The Allegories of Homer* (ch. 3), and Theon of Smyrna (*Expos.* 14. 17–16. 2 Hiller), that of the 'mysteries of philosophy'. A. here makes the 'encyclic studies' of music, arithmetic, astronomy, geometry (for the soul), and gymnastic (for the body), the 'introductory ceremonies' (*proteleia*) and 'preliminary purifications' (*prokatharsia*) which prepare us for initiation into the Greater Mysteries.

In his discussion of virtue and the virtues (chs. 29–30), A. presents, in non-controversial terms, basic Middle-Platonic doctrine, which itself draws much terminology from both Aristotle and the Stoics. In chapter 29 virtue is defined, in terms borrowed from Aristotle, as a 'perfect and most excellent state of the soul, which makes a man, both in speech and in action, graceful, harmonious and firm, both in relation to himself and to others'. We then have a description of the four cardinal virtues, based on the doctrine of the *Republic*, but reflecting centuries of scholastic definition. The conclusion drawn from this doctrine, however, is expressed in Stoic terms, that the virtues are mutually interdependent (*antakolouthein*). In their developed, rational form, the virtues all involve 'right reason' (*orthos logos*); one cannot possess, for instance, rational courage without having also rational moderation, and so on. While the technical term *antakolouthia* is Stoic in origin, the doctrine itself may be found already in Plato's *Protagoras*, and this is A.'s justification for using it here.

What one might call 'natural virtues', however, such as appear in unreflective persons, children, or animals, are not true virtues at all, and do not imply each other. The valour of the average soldier, for instance, is not generally accompanied by temperance. For these A. employs both the Aristotelian term 'good natural dispositions' (*euphyiai*, cf. *EN* 1114^{b}12) and the Stoic term 'progressions (towards virtue)' (*prokopai*). In chapter 30 he discusses first these, then the vices, and then the doctrine of virtue as a mean, depending here again on the *Nicomachean Ethics*. Here we find him uttering what seems to be common Middle-Platonic doctrine, arising from a remark of Aristotle's (*EN* 1107^{a}23) that the virtues, while being 'means', are also in a way 'summits' or 'extremes' (184. 14 ff.). He goes on to adopt the doctrine of moderation of the emotions (*metriopatheia*) as opposed to their extirpation (*apatheia*), thus setting himself at odds with Stoicism. Lack of emotion A. regards as being just as much a vice as excessive emotion (184. 20–1). Here he is in complete agreement with Plutarch and Taurus. What Atticus had to say on this question we do not know, but it is a reasonable guess that he took the Stoic line.

A. opposes also the extreme Stoic view that men must be either good or bad absolutely (the vast majority being, of course, bad). One cannot switch immediately from vice to virtue, he says (183. 33 ff.), so that most people are in a state (or process) of *prokopē*, '(moral) progress', and that is a truly intermediate state, not a condition *within* absolute badness, as orthodox Stoics maintained.

Chapter 31 comprises a discussion of the Socratic paradox of the involuntariness of vice. The *Gorgias* is the chief influence here. A. is careful also to make the point that, although vice is in the strict intellectualist sense involuntary, yet punishment is in order, since ignorance and emotion can be 'rubbed away' by remedial training (185. 12 ff.). Otherwise it would be liable to the same charge as was brought against the Stoics in consequence of their theory of fate, of having no reason to punish wrongdoing.

The mention of crime due to the emotions leads to a chapter on the emotions (ch. 32). Here the Old Stoic view that the emotions are judgements or opinions, already abandoned long since by Posidonius, but perhaps not by more faithful Stoics, is dismissed, as failing to take account of an irrational part of the soul. This line is taken also by Plutarch in his essay *On Moral Virtue*.

As against the Stoic theory of four basic emotions, A. asserts that there are really only two, pleasure and distress, here relying on various passages of Plato, but in particular *Philebus* 44b ff. To these, fear and desire are only secondary. There follows a division of emotions into 'wild' and 'tame', derived from *Republic* 9. 589b, which must have been popular in the Middle-Platonic period, since it turns up, for instance, in Philo, *Quaestiones in Genesim* 2. 57, in connection with his (Stoicizing) distinction of the emotions proper from the *eupatheiai*, or Stoic 'equable states'. A. does not make use of that distinction here, but he distinguishes between natural degrees of the emotions, and excessive, unmeasured degrees, which comes to something like the same thing. The natural condition for man, though, he describes, following *Philebus* 33a, as 'the mean between distress and pleasure, being the same as neither of them' (186. 33–5). He thus rejects Aristotle's view of pleasure (presented in *EN* 10. 4–5) as the natural accompaniment of happiness, using to describe it, curiously, the term, 'supervenient' (*epigennēmatikē*), which for Aristotle would not have been a negative description, but for the Stoics, from whom the term is here borrowed, it was.

After the discussion of pleasure, we find a chapter (33) on friendship (*philia*). This actually follows Aristotle's order of subjects in the *Nicomachean Ethics* (from the latter half of book 7 to book 10), and is indeed thoroughly Aristotelian in influence, though at the same time containing nothing un-Platonic. The discussion of three kinds of love, noble (*asteia*), wicked (*phaulē*), and 'middling' (*mesē*) is based on *Laws* 837b–d, but employs Stoic terminology. Of the noble form of love it is possible to have an art (*technē*); it has *theōrēmata*, to wit, how to recognize the worthy object of love, how to gain it, and how to behave with it. It seems to me that this essay at a Platonist *ars amatoria* is based on a scholastic exegesis of the *First Alcibiades*, Socrates' relationship with Alcibiades being taken as paradigmatic of how the wise man should behave in love.

The topic of friendship leads for A., as it does for Aristotle, from the study of ethics to that of politics, since friendship concerns relations of various sorts within civil society. The main aspect of interest in A.'s treatment of political theory is a distinction which he makes, of rather mysterious provenance, between the types of state which Plato describes in his works, the 'non-hypothetical' and the 'hypothetical'. The former category comprises the various levels of state described in the *Republic*, from the 'city of pigs' on up to the state ruled over by the Guardians, the latter the ideal states of the *Laws* and of the *Eighth Platonic Letter*. The distinction presumably lies in the fact that the schemes outlined in the *Republic* do not specify any material preconditions for their realization, whereas those of the *Laws* and of *Letter* 8 assume a new foundation in a certain place under certain definite conditions. The distinction turns up again, much later, in the sixth-century anonymous *Prolegomena to Platonic Philosophy*, but it seems to be reflected also in a distinction made by Apuleius in *de Platone* 2. 26, so it certainly antedates A.

He ends the chapter with a definition of politics (189. 5 ff.): 'Politics, then, is a virtue which is both theoretical and practical, the aim of which is to render a state good, happy, harmonious, and concordant. It exercises a directive role, and has as subordinate to it the sciences or war and generalship and the administration of justice'—a passage that draws a good deal of its inspiration from *Politicus* 303d–305e.

The treatise ends with a comparison of the true philosopher with the sophist (ch. 35), based, naturally, on Plato's *Sophist*, and a little epilogue, which I mentioned at the outset, apologizing to the reader for any failings in organization that may have appeared in the course of the work.

3. Stylistic and Structural Features of the Treatise: The Question of Sources

A few words may be said here about certain distinctive features of A.'s style and method of procedure in the *Didaskalikos*. These have been discussed very fully by John Whittaker in the introduction to his Budé edition of the work (pp. xvii–xxxi), and in Whittaker (1989), to both of which I would refer the reader for a more comprehensive account.

First of all, there is the question of his use of Plato. The most obvious feature of this is one that is brought to our attention at the very beginning of the treatise, his treatment of Plato's work as *a body of doctrine* (*dogmata*). In this connection, we must realize that A. is heir to a centuries-long tradition of scholastic systemization and interpretation of Plato, which may go back even to Xenocrates, third head of the Academy (339–314 BC), to whom we perhaps owe the first definitive collected edition of Plato's dialogues.[6] Many of the titles of Xenocrates' works (all of which are unfortunately lost) seem to indicate a tendency to systematize Plato's doctrine, with or without directly quoting from the dialogues—titles such as *On Nature, On Wisdom, On Being, On Fate, On Virtue, On Ideas, On the Gods, On the Soul, On the Good*. It was Xenocrates also, if we may credit Posidonius (Fr. 88 Edelstein–Kidd = Xenocr. Fr. I Heinze), who first explicitly divided the subject-matter of philosophy into the three domains of physics, ethics, and logic. All indications are, then, that the systematization of Platonic philosophy begins with Xenocrates (though works such as that of Hermodorus, *On Plato*, may have played some part in this also).

We cannot, I think, presume that much further systematizing went on under the New Academy from Arcesilaus to Carneades, but after dogmatism was re-established in the Platonist tradition under Antiochus of Ascalon in the early first century BC the work of systematizing was renewed, and perhaps only now are many of the doctrines and formulations of Aristotle, Theophrastus, and the Stoics incorporated into the

---

[6] See on this H. Alline (1915: ch. 2, esp. pp. 46–56), though there is really very little hard evidence for the scenario that he presents. There is an interesting passage on this question in the Anonymous *Theaetetus* Commentary, 54. 38 ff., where the problem of whether Plato propounded *dogmata* is discussed, or at least alluded to. The author, not surprisingly, feels that he did, adducing the argument that the great majority of Academic philosophers believed that he did.

mix which is to become 'Middle Platonism'.[7] Antiochus himself, however, was more attached to Stoic materialism than was the mainstream of the Middle-Platonic tradition as it subsequently emerged, and a further infusion of Pythagoreanism (a spin-off of the general revival of interest in the Pythagorean tradition that is evident in the first century BC) was required to produce the distinctive lineaments of the Platonism of the first and second centuries AD.

An important influence in this further development seems to be the figure of Eudorus of Alexandria,[8] whose work *A Division of the Subject-Matter of Philosophy* (if that is a reasonable rendering of *Diairesis tou kata philosophian logou*) is highly praised by Arius Didymus (*ap.* Stob. *Ecl.* 2. 42. 7 ff. Wachsmuth), who makes use of the section on Ethics in his handbook on Ethics (to which we shall turn in a moment). Eudorus also wrote a commentary on the *Timaeus* (drawn on by Plutarch in his treatise *On the Creation of the Soul in the Timaeus*), which provided a synthesis of the Old Academic authorities Xenocrates and Crantor on certain key questions.

An important influence, however, on the composition of A.'s own work would seem to have been the handbook of Arius Didymus just mentioned. Arius, who became court philosopher to the Emperor Augustus, seems to have professed Stoicism rather than Platonism, but composed a comprehensive survey of philosophy (or at least the ethical and physical divisions of it),[9] giving a reasonably impartial account of Platonism and Aristotelianism as well as Stoicism. For his account of Platonism, Arius may have drawn exclusively on Eudorus, or he may also have referred back to sources in the Old Academy, but his use of a single source, if a comprehensive one was to hand, seems more likely.[10]

The question of A.'s relation to Arius is given sharp focus by a passage at the beginning of ch. 12 of the *Didaskalikos*, which reproduces virtually verbatim (though with some interesting small alterations) a passage of Arius' account of Platonic doctrine on the soul which happens to survive (see Commentary). Scholarly opinion is divided as to whether this is to be regarded as a flash in the pan, or

---

[7] On this process I may refer the reader to ch. 2 of Dillon (1977), and now to the excellent discussion of Jonathan Barnes (1989).

[8] On whom see Dillon (1977), ch. 3, and P. Moraux (1984), 509–27.

[9] He may have dealt with logic also, and with the Epicureans, but if so, we have no evidence of it.

[10] He does, it must be said, just before his account of Eudorus' division of philosophy, give that of Philo of Larisa; but he seems to prefer Eudorus.

the tip of the iceberg. I am on record (1977: 269) as suggesting that the *Didaskalikos* is no more than a 'new edition' of the work of Arius, with the proviso that it should probably be seen as a new, *revised* edition. This view has been criticized recently by John Whittaker (1989: 68 n. 10), but I do not think we are necessarily seriously at odds. In the introduction to his edition (pp. xvi–xvii), he concedes that A. is basing himself 'entirely on the work of his predecessors', rather than aspiring to any degree of originality. I would quite agree, but would tend to see these predecessors as extending in chronological sequence from Arius to A., rather than being a range of alternatives from which A. is picking and choosing. In other words, while it may be an oversimplification to regard Arius as *the* source of A.'s work, it seems not unreasonable to see him as at least the penultimate link in a chain of pretty conservative scholastic doxographers on which A. is drawing.

This may also be the best approach to the problem of the relationship of the handbooks of A. and of his approximate contemporary, the North African rhetorician Apuleius of Madaura, as I have mentioned above (Sect. 1). A better solution seems to be to view these two documents as cousins, rather than sisters, dependent, perhaps, on the same *penultimate* source, whether that be Arius or another, but not really adding up to the doctrine of a definite 'school' within second-century Platonism. What needs to be emphasized, I think, is that there was a great deal more going on in the three centuries from 80 BC onwards in the way of the reproduction of handbooks of Platonism (mostly not for 'publication', but rather for personal use) than we have any evidence for.

All this by way of background to the observation that what we find in the *Didaskalikos* is not so much the direct utilization of Plato's dialogues as the relaying of a formalized distillation of them into *dogmata* which had been completed long before A.'s time. Many indications of this process will have attention drawn to them in the commentary. Notable characteristics are: (1) the splicing together of various Platonic passages dealing with the same topic to give a coherent whole, or alternatively, the incorporation of a phrase from one dialogue into a passage which is primarily borrowed from another (e.g. a phrase from the *Phaedo* or the *Laws* into a passage mainly dependent on the *Republic* or the *Timaeus*);[11] (2) a tendency to alter the language

[11] e.g. 179. 9–11 (*Phdr.* 248c with *R.* 10. 617d ff.); 180. 16–28 (*L.* 631b with. *Phdr.* 247a–248b and *R.* 7. 527d–e); 188. 22–5 (*R.* 5. 473d with *Ep.* 7. 326a–b).

of a Platonic passage, either for purely stylistic reasons, or in the interest of introducing 'modernized'—perhaps Peripatetic or Stoic—terminology. An interesting subclass of the former type of alteration is A.'s habit, well identified and discussed by Whittaker (both in (1989) and in the introduction to his edition, pp. xviii ff.), of switching a given pair of words used by Plato (verbs, nouns, adjectives, and adverbs all figure in this connection) when utilizing a Platonic passage. This device of 'mirror' quotation must be deliberate, introduced, no doubt, to *avoid* direct quotation.[12]

This *may* be a stylistic quirk peculiar to A., but all the other features mentioned can be matched in such authors as Philo of Alexandria, 'Timaeus of Locri', Arius Didymus, Plutarch, Numenius, Clement of Alexandria, the anonymous *Theaetetus* Commentator, and later, in Plotinus—and, in Latin translation, in Apuleius and in Calcidius—showing that we are in the presence of a widespread tradition. Instances will be noticed on nearly every page of the Commentary. Dwelling on them may seem pedantic, but the purpose is to remind the reader that A. is simply a modest member of a great tradition.

4. The *Didaskalikos* in Context: The Middle-Platonic Background

It may now be helpful to sketch in something of the philosophical background to A.'s handbook by looking at the growth of Platonist doctrine over the preceding few centuries, so far as we can recover it from the very fragmentary evidence available to us. I will cover the main topics in the order in which A. treats them, logic, 'physics' (including what we would regard as metaphysics), and ethics.[13]

4.1 Logic

In the field of logic, the primary 'achievement' of the Middle Platonists was to appropriate Aristotelian logic, together with the developments attributable to Theophrastus and Eudemus, for Plato.

---

[12] e.g. 154. 29–30 (*Ti.* 29b5–6); 167. 12 (*Ti.* 30a4–5); 167. 35 (*Ti.* 33a2); 172. 28–9 (*Ti.* 73b6); 172. 33 (*Ti.* 74c7).

[13] I will be drawing here, inevitably, on my own previous survey in *The Middle Platonists*, 43–51, though with updating and correction where necessary.

Theophrastus and Eudemus had developed a system of hypothetical syllogisms, which had been more or less ignored by Aristotle,[14] distinguishing 'pure' and 'mixed' hypotheticals, the latter being those adopted later by the Stoics. In so far, then, as the Platonists borrowed from Stoic logic, they felt justified in this by finding it prefigured in Theophrastus. We find this synthesis exhibited in ch. 6 of A.'s work, where both categorical and hypothetical syllogisms are discerned in the dialogues, particularly the *Parmenides*. Plato is also credited with knowledge of the ten Categories, which A. discerns in the *Parmenides*, while Plutarch (*An. Proc.* 1023e) sees them operating in *Timaeus* (37a–b).

The process of synthesis, though with explicit dependence upon Stoic logic, can be seen already established in such a text as Cicero's *Topica*, so that it may be attributed with some probability to Antiochus of Ascalon—although Aristotelian–Theophrastean logic may have been accepted already into the New Academy. At any rate, the Old Academic loyalty to diaeresis and the two basic categories of 'absolute' and 'relative' has been abandoned in our period. In an important article, Michael Frede (1974) has shown that the distinction which we make between the logic of terms (Aristotelian) and the logic of propositions (Stoic) was not obvious to the ancients, and that their mutual exclusivity was argued for on other and more trivial grounds. Certainly the Middle Platonists saw no incompatibility between the two logics, and were happy to view Plato as the father of both.

It cannot be said, however, that the Middle Platonists added much that is valuable to the science of logic (though the Peripatetic Ariston of Alexandria, a contemporary of Eudorus, can be credited, perhaps, with some development in syllogistic[15]). There are a few lost works of Plutarch, such as *A Reply to Chrysippus on the First Consequent*, *A Lecture on the Ten Categories*, *A Discourse on Hypothesis*, and *On Tautology*, which sound interesting, but there is little reason to suppose, on the basis of Plutarch's surviving remarks, that they contributed anything of basic importance.

4.2 Physics

In the sphere of 'physics', however, there is more to be said. Throughout our period, the question of the nature and activity of the

---

[14] Alexander, *in APr.* (326. 20 ff., 389. 32 ff. = Fr. 30 Graeser); cf. Graeser (1973: 97–100), and Barnes (1985).   [15] See Moraux (1973), 181–93.

supreme principle, or God, is dominant. Later Platonists preserved
the Old Academic opposition of monad, or One, and dyad, though
they varied in the relationship that they postulated between these two.
Antiochus of Ascalon, indeed, seems simply to accept the Stoic pair
of an active and a passive principle.[16] It is not even clear that he recognized any transcendent, immaterial principle in the world at all.
Eudorus of Alexandria, however, in the next generation, while re-
establishing the Old Academic and Pythagorean monad and dyad as
transcendent principles, places above them both a supreme One,[17]
possibly drawing some inspiration here from the metaphysical scheme
of the *Philebus* (26e–30e). With Plutarch, in the late first century, we
are back to the basic duality, but he, and his follower Atticus (late
2nd cent.), grant the dyadic element rather more independence than
orthodox Platonism would allow. In such passages as *de Defectu
Oraculorum* 428f–429a, *de Iside et Osiride* 369e–370e, or *de Animae
Procreatione in Timaeo* 1027a, Plutarch exhibits a degree of dualism
which, despite his claims, is not truly Platonic, and may owe something to Zoroastrian influences.

For A., by contrast, God is dominant and matter is simply passive.
Neither in the metaphysical scheme presented in ch. 10 nor elsewhere
in the work is any use made of an indefinite dyad, or of any positively
evil principle. In the Neopythagoreanism of another approximate contemporary of his, Numenius, however, a radical dualism does seem to
be asserting itself, though partially held in check by the influence of
orthodox Platonism, as shown in his treatment of matter (*ap.*
Calcidius, *in Tim.* 295–9 = *Fr.* 52 Des Places).

Besides these first principles, there is, as an intermediate and medi-
ating entity, the world-soul. This is basically the entity whose creation is described in the *Timaeus* (35a ff.), but traces appear, in such
men as Philo of Alexandria (1st cent. BC) and Plutarch, of a rather
more august figure, which seems to owe something to the Old
Academic (Speusippean) dyad, a figure not positively evil, but simply
responsible for multiplicity, and thus for all creation. In Philo this
appears as the figure of Sophia, God's Wisdom (e.g. *Fug.* 109; *Quod
Det.* 116–18), and Plutarch, both in the preface of *de Iside et Osiride*

---

[16] Cf. Varro's account of Antiochus' position in Cicero, *Acad. Post.* 17 ff.

[17] As reported by Simplicius, *in Phys.* 181. 10 ff. Diels. On the face of it, Eudorus is
here simply reporting the views of 'the Pythagoreans', but it is a reasonable assumption, I think, that he subscribes to them himself, especially since his scheme is *not*
attested for any known Pythagoreans.

and later in the treatise (372e), seems to describe such a figure, whom he identifies with Isis.[18] Elsewhere, as in the *Didaskalikos* (chs. 10 and 14), the world-soul is depicted as an irrational entity, requiring 'awakening' by the Demiurge, and even in the latter part of *de Iside et Osiride* (369 ff.) Plutarch makes Isis rejoice at 'impregnation' by the *logos* of God, thus producing somewhat of a discrepancy with the portrayal in the preface.

The reason for the vacillation as regards the status of this figure seems to lie in another development characteristic of Middle Platonism, deriving not from the Old Academy but rather, it would seem, arising as a development from Stoicism, that is, the distinguishing of a first and second god. The distinction is between a completely transcendent, self-intelligizing figure, and an active, demiurgic one. The later Platonists, from Antiochus on, adopted the Stoic *logos* into their system as the active aspect of God in the world, and when they reinstated a transcendent, immaterial first principle, as did Eudorus and later thinkers, they arrived at two entities, basically the Demiurge of the *Timaeus*, the other the Good of the *Republic* and the One of the first hypothesis of the *Parmenides*. In Philo, partly, no doubt, because of his strong monotheistic inclinations, we have a contrast rather between God and his *logos* than between a first and second god, but later Platonists such as Apuleius (e.g. *de Plat.* 1. 6. 193), Numenius (Frs. 12 and 16, Des Places), or A. himself, postulate two distinct gods, both intellects, certainly, but one in repose and turned in upon itself, the other in motion and directed outwards, both above and below itself. Some Neopythagoreans, such as Moderatus of Gades (late 1st cent. AD)[19] and Numenius, go further and postulate a triad of 'ones' or gods in descending order, deriving the inspiration for this, perhaps, from a curious passage of the *Second Platonic Letter* (312e), but also, in all probability, from a metaphysical interpretation of the first three hypotheses of the second part of the *Parmenides*. In either case, however, the third member of the trio turns out to be the world-soul, so that the basic metaphysical scheme is unchanged.

Besides these basic entities, the Platonist cosmos was filled with subordinate, intermediate beings, the race of daemons, which A. notices briefly in chapter 15 of his treatise. There are broadly two theories on the nature of daemons, one static, so to speak, the other

[18] See my article, 'Female Principles in Platonism', (1986: 107–23), now repr. in Dillon (1991).
[19] For Moderatus, see E. R. Dodds (1928: 129–42), and J. M. Rist (1962: 389–401).

dynamic, and both are represented within the period of Middle Platonism, though A. seems to adhere rather to the former view.

Xenocrates, in the Old Academy, had already elaborated on Plato's doctrine of the intermediate nature of daemons (as propounded in *Symp.* 202e–203e), expressing it in geometrical terms (*ap.* Plut. *Def. Or.* 416c–d). Such daemons sound like permanent fixtures in the universe, though the question of their relationship with disembodied souls is unclear in the evidence available to us. The alternative theory, represented by Plutarch and by Apuleius (particularly in the *de Deo Socratis*), is the one according to which daemons are in fact souls, either on their way up or on their way down the scale of being, either heading for complete purification (and thus divinization) in the sun, or for embodiment on the earth (*Def. Or.* 415b). For this theory Plutarch could appeal back to the authority of Empedocles (*de Is. et Os.* 361c).

The theory is not presented by Plutarch with complete coherence, however; the static theory also appears. In particular, evil daemons are recognized, as they were by Xenocrates. Are these daemons permanent elements in the universe, or are they souls in the process of being punished for misdeeds committed during incarnation? Both possibilities seem to be entertained by Plutarch.[20] Truly evil daemons, as opposed to avenging agencies of God, are not a properly Platonic conception, but rather a concession to popular belief, or perhaps an influence from Persian dualism. 'Avenging' daemons, on the other hand, are a more acceptable idea, since they are subordinate to God, and their activity is ultimately beneficent. Even Philo of Alexandria finds such entities compatible with his monotheism (e.g. *de Gig.* 6–9; 12; 16; *Somn.* 1. 134–5; 141–2).

Besides daemons proper, there is also mention made of heroes and angels, the latter possibly in origin non-Hellenic, but certainly accepted in Neoplatonism into the Platonic universe. Heroes are more respectable, but the distinction between them and daemons in the Middle-Platonic period is not quite clear. The Stoic Posidonius wrote a treatise on the subject, but it is lost. One distinction can be that heroes are souls formerly embodied, but this distinction assumes a permanent class of non-embodied souls, which is only acceptable on the 'static' theory. Whatever the differences in detail, however, it is

---

[20] On the knotty problem of Plutarch's demonology, see the comprehensive study of F. E. Brenk, *In Mist Apparelled* (1977).

common ground for all Platonists that between God and man there must be a host of intermediaries, that God may not be contaminated or disturbed by too close an involvement with matter.

The Platonic theory of forms suffered various transformations during our period. We are hampered, of course, by not really knowing what stage the theory of forms had reached in Plato's maturest thought. It is probable, however, that already for Plato, by the end of his life, the forms were quasi-numerical entities, though being explicitly differentiated from mathematical numbers by being unique in their kinds. Neither Speusippus nor Xenocrates liked the distinction between forms and 'mathematicals', and each collapsed it in different directions, Speusippus rejecting the 'form-numbers' (though apparently postulating many other layers of reality, Fr. 29 Tarán), Xenocrates declaring forms to be numbers (Fr. 34 Heinze), but rejecting mathematicals. The definitive Platonist doctrine on the question 'of what things there are forms', which we see set out in chapter 9 of the *Didaskalikos*, may very well be due to Xenocrates.

When the theory of forms surfaces again with Antiochus of Ascalon, it looks very much as though they have become assimilated in his mind to the Stoic 'common notions' (*koinai ennoiai*), which would dispose of their transcendental aspect (cf. Cicero, *Acad. Post.* 30 ff.). For the source behind Cicero's *Tusculan Disputations*, book 1, admittedly, they still seem to be transcendent entities; there is 'recollection' of them, which involves their existence outside the human mind (sect. 57). But it is not certain that the source of *Tusc.* 1 is Antiochus, and even there it is by no means clear that we are dealing with the Platonic forms in their pristine guise; it is much more probable that they are to be seen by this time as thoughts in the mind of God.

With the assimilation of the Platonic Demiurge to the Stoic Logos, the situating of the forms in the mind of God becomes more or less inevitable (though the influence of Aristotle, who explains technical production precisely in terms of the presence of the form of the artefact in the soul, may have some influence here as well). When the distinction is later made between a first and a second god, the forms gravitate towards the mind of the second, demiurgic god. It seems also as if they were thought to exist in the world-soul in a secondary, 'extended' form; at least we find in Plutarch and the later Pythagoreans the equation of the soul with the Platonic 'mathematicals', which in the context of Middle Platonism correspond to something intermediate between forms proper and sensible objects.[21] But if there was significant theorizing in the Middle-Platonic period on the theory of forms, not much sign of it has survived. A. summarizes, in chapter 9 of his work, the accepted Middle-Platonic doctrines as to what there are forms of, and what relationship they have to other entities, such as God and the physical cosmos, but he gives little hint of serious thought as to their nature or their relevance to a theory of knowledge. Plutarch wrote a work (now lost) entitled *Where are the Forms Situated?* (*Catalogue of Lamprias* 67), but it probably did not raise any really basic questions. The complacency of the later Platonists about the theory of forms is, on the face of it, extraordinary, considering the powerful arguments that Aristotle had directed against it. Only, perhaps, in the first part of Plotinus' *Ennead* 6. 7 (chs. 1–15) do we get something like a searching analysis of the topic.

Another issue that surely merited serious questioning, but does not seem to have received it, is that of the relationship of the forms to matter, and the related question of the creation of the physical world out of the basic atomic triangles. I can discern no sign of philosophic questioning behind A.'s summary of Platonic physical theory in chapters 12–13 of the *Didaskalikos*, which may be taken to represent the established second-century AD position on these questions.

For Antiochus, who accepted Stoic materialism, the problem of the relation of the immaterial to the material did not arise, but for all subsequent Platonists it was, one would think, a very serious issue. We do have the title of a work by Plutarch (*Catalogue of Lamprias* 68), *The Manner of the Participation of Matter in the Forms, namely that it constitutes the Primary Bodies*, but we have no idea what was in it, other than what is suggested by the title. As for A., he simply summarizes the *Timaeus*, and leaves it at that.

The only issue on which we find much dispute in this area (and even this disagreement is partly vacillation) is whether we are to accept a four-element or a five-element universe, rejecting or accepting Aristotle's theory of ether as the element proper to the heavenly realm. Even this tends to dissolve into a dispute about formulations. Many Platonists assimilated Aristotle's ether to the Stoic pure fire, and the Stoics recognized that the fire of the heavenly realm was of a superior type to that of our experience, though they were not specific as to its innate circular motion. We can observe men like Philo of

---

[21] For Plutarch, cf. *de An. Proc.* 1013d; 1023b; for the Neopythagoreans Moderatus of Gades and Nicomachus of Gerasa, see the passages quoted by Merlan (1968), 12–33.

Alexandria (e.g. *de Plant.* 1–8; *Heres* 283; *QG* 4. 8), Plutarch (e.g. *de Fac.* 930e, 943d–e; *de E.* 390b), and Apuleius (*de Deo Socratis*, 8), apparently veering back and forth on this question within one and the same treatise, which seems to indicate that they found the two theories compatible—perhaps by equating Aristotelian ether with the purest form of fire, the Stoic *pyr tekhnikon*. A. himself seems to vacillate in this way between chapters 13 and 15 of the *Didaskalikos*, and this presumably is the explanation (see Commentary ad loc.). On one basic issue all were agreed, however, that the heavenly realm was qualitatively different from our own—intermediate, indeed, between the sublunar and the intelligible realms, a place of unchanging divine entities pursuing perfectly regular courses. Once this is agreed, the issue of four or five elements becomes secondary.

If the Middle Platonists seem uninterested in questions of what we would term 'physics', they are after all only reflecting the non-scientific bias of the age in which they lived. After the active period of Alexandrian scientific speculation, the civilized world relapsed into an attitude so anti-experimental that a man such as Plutarch, if he wished to find out the answer to some practical question, would turn instinctively to some 'authority', such as the pseudo-Aristotelian *Problems*, rather than conduct an experiment himself. His *Quaestiones Conviviales* are full of futile discussions on matters of this sort, with the learned disputants quoting ancient authorities at each other on practical questions which could only be solved by experiment. Only in the field of medicine, in the person of Galen, and to some extent in the field of astronomy, in the person of Ptolemy, does one find a refreshing reliance on experiment and first-hand observation—though neither Galen nor Ptolemy should be thought of as isolated figures within their disciplines. It is rather the case that the philosophers seem to lose interest in scientific enquiry than that the scientists lose interest in experimenting.

4.3 Ethics

All the main concerns of ethics had appeared already in the Old Academy, but they acquire new ramifications in the Middle-Platonic period. The first issue is, logically, the purpose of life, or, as it was termed, 'the end of goods' (*telos agathōn*). This can also be taken as the definition of happiness,[22] although A. accords these topics

---

[22] Cf. Arius Didymus (*ap.* Stob. 2. 48. 6), who tells us that the Platonists say that happiness is synonymous with the *telos*.

separate chapters (27 and 28), taking happiness first. Definitions of happiness were attributed to all the heads of the Old Academy, Speusippus, Xenocrates, and Polemon. Speusippus defined it as 'the state of perfection in things natural' (Fr. 77 Tarán); Xenocrates as 'the possession of the excellence (*aretē*) proper to us and of the power subservient to it' (Fr. 77 Heinze); and Polemon as 'a self-sufficiency (*autarkeia*) in respect of all, or at least of the most and greatest goods' (*ap.* Clement of Alexandria, *Strom.* 7. 32). For Speusippus, the *telos* was reported to be 'freedom from disturbance' (*aokhlēsia*, Fr. 77 Tarán); for Xenocrates, 'the elimination of all causes of disturbance in life' (Fr. 4 Heinze); and for Polemon, 'living a virtuous life while enjoying those primary things that nature recommends to man'. This last definition is relayed to us by Antiochus, via Cicero (*Tusc.* 5. 39; *Fin.* 4. 14; *Acad.* 2. 131), and so may be suspected of being doctored in the direction of Stoicism, but it seems to me equally plausible that Polemon in his ethics largely anticipated, or at least agreed with, the Stoics. What seems to emerge from the Old Academy, then, is a distinctly this-worldly emphasis when discussing the purpose of life, and that is what we find also in Antiochus.·

When we turn later to Alexandrian Platonism, however, in the person of Eudorus, we find that the Stoicizing definition of 'life in accordance with nature' adopted by Antiochus has been abandoned in favour of a more spiritual, and perhaps more truly Platonic, ideal of 'likeness to God' (*homoiōsis theōi*), derived from the famous passage of the *Theaetetus* (176b), and this formula remained the distinctive Platonist definition of the *telos* ever afterward, appearing duly in chapter 28 of the *Didaskalikos*.

A second key issue is whether virtue is sufficient to happiness. By Antiochus' time the battle lines on this issue had already been clearly drawn between the Peripatetics and the Stoics, and the Platonists had to take their pick, there being proof-texts in the dialogues to support either position. Antiochus, although Stoic in all else, sided here with the Peripatetics (and the Old Academy), declaring that for complete happiness all three classes of good were required in some measure, goods of the body and external goods as well as the virtues (cf. e.g. Cic. *Fin.* 5. 26–7; *Acad. Post.* 22–3). Once again, he was opposed by Eudorus, who declared that the two inferior classes of good could not be accounted an integral part of happiness, or the *telos*, thus siding with the Stoics (*ap.* Stob. *Anth.* 2. 55. 22 ff. Wachs.).[23] This time,

---

[23] If we may assume, as I think (cf. Dillon 1977: 116), that Arius is here taking his account of Platonic doctrine from Eudorus.

however, the argument was not over. All through the Middle-Platonic period the two alternatives secured adherents, Plutarch (in *de Virtute Morali*) and Calvenus Taurus (*ap.* Aulus Gellius, *NA* 12. 5), for instance, agreeing with Antiochus and the Peripatetics, Atticus (*Fr.* 2 Des Places) with the Stoics. A. himself, in chapter 27, takes up a distinctly Stoicizing position. Along with this taking of sides there often went a certain amount of polemic, anti-Stoic or anti-Aristotelian, as the case might be.

A question with considerable consequences for ethics, though it also has aspects belonging, in the ancient classification, to 'physics', is that of free will and necessity.[24] Before the Stoics, and in particular Chrysippus, had stated the problem of determinism in its starkest form, the question had not been one of great urgency. Plato treats of it only in rather poetical form, in the myths of the *Republic* and the *Phaedrus*, as well as in book 10 of the *Laws*, and raises more problems than he solves, but, as does Aristotle, he maintains a belief in personal freedom of choice. Aristotle, in the *Nicomachean Ethics*, book 3, treats the suggestion that there is no such thing as freedom of choice as a mere sophistic paradox. As for the Old Academy, Xenocrates did write an essay *On Fate*, but we do not know what he said in it. However, he can hardly have seriously addressed the problem of determinism.

For the Middle Platonists, on the other hand, the problem of free will and necessity, with which is linked up that of God's providence (*pronoia*), could not be dismissed so easily, and they did not find much help in Plato or Aristotle, though they did make appeal to key passages of both—in particular to the speech of Adrasteia in *Republic* 10 (617d–e). We cannot be sure what Antiochus' stance was, as the source or sources on which Cicero is drawing in *de Fato* are uncertain, nor can we say anything about Eudorus' position. It is Philo, in fact, who gives us the first defence of the Platonist position (in the *de Providentia* I; cf. also *Deus* 47–8), which asserts both the freedom of the will and the existence of providence against the Stoic doctrine of fate (*heimarmenē*), though with more rhetorical vigour than logical force. Plutarch also touches on the theme repeatedly, though his most serious discussions of the subject have not survived. The document *On Fate* surviving under his name is certainly not by him, but it is of great interest, as containing a most elaborate scholastic theory of fate,

---

[24] See the useful discussion by R. W. Sharples in the introduction to his edition of Alexander of Aphrodisias, *On Fate* (1983: 3–14).

of which reflections can be found in Apuleius, *de Platone* 1. 12, Calcidius' *Commentary on the Timaeus* (chs. 142–90), and Nemesius, *On the Nature of Man* (ch. 38), though *not*, we may note, in the *Didaskalikos* (ch. 26), where A. gives a summary of what seems to be the main-line Platonist position. All in all, however, the Middle Platonists, though producing many scholastic formulae of considerable subtlety, failed to solve the problem, and bequeathed it in all its complexity to Plotinus, who composed a magnificent, if inconclusive treatise on the topic in *Enneads* 3. 2–3.

4.4 Conclusion

Throughout the Middle-Platonic period (approx. 80 BC to AD 250), we find philosophers oscillating between the twin poles of attraction constituted by Peripateticism and Stoicism, but adding to the mixture of these influences a strong commitment (after Antiochus, at least) to a transcendent supreme principle, and a non-material intelligible world above and beyond this one, which stands as a paradigm for it. The influence of Pythagoras and what was believed to be his doctrine was also powerful throughout the period, though particularly so on those thinkers who liked to think of themselves as 'Pythagoreans', such as Moderatus of Gades, Nicomachus of Gerasa, and Numenius of Apamea. A. shows not much trace of this.

On most topics, as we have seen, particularly in the sphere of ethics, no strict canons of orthodoxy prevailed. What we find rather is a spectrum of acceptable Platonist positions, among which an individual philosopher might pick and choose while still remaining part of the tradition. Nevertheless, despite all the variations in doctrine that emerge in the Middle-Platonic period, we can observe the growth of a consistent body of thought, constituting a Platonic heritage that could be handed on, first to Plotinus and his followers, and then to later ages. Of this heritage, A.'s little handbook is, for us at least, to whom so much else is lost, an important part—irrespective of what influence it may have had among its contemporaries, which was probably not great.

5. A Note on the Manuscript Tradition, and on Previous Editions and Translations

5.1 The Manuscript

The oldest and best manuscripts of the *Didaskalikos* are the Parisinus graecus 1962 (P), dating from the ninth century (but split up in the thirteenth, when certain works mentioned in the Table of Contents, including some works of Albinus, were lost); and the Vindobonensis philosophicus graecus 314 (V), copied in the year 925 by a certain John the Grammarian from a manuscript owned by Bishop Arethas of Caesarea. V, though most interesting in its provenance, is rather carelessly copied (perhaps in some haste), and so somewhat less valuable than P. On the basis of their many similarities, both in the text and in the scholia, Whittaker (1990, intro. p. xxxix) conjectures that Arethas' manuscript is itself a copy of P.

At any rate, all the other manuscripts, of which the oldest are Vat. gr. 1390 and Vat. gr. 1144 (both of the thirteenth or fourteenth century), are copies of P, and thus of no independent importance, though sometimes useful for conjectures. Whittaker lists twenty-seven, dating from the fourteenth to the sixteenth century, attesting to the popularity of the treatise in the Renaissance.

5.2 Printed Texts

The first printed edition of the *Didaskalikos* was that published as an appendix to the Aldine edition of Apuleius edited by Francesco D'Asola, brother-in-law of Aldus Manutius. It seems to have been based on a descendant of Vat. gr. 1144, though revised with the aid of a manuscript from the family of Vat. gr. 1390. This text was reprinted in Paris in 1532 by Michael Vascosanus, together with the translation of Marsilio Ficino. (A previous Latin translation had been made by Pietro Balbi already by 1460, and published in Rome in 1469 by Sweynheim and Pannartz, also as an appendix to the works of Apuleius, thus making A. the first Greek author to receive a printed edition, albeit in Latin translation!)

A new edition, prepared by Arsenius Apostolides, was published in Venice in 1535 by Stefano di Sabbio. It was based on a lost descendant of Vat. gr. 1390. Then in 1567 Dionysius Lambinus published in

Paris a text with translation and commentary, essentially a revision of the Aldine edition, but adorned with many useful conjectures.

In the next century, Daniel Heinsius published two editions of the *Didaskalikos*, both as appendices to editions of Maximus of Tyre (Leiden, 1607 and 1614), basing himself on the Aldine edition, and to a lesser extent on that of Lambinus, but also making some use (though not as much as he should) of the best manuscript P, which had recently entered the royal collection in Paris.

An edition by John Fell in Oxford in 1667 largely reproduces the second edition of Heinsius, as do those of Bortoli in Venice (1748) and Fischer in Leipzig (1783). Fischer is actually the first editor to mention V, but he makes no apparent use of it.

The first modern edition, and the one which remained basic until the recent Budé edition of John Whittaker, is the Teubner edition of C. F. Hermann (Leipzig, 1853), who prints the text of the *Didaskalikos* in volume vi of his collected edition of Plato's works. Hermann did not himself examine manuscripts, but relied on collations by colleagues of P and Par. gr. 1309 (a descendant of Vat. gr. 1390). His is a far superior edition to that of Heinsius, however, since he made proper use of what is in fact the best manuscript.

The edition of Fr. Dübner (Firmin-Didot, Paris, 1873) is no improvement on that of Hermann, which it follows very closely, nor really was the Budé edition of Pierre Louis (Paris, 1945), though it did provide a translation and some useful notes.

John Whittaker, in his new Budé edition (Paris, 1990—the French translation is provided by Pierre Louis), has undertaken complete collations of all twenty-seven manuscripts (some of which are fragmentary), and has set the text on a footing that is hardly likely to call for much revision in the future. He was able also to make use of an unpublished edition prepared in the 1930s by R. E. Witt (author of *Albinus and the History of Middle Platonism*), which has the distinction of being the first to give due weight to the readings of V. I have very largely accepted the text of Whittaker, but in a number of places have ventured to adopt readings different from his, for some of which I am indebted to Professor Matthias Baltes of Münster, who has kindly communicated to me his annotations on the text.

5.3 Translations

Apart from the early Latin translations of Balbi, Ficino, and Lambinus mentioned above, the *Didaskalikos* has been translated into modern tongues as follows: into English, by Thomas Stanley, as part of an ambitious work entitled *The History of Philosophy: containing the lives, opinions, actions and discourse of the philosophers of every sect* (London, 1656); and by George Burges, as an appendix to a translation of the works of Plato (London, 1854);[25] into French by J.-J. Combes-Doumous (Paris, 1800), and by Pierre Louis, in both the above-mentioned Budé editions; into Italian, by Giuseppe Invernizzi (Rome, 1976), in a two-volume work which also comprises a set of introductory essays and useful, if brief, notes.

There is also the unpublished translation of R. E. Witt, which has been kindly communicated to me by John Whittaker. We should note in addition the useful French translation of chapter 10, with comments, by A.-J. Festugière, in volume iv of his great work *La Révélation d'Hermès Trismégiste* (Paris, 1954), 161–2.

In the composition of the present work, I have been content to rely on the text and apparatus of Whittaker, and have derived great benefit also from his notes. The notes and essays of Invernizzi have also frequently been helpful, as has the unpublished translation of Witt.

The page numbers in the present translation are those of Hermann's edition, but the line numbers are co-ordinated with those of Whittaker, who uses Hermann's page numbers, but supplies his own line numbers.

---

[25] There is also a translation by Jeremiah Reedy (Grand Rapids, Mich., 1991).

TRANSLATION

1. Definition of Philosophy and the Philosopher

1. The following is a presentation of the principal doctrines of Plato. Philosophy is a striving for wisdom, *or* the freeing and turning around of the soul from the body, when we turn towards the intelligible and what truly is; and wisdom is the science of things divine and human.

2. The term 'philosopher' is derived from 'philosophy' in the same way as 'musician' from 'music'. The first necessity is that he be naturally apt at those branches of learning which have the capacity to fit him for, and lead him towards, the knowledge of intelligible being, which is not subject to error or change. Next, he must be enamoured of the truth, and in no way tolerate falsehood. Furthermore, he must also be endowed with a temperate nature, and, in relation to the passionate part of the soul, he must be naturally restrained. For he who devotes himself to the study of reality and turns his desires in that direction would not be impressed by (bodily) pleasures.

3. The prospective philosopher must also be endowed with liberality of mind, for nothing is so inimical as small-mindedness to a soul which is proposing to contemplate things divine and human. He must also possess natural affinity for justice, just as he must towards truth and liberality and temperance; and he should also be endowed with a ready capacity to learn and a good memory, for these too contribute to the formation of the philosopher.

4. These natural qualities, if they are combined with correct education and suitable nurturing, render one perfect in respect of virtue, but if one neglects them, they become the cause of great evils. These Plato was accustomed to name homonymously with the virtues, temperance and courage and justice.

2. The Contemplative and the Practical Life

1. There are two types of life, the theoretical and the practical. The summation of the theoretical life lies in the knowledge of the truth, while that of the practical life lies in the performance of what is counselled by reason. The theoretical life is of primary value; the practical

of secondary, and involved with necessity. The truth of this will become plain from what follows.

2. Contemplation, then, is the activity of the intellect when intelligizing the intelligibles, while action is that activity of a rational soul which takes place by way of the body. The soul engaged in contemplation of the divine and the thoughts of the divine is said to be in a good state, and this state of the soul is called 'wisdom', which may be asserted to be no other than likeness to the divine. For this reason such a state would be of priority, valuable, most desirable and most proper to us, free of (external) hindrance, entirely within our power, and cause of the end in life which is set before us. Action, on the other hand, and the active life, being pursued through the body, are subject to external hindrance, and would be engaged in when circumstances demand, by practising the transferral to human affairs of the visions of the contemplative life.

3. For the good man will enter upon public life whenever he sees it being conducted badly by certain parties, considering as necessitated by circumstances serving as a general, or on a jury, or as an ambassador, while he would reckon best in the sphere of action, and primary on that level, such activities as lawgiving, and the establishment of constitutions, and the education of the young. It is proper, then, on the basis of what we have said, for the philosopher by no means to abandon contemplation, but always to foster and develop this, turning to the practical life only as something secondary.

3. The Parts of Philosophy

1. The concern of the philosopher, according to Plato, would seem to be channelled in three directions: (1) the contemplation and understanding of what exists, (2) the performance of what is noble, and (3) the actual study of reason. The understanding of what exists is called 'theoretical' (philosophy), that which concerns what is to be done 'practical', and the knowledge of reason 'dialectical'.

2. This last is divided into the processes of division, definition, ⟨analysis⟩, induction, and syllogistic; and this last in turn is divided into the demonstrative, which concerns the necessary syllogism, the epicheirematic, which deals with syllogisms based on reputable opinion, and thirdly the rhetorical, which concerns the enthymeme, which

is termed an 'incomplete' syllogism; and in addition sophisms. This
latter activity is not really a primary concern of the philosopher, but
is something unavoidable.

3. Of practical philosophy, one part is concerned with the care of
morals, another with the administration of the household, another   40
with the state and its preservation. Of these the first is called ethics,
the second economics, and the third politics.

4. Of theoretical philosophy, that part which is concerned with the
motionless and primary causes and such as are divine is called theo-   154
logy; that which is concerned with the motion of the heavenly bodies,
their revolutions and periodic returns, and the constitution of the visible world is called physics; and that which makes use of geometry
and the other branches of mathematics is called mathematics.   5

5. Such, then, being the division and the partition of the various
sorts of philosophy, we must first speak of the theory of the dialectic
according to the doctrine of Plato, and first of all about the faculty of
judgement.

4. The Judging of Truth and Theory of Knowledge

1. Since there is something that judges, and there is something   10
that is judged, there must also be something that results from these,
and that may be termed judgement. In the strictest sense, one might
declare judgement to be the act of judgement, but more broadly that
which judges. This may be taken in two senses: (1) that *by the agency
of which* what is judged is judged, and (2) that *by means of which* it is   15
judged. Of these the former would be the intellect in us, while that
'by means of which' is the physical instrument which judges—primarily truth, but consequently also falsehood; and this is none other than
our reasoning faculty working on the physical level.

2. To take a clearer view of the matter, the judging agent might be
said to be the philosopher, by whom things are judged, but equally   20
well it could be taken to be the reason, by means of which the truth
is judged, and which was what we declared to be the instrument of
judgement. Reason in turn takes two forms: the one is completely
ungraspable and unerring, while the other is only free from error
when it is engaged in the cognition of reality.

25 Of these the former is possible for God, but impossible for men, while the second is possible also for men.

3. This latter, too, has two aspects: one concerned with the objects of intellection, the other with the objects of sensation. Of these, the former, that concerning the objects of intellection, is science and scientific reason, while that concerning sense-objects is opinion, and reason based on opinion. For this reason scientific reason possesses

30 stability and permanence, inasmuch as it concerns principles which are stable and permanent, while the reason based on persuasion and opinion possesses a high degree of (mere) likelihood, by reason of the fact that it is not concerned with permanent objects.

4. Science, which relates to the objects of intellection, and opinion, which relates to sense-objects, have as their originating principles intellection and sensation. Sensation is an affection of the soul

35 brought about through the medium of the body, presenting the message primarily of the faculty affected. Whenever, in the case of perception, an impression occurs in the soul through the medium of the sense-organs, which is what sensation consists in, and this impression does not subsequently fade away through passage of time, but remains

40 and is preserved, such a preservation is termed memory.

5. Opinion is the combination of memory and sensation. For when we first come up against a sense-object and a sensory perception

155 arises in us from it, and from that a memory, and then we come up against the same sense-object again, we put together the previous memory with the second sensory perception, and we say within ourselves, for instance, 'Ah, Socrates!', or 'horse', or 'fire', and so on, and it is this that is termed 'opinion', when we have put together the

5 pre-existent memory with the present sensory perception. When these two prove concordant on being juxtaposed, there arises true opinion, but when they become transposed (with something else), false opinion. For instance, if someone who possesses a memory-image of Socrates meets up with Plato, and thinks, by reason of some resem-

10 blance, that he has once again met Socrates, and then, taking the sense-impression received from Plato as being from Socrates, links it to the memory-image which he has of Socrates, the opinion arising from that will be false.

That in which memory and sense-perception come to be is likened by Plato (*Tht.* 191c) to a wax mould. When the soul, having moulded

15 its opinions out of sense-perception and memory, looks with its think-

ing faculty upon these, in the same way as upon those things from
which they derive, Plato calls such an activity 'delineation' (*Phlb.*
39b), and sometimes 'imagination' (*Tht.* 161e; *Sph.* 263d). Thinking
he declares to be the dialogue of the soul with itself (*Sph.* 263e), and .
speech to be the current proceeding from it through the mouth   20
accompanied by sound (ibid.).

6. Intellection is the activity of the intellect as it contemplates the
primary objects of intellection. There seem to be two forms of this,
the one prior to the soul's coming to be in this body, when it is contemplating by itself the objects of intellection, the other after it has
been installed in this body. Of these, the former, that which existed
before the soul came to be in the body, is called intellection in the   25
strict sense, while, once it has come to be in the body, what was then
called intellection is now called 'natural conception', being, as it were,
an intellection stored up in the soul. So when we say that intellection
is the first principle of scientific reasoning, we are not referring to
what is now called this, but rather to that which existed when the   30
soul was apart from the body, which, as we said, was in that context
called 'intellection', but in its present state 'natural conception'. The
natural concept is called by him, 'simple item of knowledge', 'the
wing of the soul' (*Phdr.* 246e), and sometimes 'memory'.

7. It is from these 'simple forms of knowledge' that natural and   35
scientific reasoning is constituted, which arises in us by nature. So
then, since reason exists on the level both of scientific knowledge and
of opinion, and since there exist both intellection and sense-perception,
there exist also objects of these, that is to say, intelligible and sensible
objects; and since of intelligible objects some are primary, such as the
(transcendent) Ideas, and others secondary, such as the forms in mat-   40
ter, which are inseparable from matter, so also intellection will be
twofold, the one kind of primary objects, the other of secondary.

And in turn, since of sense-objects some are primary, such as qual- 156
ities, e.g. colour, or whiteness, and others accidental, such as 'white'
or 'coloured', and following on these the composite entity, such as fire
or honey, even so there will be one sort of sense-perception concerned with the primary objects, called 'primary', and another con-   5
cerned with secondary, called 'secondary'.

The primary intelligibles are judged by intellection not without the
aid of scientific reason, by means of a kind of comprehension, not discursive reasoning, while the secondary are judged by scientific reason

not without the aid of intellection. The primary and secondary sensibles are judged by sense-perception not without the aid of opinion-
10 based reason, while the composite is judged by opinion-based reason, not without the aid of sense-perception.

8. Accepting that the intelligible world is the primary object of intellection, and that the sensible world is a composite, the intelligible world is judged by intellection along with reason, that is to say, not without the aid of reason, and the sensible world by opinion-based
15 reason not without the aid of sense-perception. Again, accepting the existence of contemplation and action, right reason does not judge in the same way the objects of contemplation as it does those of action, but in the case of contemplation it enquires into truth and non-truth, while in the sphere of action it enquires into what is appropriate and what is alien (to the agent), and what is the nature of the action. For
20 it is by virtue of possessing a natural concept of the fine and the good, by using our reason, and by referring to natural concepts as to definite units of measurement that we judge whether certain given actions are of one nature or another.

5. Dialectic

25   1. Dialectic, according to Plato, has as its fundamental purpose first the examination of the essence of every thing whatsoever, and then of its accidents. It enquires into the nature of each thing either 'from above', by means of division and definition, or 'from below', by means of analysis. Accidental qualities which belong to essences it examines either from the standpoint of individuals, by induction, or
30 from the standpoint of universals, by syllogistic. So, logically, dialectic comprises the procedures of division, definition, analysis, and in addition induction and syllogistic.

35   2. Division may consist in dividing a genus into species, or a whole into parts. An instance would be when we divide the soul into a rational part and a passionate part, and the passionate in turn into the spirit and the appetitive. Again, we may take the division of speech into meanings, as when one and the same word is applied to more
40 than one thing; or again, the division of accidents between different subjects, as when we say that of goods, some pertain to the soul, others to the body, and others are external; or the division of subjects

according to their various accidents, as when we say that of men some
are good, others bad, and others middling.   157

3. It is primarily, however, the division of the genus into species
that one must make use of for the purpose of discerning what each
thing is in itself by virtue of its essence. This, however, could not be
achieved without definition. Definition arises from division in the following manner: when one wants to subject a thing to definition, one   5
must first of all grasp the genus, as for instance in the case of man,
'living thing'; then one must divide this according to its proximate
differentiae until one arrives at the species, as for instance into rational and irrational, and mortal and immortal, with the result that if
the proximate differentiae are added to the genus which is composed   10
of them, the definition of man results.

4. Analysis comprises three types: the first is an ascent from sense-
objects to the primary intelligibles; the second is an ascent through
what can be demonstrated and indicated to propositions which are
indemonstrable and immediate; and the third is that which advances
upwards from a hypothesis to non-hypothetical first principles.

5. The first type is employed when, for example, we pass from that   15
beauty which is connected with bodies to the beauty in souls, and
from this to that in activities, and then from this to that manifested
in laws, and then to the 'great sea of Beauty' (*Smp.* 210d), so that by
this transition we may finally discover the Beautiful Itself.   20

The second type of analysis is as follows: one must postulate what
is being sought, and then consider what other propositions are
antecedent to it, and demonstrate these by ascending from (logically)
later propositions to more primary ones, until we come to that which   25
is (absolutely) primary and admitted (by all), and beginning from this
we will arrive at what is being sought by a procedure of synthesis.
For example, if I am enquiring whether the soul is immortal, I first
postulate this very thing, and then enquire if it is ever-moving.
Having demonstrated this, I enquire if what is ever-moving is self-
moving; and in turn, having demonstrated this, I investigate whether   30
what is self-moving is a first principle of motion; and then, whether a
first principle is ungenerated, which is taken as universally agreed, the
ungenerated being also imperishable. And starting from this proposition, which has the quality of self-evidence, I produce by synthesis
such a proof as follows: a first principle is something ungenerated and
imperishable, the first principle of motion is the self-moved; but the   35

self-moved is soul; therefore the soul is imperishable and ungenerated and immortal.

6. Analysis from a hypothesis, on the other hand, is as follows: when seeking to establish any proposition, one postulates that very thing, and then sees what follows from one's hypothesis; and after that, if one has to give an account of the hypothesis, one postulates
40 another hypothesis, and investigates in turn if the former hypothesis follows from this other, and one continues to do this until one arrives at a principle which is non-hypothetical.

158 7. Induction is any logical procedure which passes from like to like, or from the particular to the general. Induction is particularly useful for activating the natural concepts.

6. Syllogistic

5 1. That part of discourse which we call the proposition comprises two species, affirmation and negation. An example of affirmation is: 'Socrates is walking.' An example of negation is: 'Socrates is not walking.' Of affirmations and negations some are universal, others particular. An example of a particular affirmation is: 'Some pleasure is
10 good'; of a particular negation: 'Some pleasure is not good.' Of a universal affirmation an example would be: 'All that is base is evil'; of a universal negation: 'None of the things that are base is good.'

15 2. Of propositions some are categorical, others hypothetical. Categorical are simple propositions, such as: 'Everything just is fine.' Hypotheticals are those which exhibit consequentiality or incompatibility.

3. Plato employs the procedure of syllogism for the purposes both of refutation and of demonstration, refuting false statements through
20 investigation, and demonstrating true ones through a type of exposition. A syllogism is a form of words in which, when certain assumptions are made, something other than what has been assumed necessarily follows from those very assumptions. Of syllogisms, some are categorical, others hypothetical, and others a mixture of the two.
25 Those of which both the premisses and the conclusions are simple propositions are categorical, while those compounded of hypothetical premisses are hypothetical, and those which comprise both sorts are mixed.

4. Plato uses demonstrative syllogisms in his expository dialogues, syllogisms based on widely held opinion when dealing with sophists and young people, and eristic ones when dealing with those properly 30 called eristics, such as Euthydemus, for example, or Hippias.

5. There are three figures of categorical syllogisms. The first is that in which the common term is predicated of the first term, and is the subject of the other; the second is that in which the common term is predicated of both; and the third is that in which it is the subject of 35 both (by 'terms' I mean the parts of the propositions, e.g. in the proposition 'Man is an animal', we say that 'man' is a term, and also 'animal'). Plato, in propounding arguments, frequently makes use of the first figure, and also of the second and the third. He uses the first 40 figure in the *Alcibiades* (115a ff.) thus: '(All) just things are fine; (all) fine things are good; therefore (all) just things are good.' The second figure he uses in the *Parmenides* (137e), as follows: 'What does not have parts is neither straight nor curved; what partakes in shape is 159 either straight or curved; therefore what does not have parts does not partake in shape.' The third figure he uses in the same work, as follows: 'That which partakes in shape is qualified; that which partakes 5 in shape is limited; therefore something that is qualified is limited.'

6. We shall find hypothetical syllogisms used by him when propounding arguments in many of his works, and most of all in the *Parmenides* we find such arguments as the following (137d): 'If the One does not have parts, it does not have a beginning, a middle, and 10 an end; if it does not have a beginning, middle, and end, it does not have limit; if it does not have limit, it does not partake of shape; therefore, if the One does not have parts, then neither does it partake of shape.' In the second hypothetical figure, which most people 15 regard as the third, according to which the common term follows the two extremes, Plato reasons as follows, in the course of an argument (*Prm.* 137e): 'If the One does not have parts, it is neither straight nor curved; if it partakes of shape, it is either straight or curved; therefore if it does not have parts, it does not partake of shape.'

And in the third hypothetical figure (regarded by some as the sec- 20 ond), according to which the common term precedes the two extremes, in the *Phaedo* (74a–75e) he in effect argues as follows: 'If we acquired the knowledge of the equal and have not forgotten it, we know it; if we have forgotten it, then we recollect it; ⟨therefore, if we do not know it, we recollect it⟩.'

25 7. Plato also makes use of mixed syllogisms. Of those which are constructive on the basis of (logical) consequence, there is the following example (*Prm.* 145a–b): 'If the One is a whole and limited, then it has beginning and middle and end, and partakes of shape; but the former; so the latter.' Of those which are destructive on the basis of consequence . . .

8. This, then, constitutes a survey of the specific differentiae (of 30 syllogisms). When, therefore, one has acquired an accurate perception of the faculties of the soul and the differences between men, and the types of discourse which are fitted to this or that soul, and when one perceives with precision which sort of person can be persuaded by 35 what arguments and of what sort those are, such an individual, if he also picks the right opportunity for using the particular argument, will be a complete orator, and his rhetorical skill would justly be termed the science of speaking well.

9. As for the practice of sophisms, we will find that sketched out 40 by Plato in the *Euthydemus*, if we pay close attention to that book. We will find indicated in it, then, which sophisms are dependent upon words, and which are dependent upon facts, and the solutions to them.

10. Again, he gives indications of the ten categories both in the *Parmenides* and elsewhere, and in the *Cratylus* he goes thoroughly into 45 the whole topic of etymology. In general, the man was supremely 160 competent in, and a connoisseur of, the procedures of definition, division ⟨and analysis⟩, all of which demonstrate particularly well the power of dialectic.

The subject matter of the *Cratylus* is as follows. He is enquiring 5 whether names arise from nature or from convention. His view is that the correctness of names is a matter of convention, but not absolutely nor as a result of chance, but in such a way that convention arises from the nature of a given thing. Indeed, the correctness of a name is 10 nothing else than a convention which is in accord with the nature of the given thing. For neither is the arbitrary postulation of a name adequate and sufficient for its correctness, nor yet its nature and its first utterance, but rather the combination of both, so that the name of every object is fixed by its proper relationship to the nature of the 15 given thing; for, after all, it is not the case that if any name is attached to anything, it yields a correct signification, as for instance if we attach the name 'horse' to man. Speaking, after all, is a type of action, so that it would not be the case that no matter how one speaks one speaks correctly, but rather if one speaks according to the nature of things. And since naming is one part of speaking, even as the name 20 is one part of speech, so naming rightly and wrongly would not come about according to any random arrangement, but according to the natural affinity of the name to the thing; and he would be the best name-giver who indicates through the name the nature of the thing. 25 For the name is an instrument corresponding to a thing, not attached to it at random, but appropriate to it by nature. It is by means of this that we teach each other things and distinguish them, so that the name is an instrument which teaches about and distinguishes the essence of each thing, as the shuttle does for the weaving of cloth. 30

11. It is dialectic which has the job of using names rightly. For even as the weaver would use a shuttle, knowing its proper function, once the carpenter has made it, so the dialectician, once the name- 35 giver has laid down the name, would be the one to use it properly and fittingly. It is the job of the carpenter, after all, to make the tiller, but it is the job of the steersman to use it well. Even so, the name-giver would perform his fixing of names best if he did this, as it were, in the presence of the dialectician, who would know the nature of the 40 subject-matter.

7. Mathematics

1. This will suffice as a sketch of dialectic. Next let us discuss theoretical science. We have said earlier that the divisions of this are theology, physics, and mathematics. The aim of theology is know- 161 ledge of the primary, highest, and originative causes. The aim of physics is to learn what is the nature of the universe, what sort of an animal is man, and what place he has in the world, if God exercises 5 providence over all things, and if other gods are ranked beneath him, and what is the relation of men to the gods. The aim of mathematics is to examine the nature of plane and three-dimensional being, and the phenomena of change and locomotion.

2. Let us now set out in summary fashion the theory of mathemat- 10 ics. This was adopted by Plato as a means of sharpening the intellect, by honing the soul and providing it with the accuracy necessary for the examination of reality. That part of mathematics which concerns

15   number instills no slight degree of readiness for the ascent to Being,
but more or less delivers us from the error and ignorance associated
with the sensible realm, assisting us towards the knowledge of true
being; and it is also handy for the practice of war by reason of its relevance to the theory of tactics.

20   That part which concerns geometry, in its turn, is most useful also
for the knowledge of the Good, at least when one does not simply
pursue geometry for practical purposes, but makes use of it for the
ascent to the realm of eternal being, and does not waste time on what
comes to be and passes away.

25   3. Stereometry is also most useful; for after the study of the second
dimension there follows the study of this subject, which involves the
third dimension. Useful also is a fourth subject of study, astronomy,
by means of which we will study in the heaven the motions of the
30   stars and the heaven, and the creator of night and day, the months
and the years. From these studies, by a proper route, we will proceed
to the search for the creator of all things, transferring ourselves
upwards from these subjects of study as from a foundation or from
elements.

35   4. We will pay attention also to music, relating the sense of hearing
to the same objects; for even as the eyes are naturally suited to
astronomy, so is the sense of hearing to harmony; and even as in
applying our minds to astronomy we are led from visible objects to
invisible and intelligible essence, so in listening to harmonious sound
40   we in the same way transfer our attention from things audible to what
is contemplated by the mind itself; whereas if we do not approach
these studies in this way, our view of them will be imperfect and
unproductive and of no account. For one must pass swiftly from what
162 is visible and audible to those things which may be seen only by the
rational activity of the soul.

The study of mathematics, then, is as it were a prelude to the contemplation of true beings; for, as they strive to attain to Being, geo-
5   metry, arithmetic, and the arts which follow upon them have a
dream-like apprehension of Being, but are not capable of seeing it in
a waking state, since they are ignorant of the first principles and of
what are compounded from the principles, but none the less they
contrive to be most useful, in the way we have described.

10   5. It is for this reason that Plato does not call these disciplines sciences. It is the procedure of dialectic that has the capacity to ascend

from the hypotheses of geometry to primary principles not subject to hypothesis. It is for this reason that he called dialectic 'science', while he terms mathematics neither 'opinion' (for mathematical objects are more perspicuous than sense-objects), nor 'science' (since they are more obscure than the primary objects of intellection), but opinion he   15
declares to relate to bodies, and science to first principles, while to mathematical objects he assigns 'discursive reason'. He also postulates the existence of 'belief' and 'conjecture'. Of these, belief relates to sense-objects, while conjecture is of images and reflections. So, since dialectic is the more powerful discipline, inasmuch as it concerns   20
objects which are divine and permanent, it is therefore ranked above the mathematical disciplines, serving as a sort of coping-stone or guard of all the others.

8. Matter

1. Following on these topics, let us turn to a discussion of first principles and doctrines of theology, taking our start from the prim-   25
ary elements, and then descending from these to examine, first, the origin of the world, and finally the origin and nature of man. So then, let us first discuss Matter.

2. Plato calls this a 'mould' (*Ti.* 50c), 'all-receiver' (51a), 'nurse'   30
(49a, 52d, 88d), 'mother' (50d, 51a), and 'space' (52a–d), and a sub-stratum 'tangible by non-sensation' and graspable (only) 'by a bastard reasoning' (52b). He declares that it has the characteristic of receiving the whole realm of generation by performing the role of a nurse in sustaining it, and receiving all the forms, while of itself remaining   35
without shape, or quality, or form, but it can be moulded and imprinted with such impressions like a mould and shaped by these, having no shape or quality of its own. For nothing would be readily adapted to (receiving) a variety of imprints and shapes unless it were   40
itself devoid of qualities and without participation in those forms which it must itself receive. Indeed, we observe also that those who manufacture fragrant ointments on a base of oil employ for this purpose the most odourless type of oil, and that those who want to create   163
shapes out of wax or clay first smooth these out and render them as shapeless as possible.

3. It is likewise proper to all-receptive matter, if it is to receive the forms thoroughly, not to have subsistent in itself any of their nature,

5 but to be without quality or form in order to be the receptacle of the forms. And being such, it will be neither body nor incorporeal, but potentially body, just as we understand the bronze to be potentially a 10 statue, because once it has received the form it will be a statue.

9. The Forms

1. Matter constitutes one principle, but Plato postulates others also, to wit, the paradigmatic, that is the forms, and that constituted by God the father and cause of all things. Form is considered in relation 15 to God, his thinking; in relation to us, the primary object of thought; in relation to Matter, measure; in relation to the sensible world, its paradigm; and in relation to itself, essence. For in general everything that we can conceptualize must come to be in reference to something, of which the paradigm must pre-exist, just as if one thing were to be 20 derived from another, in the way that my image derives from me; and even if the paradigm does not always subsist externally, in any event every artist, having the paradigm in himself, applies the structure of it to matter.

2. Form is defined as an eternal model of things that are in accor-25 dance with nature. For most Platonists do not accept that there are forms of artificial objects, such as a shield or a lyre, nor of things that are contrary to nature, like fever or cholera, nor of individuals, like Socrates and Plato, not yet of any trivial thing, such as dirt or chaff, 30 nor of relations, such as the greater or the superior. For the forms are eternal and perfect thoughts of God.

3. They justify the existence of forms in the following way also. Whether God is an intellect or is possessed of intellect, he has thoughts, and these are eternal and unchanging; and if this is the 35 case, forms exist. For if matter is unmeasured in its own right, it needs to receive measures from something else superior to it and immaterial. But the former is true; therefore so is the latter; and if this is the case, then forms exist as a type of immaterial measure.

40 Further, if the world is not such as it is by accident, it has not only been generated *from* something, but also *by* something (or someone); and not only this, but also *with reference to* something. But what could 164 that with reference to which it is generated be other than form? So forms exist.

4. But further, if intellect differs from true opinion, then also the objects of intellection differ from the objects of opinion. But if this is the case, then there are objects of intellection distinct from objects of opinion. So there will also be primary objects of intellection, just as there are primary objects of sense-perception. But if this is so, then forms exist. But in fact intellect does differ from true opinion; so that forms exist.

10. God

1. We must next discuss the third principle, which Plato declares to be more or less beyond description. However, we might arrive by induction at some notion of it in the following fashion. If there exist objects of intellection, and these are neither sense-perceptible nor participate in what is sense-perceptible, but rather in certain primary objects of intellection, then there exist primary objects of intellection in an absolute sense, just as there exist primary objects of sense-perception. But the former is true; therefore so is the latter. Since human beings are filled with sense-impressions, with the result that even when they set out to direct their minds to the intelligible, they still retain in their imaginations sensible images, to the extent of conceiving along with it often a notion of size, or shape, or colour, it is impossible for them to acquire any pure conception of the intelligibles, but the gods are free from sense-perception, and therefore apprehend them in a pure and uncontaminated mode.

2. Since intellect is superior to soul, and superior to potential intellect there is actualized intellect, which cognizes everything simultaneously and eternally, and finer than this again is the cause of this and whatever it is that has an existence still prior to these, this it is that would be the primal God, being the cause of the eternal activity of the intellect of the whole heaven. It acts on this while remaining itself unmoved, as does the sun on vision, when this is directed towards it, and as the object of desire moves desire, while remaining motionless itself. In just this way will this intellect move the intellect of the whole heaven.

3. Since the primary intellect is the finest of things, it follows that the object of its intelligizing must also be supremely fine. But there is nothing finer than this intellect. Therefore it must be everlastingly

30 engaged in thinking of itself and its own thoughts, and this activity of
    it is Form.
       The primary god, then, is eternal, ineffable, 'self-perfect' (that is,
    deficient in no respect), 'ever-perfect' (that is, always perfect), and
    'all-perfect' (that is, perfect in all respects); divinity, essentiality,
    truth, commensurability, ⟨beauty⟩, good. I am not listing these terms
35 as being distinct from one another, but on the assumption that one
    single thing is being denoted by all of them. He is the Good, because
    he benefits all things according to their capacities, being the cause of
    all good. He is the Beautiful, because he himself by his own nature is
    perfect and commensurable; Truth, because he is the origin of all
40 truth, as the sun is of all light; he is Father through being the cause
    of all things and bestowing order on the heavenly Intellect and the
    soul of the world in accordance with himself and his own thoughts.
165 By his own will he has filled all things with himself, rousing up the
    soul of the world and turning it towards himself, as being the cause
    of its intellect. It is this latter that, set in order by the Father, itself
    imposes order on all of nature in this world.

5   4. God is ineffable and graspable only by the intellect, as we have
    said, since he is neither genus, nor species, nor differentia, nor does he
    possess any attributes, neither bad (for it is improper to utter such a
    thought), nor good (for he would be thus by participation in some-
10 thing, to wit, goodness), nor indifferent (for neither is this in accor-
    dance with the concept we have of him), nor yet qualified (for he is
    not endowed with quality, nor is his peculiar perfection due to
    qualification) nor unqualified (for he is not deprived of any quality
    which might accrue to him). Further, he is not a part of anything, nor
    is he in the position of being a whole which has parts, nor is he the
15 same as anything or different from anything; for no attribute is proper
    to him, in virtue of which he could be distinguished from other
    things. Also, he neither moves anything, nor is he himself moved.

       5. The first way of conceiving God is by abstraction of these attri-
    butes, just as we form the conception of a point by abstraction from
    sensible phenomena, conceiving first a surface, then a line, and finally
    a point.
20   The second way of conceiving him is that of analogy, as follows:
    the sun is to vision and to visible objects (it is not itself sight, but
    provides vision to sight and visibility to its objects) as the primal
    intellect is to the power of intellection in the soul and to its objects;

for it is not the power of intellection itself, but provides intellection   25
to it and intelligibility to its objects, illuminating the truth contained
in them.

6. The third way of conceiving him is the following: one contemplates first beauty in bodies, then after that turns to the beauty in
soul, then to that in customs and laws, and then to the 'great sea of   30
Beauty', after which one gains an intuition of the Good itself and the
final object of love and striving, like a light appearing and, as it were,
shining out to the soul which ascends in this way; and along with this
one also intuits God, in virtue of his pre-eminence in honour.

7. God is partless, by reason of the fact that there is nothing prior to
him. For the part, and that out of which a thing is composed, exists   35
prior to that of which it is a part; plane, for instance, is prior to body,
and line is prior to plane. Having no parts, it follows that he is motionless in respect of both locomotion and qualitative change. For if he
were subject to change, this would have to be by his own agency or
that of another. If at the hands of another, that one would be stronger   40
than him; if by his own agency, either he would be altered for the
worse or for the better; but both alternatives are absurd. From all these
considerations it becomes clear also that he is incorporeal. This can be   166
demonstrated also in the following way: if God were a body, he would
be composed of form and matter, because every body is a combination
of matter and form combined with it, which has a likeness to the forms
and participates in them in a manner difficult to express; but it is
absurd that God should be composed of matter and form (for he could   5
not then be simple or primordial); so God must be incorporeal.

8. And again: if God is body, he would be composed of matter; so
he would be either fire, or water, or earth, or air, or some composite
of these; but none of these is primordial. And anyhow, he would be   10
posterior to matter, if he were made of matter. Since these conclusions, then, are absurd, it must be accepted that he is incorporeal; and
further, if he is a body, he would be also perishable and generated
and subject to change; but each of these is absurd in his connection.

11. The Incorporeality of Qualities

1. That qualities are incorporeal might be demonstrated in the fol-   15
lowing manner. Every body is a subject; but quality is not a subject,

but an attribute; therefore quality is not a body. Every quality is in a subject; but no body is in a subject; therefore quality is not a body.
20 Further, one quality is contrary to another; but one body is not contrary to another. And one body does not differ *qua* body from any other, but differs in *quality* (certainly not in body); so therefore qualities are not bodies. It is a very reasonable argument that, just as matter is devoid of quality, so quality should be immaterial; but if quality
25 is immaterial, then it would be incorporeal. On the other hand, if qualities were bodies, then two or three bodies would be in the same place, which is completely absurd. On the other hand, if qualities are incorporeal, that which creates them must also be incorporeal.

2. Further, the active (causes) could not be other than incorporeal;
30 for bodies are passive and fluid and are never identical with themselves and in the same state, nor permanent and stable, being such that, even when they seem to be active in some respect, they are, on closer inspection, found to be passive. So then, even as there exists something purely passive, so there is necessarily also something unqualifiedly active; and this we will find to be nothing other than
35 the incorporeal.

3. Such then would be the account of the first principles, which is termed theological. We must turn now to the subject of what is called physics, making our start as follows.

12. The Generation of the World

40 1. Since of natural individual objects of sense-perception there must exist certain definite models, to wit the forms, which serve as
167 the objects of scientific knowledge and definition (for besides all (individual) men one possesses the concept of Man, and besides all (individual) horses that of Horse, and in general, beside all living things the ungenerated and indestructible form of Living Thing, just as
5 from one seal there derive many impressions, and of one man myriads upon myriads of representations, the form being the cause and principle in virtue of which each thing is such as it itself is)—since, then, that is so, it is necessary that the most beautiful of constructions, the
10 world, should have been fashioned by God looking to a form of World, that being the model of our world, which is only copied from it, and it is by assimilation to it that it is fashioned by the creator,

who proceeds through a most admirable providence and administrative care to create the world, because 'he was good' (*Ti.* 29e).   15

2. He created it, then, out of the totality of matter. This, as it moved without order and randomly, prior to the generation of the heavens, he took in hand and brought from disorder into the best order, adorning its parts with suitable numbers and shapes, with the   20 result that he distinguished off fire and earth so as to have their present relationship to air and water, whereas they previously possessed only traces and the mere capacity of receiving the potency of the elements, and agitated irrationally and immoderately that matter by which they were themselves in turn agitated. For he generated it out of all of each of the four elements, all of fire, and earth, and water,   25 and air, not leaving out any part of potency of any of them, on the consideration that, first of all, what came into being must be corporeal, and so inevitably tangible and visible. But without fire and earth it is not possible for something to be tangible and visible. So, following   30 probable reasoning, he fashioned it out of earth and fire; and since some bond was required to bring both of these together, and the divine bond is that of proportion, whose nature it is to make one both itself and what it binds together, and since the world was not a plane   35 figure (for in that case one mean would have sufficed for it), but spherical, it required two means to bring it into harmony. For this reason, then, air and water were placed between fire and earth, following the system of proportion: so, as fire is to air, so air is to water,   40 and this latter in turn to earth, and vice versa.

3. By leaving nothing outside it, he made the world both unique of its kind, and likened numerically to its form, which was itself one. In addition to this, he made it free of disease and ageing, inasmuch as nothing could approach it which would harm it; and he rendered it   45 self-sufficient and in need of no outside help. By way of shape, he bestowed on it sphericity, seeing as that is the fairest of shapes and   168 the most capacious and mobile. Since it needed neither sight nor hearing nor any other (sense-faculty), he did not attach to it the appropriate organs of these to serve it; and removing from it all other   5 types of motion, he granted it circular motion, this being that proper to intellect and thought.

13. The Formation of the Elements

1. The components out of which the world is put together are two,
10   to wit, body and soul, of which the former is visible and tangible,
while the latter is invisible and intangible, and each of them possesses
a different power and constitution. Its body is composed of fire and
earth, water and air; these four (which did not yet, we must empha-
15   size, fill the role of elements) the creator of the world took up, and
gave them shape as pyramid, cube, octahedron, icosahedron, and, on
top of everything else, the dodecahedron. In so far as matter took on
the form of a pyramid, it became fire, that being the most cutting,
and composed of the least number of triangles, and by reason of this
20   the least dense. In so far as it took on that of an octahedron, it
assumed the character of air, and as it took the imprint of an icosahedron, it took that of water, while the shape of the cube he assigned to
earth, as it was the most solid and stable. As for the dodecahedron
figure, he utilized that for the universe as a whole.

25   2. But more basic than all these figures is the nature of plane
figures; for planes precede solids. Of the plane, there are, as it were,
two ancestral elements, the most beautiful of right-angled triangles,
the scalene and the isosceles. The scalene has one angle a right angle,
30   the second two-thirds of a right angle, and the remaining angle one-
third. The former, I mean the scalene triangle, becomes the basic element of the pyramid, the octahedron, and the icosahedron, the
pyramid being composed of four equilateral triangles, each one
35   divided into six of the above-mentioned scalene triangles, the octahedron of eight equilateral triangles, of which each is divided in the
same way into six scalene triangles, and the icosahedron of twenty
equilateral triangles.

The other one, I mean the isosceles, becomes the component of the
cube; for the conjunction of four isosceles triangles makes a square,
40   and from six of these squares one gets a cube. The dodecahedron
God utilized for the universe as a whole, because one sees in the
heavens twelve zodiacal signs in the zodiacal circle, and each of them
is divided into thirty degrees, even as the dodecahedron is composed
169   of twelve pentagons each divided into five triangles, of which each in
turn is composed of six triangles, so that one finds in the dodecahedron as a whole three hundred and sixty triangles, which is the
same number as the degrees of the zodiac.

3. Matter, then, being imprinted with these traces (of Forms),   5
moved first of all in a disorderly manner, but was then brought by
God to order, through all things being harmonized with each other by
means of proportion. However, these (elements) do not remain spa-
tially separated, but experience an unceasing agitation, and communicate this to matter, because, as they are compressed and thrust   10
together by the rotation of the world, and are driven against each
other, the finer particles are carried into the interstices of the more
coarse-grained ones. For this reason no space is left empty of body,
and this persisting unevenness produces the agitation; for matter is
shaken about by these, and these in turn by it.   15

14. The Soul of the World, the Stars, the Planets

1. Having given an account of the composition of bodies, he draws
on the powers that make their appearance in the soul in presenting
his teaching about it(?). For since it is with the soul that we discern
each among existent things, it is reasonable that he should have incorporated in it the first principles of all things, in order that, perceiving   20
each of the things which fall under our notice by virtue of what is
akin to it and like it, we should realize that the essence of the soul is
in conformity with its activities.

2. Declaring that there exists an intelligible essence which is indivisible, and another which is divisible about bodies, he constructed
from these a single essence, explaining that thus it can grasp in   25
thought each of the aforesaid two essences; and seeing that sameness
and difference occur both on the level of intelligible and of divisible
things, he put the soul together out of all these things. For either like
is known by like, as is the view of the Pythagoreans, or unlike by   30
unlike, as is held by Heraclitus, the philosopher of nature.

3. When he says that the world is 'generated', one must not understand him to assert that there ever was a time when the world did not
exist; but rather that the world is perpetually in a state of becoming,
and reveals a more primordial cause of its own existence. Also, God   35
does not create the soul of the world, since it exists eternally, but he
brings it to order, and to this extent he might be said to create it, by
awakening and turning towards himself both its intellect and itself, as
out of some deep coma or sleep, so that by looking towards the   40

objects of intellection inherent in him it may receive the Forms and shapes, through striving to attain to his thoughts.

4. It is clear, then, that the world would be a living thing and possessed of intellect; for in wishing to make it best, it follows that God
170 endowed it with both a soul and an intellect, for the ensouled product in general is superior to the soulless, and the intelligent to that which lacks intelligence (the intelligence, we must presume, being unable to
5 exist without soul). Now since soul is extended from the centre to the outer limits, the result is that it binds together and encloses all around the body of the world, so that it is co-extended with the whole world, and in this way binds and holds it together, though its exterior parts have dominance over its interior ones. For the outer
10 (circuit) remained undivided, while the inner was split six ways, into seven circles, according to double and triple intervals. That part which is enclosed by the sphere which remained undivided is akin to sameness, while that which is divided is akin to otherness.

5. The motion of the heaven which encompasses everything being
15 unvarying, it is therefore single and orderly, whereas the movement of the inner (spheres) is various and diversified with risings and settings, and for this reason is called 'wandering'. The outer sphere is carried round to the right, moving from east to west, while the inner,
20 in turn, goes to the left, moving contrariwise to the world, from west to east.

6. God also fashioned the planets and the stars, and of these the latter are fixed, serving as an ornament of the heaven during the night, a vast multitude, while the former, seven in number, serve for the generation of number and time, and to reveal the existence of
25 things. For he created time as the interval of the motion of the world, as an image of eternity, which is the measure of the stability of the eternal world. The non-fixed stars do not have the same properties. The sun is the leader of all of them, indicating and illuminating everything. The moon is regarded as being in second place as regards
30 potency, and the rest of the planets follow each in proportion to its particular character. The moon creates the measure of a month, by completing her own orbit and overtaking the sun in this space of time. The sun gives measure to the year; for in making the circuit of
35 the zodiac it completes the seasons of the year. The other planets each have their own revolutions, which are not accessible to the casual observer, but only to the experts. All these revolutions combine to

produce the perfect number and time, when all the planets come
round to the same point and in an order such that, if one imagines a   40
straight line dropped perpendicularly from the sphere of the fixed
stars to the earth, it would pass through the centre of each of them.

7. Now, there being seven spheres within the 'wandering' (planet-   171
ary) sphere, God fashioned seven visible bodies, mainly composed of
fire, and fitted them to the spheres which belong to the wandering
circle of otherness. The moon, first of all, he placed in the first circle   5
from the earth, and arranged the sun in the second, while to the
'Light-Bringer' and that star called sacred to Hermes he assigned the
circle the speed of which is equal to that of the sun, but which goes
in the opposite direction. Above these he arranged the others each in
their proper sphere: the slowest of them, which some call the star of   10
Kronos, lies just beneath the sphere of the fixed stars; the second
slowest, called after Zeus, comes after this, and after that the star of
Ares; and in eighth place the highest power encompasses all the
others. And all of these are living beings endowed with intelligence
and gods, and they are spherical in shape.

15. The Created Gods

1. There are, furthermore, other divinities, the daemons, whom one   15
could also term 'created gods', present in each of the elements, some
of them visible, others invisible, in ether, and fire, and air, and water,
so that no part of the world should be without a share in soul or in a
living being superior to mortal nature. To their administration the   20
whole sublunar and terrestrial sphere has been assigned.

2. God is in fact himself the creator of the universe, and of the
gods and daemons, and by his will this universe admits of no dissolution. The rest is ruled over by his children, who do everything that
they do in accordance with his command and in imitation of him.   25
From them derive omens and presages, dreams and oracles, and all
artificial divination performed by mortals.

3. The earth lies in the middle of the universe, compressed around
the pole which extends through all, guardian of night and day, eldest
of the gods within the heaven (at least after the soul of the world),   30
and providing us with abundant nourishment. Around this the world
turns, itself being a star in a sense, but immobile through being a

thing situated in a state of equilibrium in the middle, with its sur-
roundings equal (in all directions).

4. The ether, finally, is in the outermost position, divided into the
35   sphere of the fixed stars and that of the planets. Following on these is
the region of air, and in the middle is the earth, with its wet element.

16. Creation of Man and Other Living Beings

1. When God had imposed order upon the universe as a whole,
there were still left (uncreated) the three classes of living being which
40   were going to be mortal, the winged, the aquatic, and those that go
on land. The creation of these he now entrusted to the gods who
were his offspring, to avoid the consequence that, if they were made
172   by him, they would be immortal. These, then, borrowed certain portions from primal matter for fixed periods, with a view to returning
them to it again, and thus created mortal animals.

2. As for the human race, since there was special concern on the
part of the father of all and of the gods who are his offspring for this,
5   as being most akin to the gods, the creator of the universe sent down
to earth the souls of this race in number equal to the stars, and
mounting each upon its kindred star as upon a chariot, he expounded
10   to them the laws of fate, in the manner of a lawgiver, in order that he
might be free from blame. (He told them) that affections connected
with mortality would attach themselves to them from the body—in
the first place sensations, and thereafter pleasure and pain, fear and
anger. Souls which achieved dominance over these affections and were
15   in no way constrained by them would live justly and return to their
kindred star; while others who had been overcome by injustice would
come on their second birth to the life of a woman, and, if they did
not mend their ways at that stage, would come ultimately to the
nature of a wild beast. The end of their toils would be the overcom-
ing of those elements which attached themselves to them, and their
return to their proper state.

17. The Construction of the Human Body

20   1. The gods moulded man primarily out of earth, fire, air, and
water, borrowing certain portions with a view to their return. Fitting

it together with invisible pegs, and thus constructing one, single body, they placed the ruling part of the soul which had been sent down in the head, establishing the brain as a sort of field for it, while around the face they set the organs of perception, to perform each their appropriate service. They compounded the marrow from those tri- angles which were smooth and unwarped, out of which the elements were produced, to be the origin of seed. Bone they made of earth and marrow, moistened and repeatedly tempered in water and fire; the sinews were fashioned out of bone and flesh; and flesh itself was made of a sort of fermentation of salty and acidic elements.

2. They enclosed the marrow in bone, and the bones, in order to bind them together, by sinews. The sinews enabled the limbs to bend and connect with each other, and the flesh provided them with cover- ing, plastered over it, as it were, now whiter, now darker, for the greater benefit of the body.

3. These same tissues also served for the weaving together of the bowels, the belly, and the intestines wound about it, and, descending from the mouth to the stomach and the lungs respectively, the wind- pipe and the pharynx. Food is digested in the stomach by being cut up and softened by breath and heat, and thus distributed throughout the body, in the changed form suitable to each part; and two veins, running along the spine and crossing over each other, meet up and bind down the head, and then divide from there into many branches.

4. When the gods had thus constructed man, and had bound into his body the soul which was to be its master, with good reason they established the ruling part of it in the head, where are to be found the starting-points of the marrow and of the nerves, and it is here that losses of reason occur, occasioned by accidents. All round the head are stationed the senses, acting as bodyguards, as it were, for the ruling element. Here also are lodged the organs of reasoning, judge- ment, and speculation, while the affective part of the soul they placed lower down, the spirited element round the heart and the appetitive around the abdomen and the parts about the navel, about which more will be said below.

18. The Sense of Sight

1. Having placed upon the face the light-bearing eyes, the gods enclosed in them the luminous aspect of fire, which, since it is

smooth and dense, they considered would be akin to the light of day.
20 This flows out with the greatest ease through the whole of the eyes,
but especially through the mid-part of them, which is the purest and
most refined. This becomes blended with the external light, like to
like, and produces the sensation of sight. For this reason, when at
night the light departs or is obscured, the stream from within us no
25 longer coalesces with the adjacent air, but is kept within, and
smoothes out and dissolves our internal movements, and becomes an
inducement to sleep; and that is why the eyelids close.

2. If a deep level of repose comes about, sleep ensues which has
30 minimal dreams, while if some motions persist, numerous images
appear to us. It is thus that are formed those images which appear to
us directly both waking and asleep. Following on these, there arise
also images formed in mirrors and other surfaces which are translu-
35 cent and smooth, by a process of refraction, according as the mirror is
convex or concave or placed lengthwise; for the images will be
different according as the rays are thrust back in different directions,
sliding off a convex surface, but being concentrated into a concave
40 one. It is thus that in some mirrors left and right appear reversed,
while in others they remain as they were, and in others again up and
down are reversed.

19. Hearing, Smell, Taste, Touch

1. The sense of hearing has come into being for the cognizance of
174 sound, beginning from a movement situated in the head, and termi-
nating in the seat of the liver. Sound is a blow transmitted through
the ears, the brain, and the blood, and penetrating as far as the soul,
5 'shrill' when it is a rapid movement, 'deep' when it is a slow one,
'loud' when the movement is large, 'soft' when it is small.

2. Following on this, the power of the nostrils was established for
the perception of smells. Smell is a sensation which comes down from
10 the veins in the nostrils as far as the region of the navel. The species
of this do not have names, other than the two most general, good
smell and bad smell, which are the names corresponding to the pleasant and the unpleasant (olfactory sensation). All odour is thicker than
15 air and thinner than water. Indeed, the class of odours has reasonably
been termed a 'half-breed' class, because it concerns things which

have not yet undergone complete transformation, but are intermediate between air and water, in the form of smoke and mist; for it is as these (elements) are changing into each other that the sensation of smell comes about.

3. The tongue was constructed by the gods as the appraiser of a   20
very wide variety of tastes, for which purpose they extended veins from it as far as the heart, to be the tests and criteria of flavours. These, by their contractions and dilations in response to the onset of   25
flavours, distinguish the differences between them.

4. The varieties of flavour are seven: sweet, acid, astringent, dry, salty, pungent, bitter. Of these, the sweet has a nature opposite to that of all the others, diffusing in a naturally agreeable way the mois-   30
ture on the tongue. As for the others, the acid are those which stir up and tear the tongue, the astringent those which heat it and rise upwards, the bitter are those which have such a strong detergent action as to dissolve (the surface of the tongue), while those which only gently clean and purge it are the salty. Of those which contract   35
and close the pores, the rougher ones are the astringent, and those which produce this effect to a lesser degree are the dry.

5. The faculty of touch is the sense constructed by the gods to be perceptive of hot and cold, soft and hard, light and heavy, and   40
smooth and rough, in such a way as to be able to judge also the differences within each of these. Those things which give way to the touch we call 'yielding'; those which are unyielding we describe as 'resistant'. This quality depends on the bases from which the bodies   175
themselves are constructed; those with larger bases are solid and stable, while those on small bases are yielding and soft and easily altered. Unevenness combined with hardness produces the rough, evenness and compactness the smooth. Further, the experiences of   5
cold and hot, being diametrical opposites, are the products of opposite causes. The one, cutting by virtue of the sharpness and rapid move-ment of its particles, produces the sensation of heat; while cold is produced by thicker particles thrusting out by their intrusion the lesser number of smaller particles, and forcing their way in in their   10
place. A quaking and trembling then supervenes, and the resultant sensation in bodies is that of shivering.

20. Heaviness and Lightness

It is quite improper to define heavy and light in terms of 'above'
15 and 'below', for there is really no such thing as above and below. For
since the heaven as a whole is spherical and worked to perfect homo-
geneity on its outer surface, one has no right to speak of above and
below, as some do. In fact, 'heavy' is that which is with difficulty
drawn into a place other than its natural one, while 'light' is what is
20 easily so drawn; or again, the heavy is that which is compounded of
more parts, the light from the minimum amount.

21. Breathing

We breathe in the following way. We are surrounded outside us by
an abundance of air, which enters our body through the mouth and
25 the nostrils and other pores of the body which we are acquainted with
only through reasoning. Once warmed, it rushes outwards towards its
kindred element; and by whatever part it exits, it thrusts back the
outside air in turn into the spaces inside. This cyclic process continues unceasingly, and it is this that constitutes inhalation and exha-
lation.

22. The Diseases of Man and Their Causes

30   The causes of disease he declares to be many. First of all, there is
the deficiency and excess of the various elements, or their shifting
into places not proper to them. Secondly, the inverse production of
homogeneous parts, as when flesh turns into blood or bile or phlegm;
35 for all these things are nothing else than instances of decomposition.
Thus phlegm results from the decomposition of new flesh, and sweat
and tears are as it were the 'whey' of phlegm. When phlegm is
extruded to the surface of the body, it produces pimples and spots,
whereas when it is kept inside and mixed with black bile it brings on
40 the so-called 'sacred disease'; and acid and saline phlegm is responsible for all diseases involving flux or catarrh. All parts of the body
176 which are subject to inflammation owe this to bile. In fact, a vast
amount of different diseases are caused by bile and phlegm.

As for fevers, a constant fever arises from an excess of fire, a quo-
tidian fever from an excess of air; a tertian from an excess of water,   5
and a quartan from an excess of earth.

23. The Soul in Relation to the Body

1. We must next speak of the soul, resuming our discussion at the
following point, even if we seem to be repeating ourselves. When they
received the human soul in its immortal aspect from the primal god,
as we shall show presently, the gods who fashion the mortal classes of   10
being added to it two mortal parts. However, in order that the divine
and immortal part of it should not be filled with mortal rubbish, they
placed it on the citadel, as it were, of the body, designating it as the
ruling and kingly element, and assigning it to the head, which has a   15
shape which imitates that of the universe as a whole. They subordin-
ated the rest of the body to its service by attaching it to it as a
vehicle, and apportioned to each of the mortal parts of the soul a
different dwelling place.

2. The spirited part they established in the heart, and the appetit-   20
ive in the area between the midriff and the boundary at the navel,
binding it down like a raging and savage beast. They fashioned the
lungs for the sake of the heart as soft and bloodless, and furthermore
full of cavities like a sponge, so that the heart, when pounding in the   25
heat of anger, might have some padding round it. The liver has as its
purpose the stirring up and calming down of the soul, being endowed
for this purpose with both sweetness and bitterness.

It has also the role of conveying divinatory messages through
dreams; for by virtue of its smoothness and solidity and brightness   30
there appears in it the power proceeding from the intellect. The
spleen exists for the sake of the liver, to purify it and keep it bright.
It is this which receives the impurities which accumulate about the
liver due to various diseases.

24. The Soul and Its Parts

1. That the soul is divided into three parts corresponding to its   35
potencies, and that its parts are distributed rationally into their proper
places, we will learn from what follows. First of all, things which are

naturally separated are different. Now the affective and the rational parts are naturally separated, seeing as the latter is concerned with
40 intelligible reality, while the former is concerned with what is pleasurable and painful. And furthermore, the affective part is found also in other animals.

2. Then, since the affective and the rational parts are different in nature, it is proper that they occupy different locations; for they are
177 found to conflict with one another. But any single thing cannot be in conflict with itself, nor can things which are in opposition to each other occupy the same place at the same time.

3. One can see in the character of Medea the spirited element in
5 conflict with reason:

> I know what evil I am about to do
> But anger overcomes my resolutions.
>
> (Euripides, *Med.* 1078–9).

And similarly in the case of Laius, when he abducted Chrysippus, we see desire struggling with reason; for he speaks as follows:

10 Alas, alas, for mortals this is an evil sent from God,
When one sees the good, but makes no use of it.

> (Euripides, *Fr.* 841 N^2)

4. A further proof of the difference between the reason and the affective part of the soul is the fact that the cultivation of the reason is different from that of the affective part; for the former is cultivated
15 through teaching, the latter through the training of one's habitual behaviour.

25. The Immortality of the Soul

1. That the soul is immortal he demonstrates by proceeding in the following way. To whatever it attaches itself, soul brings life, as naturally associated with itself. But that which brings life to something is
20 itself non-receptive of death; and such a thing is immortal. But if the soul is immortal, it would also be imperishable; for it is an incorporeal essence, unchanging in its substance and intelligible, and invisible, and uniform. So therefore it is incomposite, indissoluble,

indispersible. Body, on the other hand, is quite the contrary—sense-   25
perceptible, visible, dispersible, composite, multiform. Further, when
the soul, through the intermediacy of the body, comes to exist in the
sensible realm, it becomes dizzy and is thrown into confusion and
becomes, as it were, drunk, while when it comes to be on its own in
the intelligible realm it comes to stability and enjoys calm. Now if it   30
is thrown into confusion by contact with something, it is not akin to
that thing. So it is akin rather to the intelligible, and the intelligible is
by nature indispersible and indestructible.

And again, it is the soul's nature to rule. But that whose nature it
is to rule is akin to the divine. So the soul, being akin to the divine,
would be imperishable and indestructible.   35

2. Things which are direct contraries of one another, not in themselves but in virtue of the accidents they contain, naturally come to
be from one another. Now the opposite of what men call living is
being dead. So then even as death is the separation of the soul from
the body, so life is the union of soul (which obviously had a previous   40
existence) with body. If the soul must exist after death, and existed
before falling in with the body, then it becomes most probable that it
is eternal, for it is not possible to conceive of anything that could
destroy it.

3. If, again, acts of learning are instances of remembering, then the   45
soul is immortal. That learning is remembering we may infer as fol-   178
lows. Learning cannot arise in any other way than by remembering
what was formerly known. If we had in fact to start from particulars
in forming our conception of common qualities, how could we ever   5
traverse the infinite series of particulars, or alternatively how could we
form such a conception on the basis of a small number (for we could
be deceived, as for instance if we came to the conclusion that only
that which breathed was an animal); or how could concepts have the
dominant role that they do have? So we derive our thoughts through
recollection, on the basis of small sparks, under the stimulus of certain particular impressions remembering what we knew long ago, but   10
suffered forgetfulness of at the time of our embodiment.

4. Again, if the soul is not destroyed by its own proper vice, it is
not going to be destroyed by that of anything else, nor in general by
anything else; and being thus constituted it would follow that it is   15
indestructible. Furthermore, that which is self-moving primordially
is eternally moving, and such a thing is immortal; but the soul is

self-moving. Again, that which is self-moving is the first principle of all motion and generation; and a first principle is ungenerated and indestructible; so both the soul of the universe and the soul of man would be such, since both partake of the same mixture. Plato says that the soul is self-moving, because it has life as something innate in it, eternally active in itself.

5. That Plato holds rational souls to be immortal is something that one may affirm; whether irrational ones are as well, however, is a matter of dispute. For it is plausible that irrational souls, driven as they are by mere representations, and not making use of reason or judgement, nor of theorems and the assembling of these into systems, nor yet of general concepts, nor having any conception at all of intelligible reality, should not be of the same essence as rational souls, and should be mortal and perishable.

6. It follows from the proposition that souls are immortal that they should enter into bodies, following upon the natural processes which form the embryo, and that they should pass through many bodies both human and non-human, either following their turn in a numbered sequence, or by the will of the gods, or through intemperance, or through love of the body; body and soul, after all, have a certain affinity for one another, like fire and asphalt.

7. The souls of the gods too possess both a critical element, which might also be called cognitive, and further an appetitive element, which one might term also dispositional, and an appropriative element. These are to be found also as faculties in human souls, but after embodiment the latter two suffer alteration, the appropriative faculty into the libidinous, and the appetitive into the spirited.

26. Man and Fate

1. On the subject of fate, Plato's views are roughly as follows. All things, he says, are within the sphere of fate, but not all things are fated. Fate, in fact, has the status of a law. It does not say, as it were, that such and such a person will do this, and that such and such another will suffer that, for that would result in an infinity of possibilities, since the number of people who come into being is infinite, and the things that happen to them are also infinite; and then the concept of what is in our power would go out of the window, and so

would praise and blame, and everything like that. But fate consists
rather in the fact that if a soul chooses a given type of life and performs such-and-such actions, such-and-such consequences will follow   10
for it.

2. The soul, therefore, owns no master, and it is in its power to act
or not, and it is not compelled to this, but the consequences of the
action will be fulfilled in accordance with fate. For example, from the
fact that Paris will steal away Helen, this being a voluntary action of
his, there will follow that the Greeks will go to war about Helen.   15
This is, after all, how Apollo put it to Laius: 'If you beget a son, that
offspring will kill you' (Euripides, *Ph.* 19). Here, in the oracle, Laius
and his begetting a son are taken as premisses, and the consequence is
fated.

3. The nature of the possible falls somehow between the true and   20
the false, and being by nature undetermined it becomes the sphere of
operation of our free will. Whatever results from a choice on our part,
on the other hand, will be either true or false. That which is potentially is different from what is said to be in a realized state or in actuality. Potentiality, after all, indicates a certain aptitude in something   25
which does not yet possess the corresponding realized state; as, for
instance, a boy will be said to be potentially a scholar, or a flautist, or
a carpenter, but only then will be 'in the state' of being one or two of
these, when he learns and acquires one of these skills. He will possess   30
them in actuality, on the other hand, when he acts on the basis of
that state which he has attained. The possible, however, is none of
these, but remains indefinite, and takes on truth or falsity in consequence of the inclination in either direction of our free will.

27. The Highest Good and Happiness

1. We must next deal summarily with the ethical doctrines of Plato.   35
The most valuable and greatest good he considered to be neither easy
to discover, nor, when discovered, to be such as to be safely revealed
to all. Certainly he only imparted his views on the good to a very
small, select group of his associates. However, if one examines his
works with care, one will see that he placed the good for us in the   40
knowledge and contemplation of the primal good, which one may
term God and the primal intellect.

180   2. All those things considered good among men he assumed to
acquire this title from their participation, to some degree or other, in
that primal and most valuable good, even as sweet things and hot
5   things gain their title by participating in their respective primal entities. The only elements in us, in his view, which can attain to likeness
with it are intellect and reason, for which reason our good is 'fine,
noble, divine, lovely, well proportioned, and may be called, in a man-
10   ner of speaking 'daemonic'(?). As for those things that are called good
by the many, such as health, beauty, strength, wealth, and suchlike,
none of these, he says, is ever good, unless their use is linked to
virtue. Apart from this, they have the role simply of matter, and can
15   come to be evils for those who make bad use of them. Sometimes he
also calls them 'mortal goods' (*Lg.* 1. 631b).

3. Happiness he considered not to be found in human goods, but
in the divine and blessed ones. For this reason he asserted that truly
philosophical souls are filled with great and marvellous things and
20   that after the dissolution of the body they will enter the society of the
gods and journey about with them and gaze upon 'the Plain of Truth'
(*Phdr.* 248b), since already during their lives they had longed for
knowledge and had preferred the pursuit of it to any other thing, as
being something by virtue of which, when they had purified and
25   rekindled, as it were, 'the eye of the soul' (*R.* 7. 533d), after it had
been destroyed and blinded—something more worth saving than ten
thousand eyes (*R.* 7. 527d–e)—they would become capable of grasping
the nature of all that is rational.

30   4. Those devoid of wisdom he compared to men living beneath the
earth who have never seen the light of day, but see only dim shadows
of the bodies in our realm, while thinking that they have a clear grasp
of reality. For even as those in this situation, when they come upon a
way upwards from their darkness and come out into the pure light,
understandably tend to reject what they previously saw and to despise
35   themselves for having been deceived, so those who advance from the
murk of everyday existence to what is truly divine and noble tend to
look with contempt on all they had previously admired, and to
acquire an even stronger urge to contemplate these latter objects. It is
40   in accord with this, then, to declare that only the noble is good, and
that virtue is sufficient for happiness. That the good consists in the
knowledge of the first principle is demonstrated throughout whole
treatises, while the things that are good by participation in it he

describes in book 1 of the *Laws* as follows (631b): 'Now goods are of 181
two kinds, human and divine' . . . and so on. If, on the contrary,
something is separated from, and has no participation in, the essence
of the first principle, and this is called good by the witless, this he
declares in the *Euthydemus* (281d–e) to be a greater evil for its posses- 5
sor (than the opposite).

5. The principle that the virtues are choiceworthy in themselves
may be seen as following from his view that only the noble is good.
This doctrine of his is presented in very many of his works, but particularly in the whole of the *Republic*. The man who possesses the
knowledge that we have just been discussing he holds to be 10
supremely fortunate and happy, not because of the honours or
rewards that will come his way through being such as he is, but even
if no one recognizes his true nature, and he is afflicted with all those
things that are commonly called evils, such as disfranchisement, exile,
and death. On the other hand, someone who acquires all the com- 15
monly accepted goods, such as wealth and monarchy on a grand scale
and bodily health and physical strength and beauty, without possessing this knowledge, is no whit the more happy because of it.

28. The End for Man: Likeness to God

1. Following from all this, he proposed as the end (of human striving) 'likeness to God in so far as is possible'. This idea he presents in 20
various forms. Sometimes he declares that likeness to God consists in
being intelligent, and just, and pious, as in the *Theaetetus* (176a–b):
'For this reason one should strive to escape from here to there as
quickly as possible. Now the way to escape is to become as nearly as
possible like to God; and to become like God is to become just and 25
pious, with the accompaniment of intelligence.' Elsewhere he asserts
that it consists only in being just, as in the last book of the *Republic*
(613a): 'For, by the gods, that man will never be neglected who is
willing and eager to be just, and by the practice of virtue to be
likened to God so far as that is possible for man.' 30

2. In the *Phaedo*, further, he declares that likeness to God consists
in becoming self-controlled and just, in more or less these words
(82a–b): 'So then, said he, the happiest and (truly) blessed, and those

who go to the best place, are those who have practised the social and
35 civil virtues, which they call self-control and justice.'

3. Sometimes he says that the end is to liken oneself to God, but
sometimes that it consists in following him, as when he says (*Lg.* 4.
715e): 'God who, as old tradition has it, holds the beginning and the
40 end', etc.; and sometimes both, as when he says (*Phdr.* 248a): 'The
soul that follows and likens itself to God', and so on. For certainly
the beginning of advantage is the good, and this is dependent on
God; so, following on from this beginning, the end would be likening
oneself to God—by which we mean, obviously, the god *in* the heavens,
45 not, of course, the God above the heavens, who does not possess
182 virtue, being superior to this. For this reason one would be right in
saying that ill fortune is properly the ill state of one's guardian spirit,
while good fortune is the good state of the same guardian spirit.

4. We can attain likeness to God, first of all, if we are endowed
with a suitable nature, then if we develop proper habits, way of life,
5 and good practice according to law, and, most importantly, if we use
reason, and education, and the correct philosophical tradition, in such
a way as to distance ourselves from the great majority of human concerns, and always to be in close contact with intelligible reality.

The introductory ceremonies, so to speak, and preliminary
purifications of our innate spirit, if one is to be initiated into the
10 greater sciences, will be constituted by music, arithmetic, astronomy,
and geometry, while at the same time we must care for our body by
means of gymnastics, which will prepare the body properly for the
demands of both war and peace.

29. Virtue

15 1. Virtue is a divine thing, being the perfect and most excellent
state of the soul, which makes a man, both in speech and in action,
graceful, harmonious, and firm, both in relation to himself and to
others. ?There are two species of it, the rational(?), and those (virtues)
20 which are concerned with the irrational part of the soul, to wit,
courage and self-control, courage being concerned with the spirited
part, self-control with the appetitive; for since the rational, and the
spirited, and the appetitive are distinct, the perfection of each should

be different. The perfection of the rational part, then, is wisdom; of   25
the spirited part, courage; and of the appetitive, self-control.

2. Wisdom is the science of what is good and evil, and what is neither, while self-control is a sense of order in relation to desires and
impulses and their submission to the ruling element, which is the rea-   30
son. When we speak of self-control being a kind of order and submission what we mean to convey is that it is a faculty in virtue of which
the impulses are brought to order and submission in relation to that
element which is their natural master, that is, the reason.   35

3. Courage is the maintenance of a law-abiding opinion as to what
is and what is not to be feared, that is to say, the capacity to maintain
a law-abiding doctrine.

As for justice, it is a kind of harmonization of these three with one
another, being a capacity in virtue of which the three parts of the soul
agree and harmonize with one another, while each of them fulfils the   40
function which is proper to it and falls to it as its due, in such a way
as to constitute the supreme perfection of the three other virtues, wisdom, courage, and self-control. Since, then, the rational element exercises rule, while the other two parts of the soul are brought into   183
submission by the reason according to their respective characteristics,
and yield obedience to it, on these terms one may accept the doctrine
of the mutual implication of the virtues.

4. Courage, then, being the 'maintaining of law-abiding opinion', is   5
thereby also the maintaining of right reason; for law-abiding opinion
is a sort of right reason, and right reason arises from wisdom. But
wisdom in turn is involved with courage; for it is knowledge of what
is good, but no one can see the good if his view is obscured by cowardice and the feelings that follow upon cowardice. Likewise, no one   10
can be wise if he is possessed of intemperance, and in general if
someone does something contrary to right reason through being overcome by passion, Plato says that he does this by reason of ignorance
and folly. So one cannot possess wisdom if one is intemperate and   15
cowardly. The virtues, therefore, in their perfect forms, are inseparable from one another.

30. Good Natural Dispositions and Progress
towards Virtue

1. One gives the name of virtue also in a different sense to what are called 'good natural dispositions' and stages of progress towards virtue, which are given the same names as the respective virtues by reason of their similarity to them. It is in this sense that we call certain soldiers 'brave', and even on occasion say that some people who are foolish are brave, but in these cases we are referring to nonperfect virtues. As for perfect virtues, it is clear that they are not subject to higher or lower levels of intensity, whereas vices exhibit both increase and decrease; for one person can be more foolish or unjust than another. But on the other hand, vices are not reciprocal with one another; for some are actually incompatible, and cannot be found together in the same person. Such, for example, is the relation of recklessness to cowardice, or libertinism to miserliness. In any case, it is not possible for any one man to possess all the vices; for it is not possible for a body to contain all the bodily vices within itself.

2. It must also be recognised that there exists an intermediate disposition which is neither vicious nor virtuous; for not all men are either virtuous or vicious. In fact only those are such (sc. virtuous) who have progressed to this state over a sufficient period; for it is not easy to transfer all at once from vice to virtue, since there is a great distance and mutual opposition between these two extremes.

3. It must be noted also that, among the virtues, some have a predominant role, others a subsidiary. Predominant are those which belong to the reasoning element in the soul, from which the rest also take their perfection, while those are subsidiary which pertain to the appetitive element. These latter achieve noble acts when they are in accord with reason, not, however, reason inherent in themselves (for they have none), but in accord with that which wisdom grants them, and which they acquire through habituation and practice. And because there exists neither science nor art in any other part of the soul than the reasoning element, the virtues that relate to the appetitive part are not such as to be teachable, because they are neither arts nor sciences (for they have no proper object of study). Indeed wisdom, in its capacity as science, bestows on each of the other virtues their proper objects, even as the helmsman instructs the sailors about

certain things that are not visible to them, and they obey him; and
the same applies to the soldier and the general.   10

4. Since vices are subject to degrees of intensity, misdeeds will not
be equal either, but some are more serious, others less; in consequence of which legislators provide greater punishments for some
than for others. As for the virtues, although they are extremes inasmuch as they are perfect and resemble the straight line, yet in   15
another way they can be seen as means, by virtue of the fact that all
or at least most of them may be viewed as having on either side of
them two vices, one on the side of excess, the other of deficiency. For
instance, in the case of generosity, there can be seen on the one side
of it meanness, and on the other prodigality.   20

5. Passions may show lack of measure either by overstepping what
is proper or by falling short of it. For neither would someone who
failed to become angry even at an insult to his parents, nor yet someone who became angry at every provocation, even the most trivial, be
regarded as being moderate in his passions, but quite the reverse.
And again, similarly, someone who shows no grief even at the death   25
of his parents is seen as insensible, while someone who seems like to
waste away with grief is held to be over-sensitive and immoderate in
his passions, but he who grieves, but does so to a moderate extent, is
seen as moderate in his passions.

6. Further, someone who is afraid of everything, and is so beyond
measure, is cowardly, while he who fears nothing is rash, but brave is 30
he who preserves due measure in respect of confidence and fear; and
the same goes for the rest. So since in the case of the passions due
measure is best, and measure is nothing else than the mean between
excess and deficiency, for this reason such virtues are means, because 35
they render us moderate in our passions.

31. The Involuntariness of Vice

1. Furthermore, since, if there is anything that is within our power
and which 'owns no master' (*R.* 10. 617e), such a thing would be
virtue (for there would be no reason to praise noble activity if it came
about by nature or by some divine influence), it follows that virtue   40
would also be a voluntary thing, arising from some ardent, and noble,
and abiding impulse. But from the fact that virtue is a voluntary

thing, it follows that vice is involuntary; for who would willingly choose to possess, in the noblest and most valuable part of himself, 185 the greatest of evils? If someone turns to vice, then, first of all he will not turn to it as to an evil, but on the assumption that it is a good; and if someone falls into vice, such a person must inevitably be deceived into imagining that he can by involving himself in some 5 lesser evil divest himself of a greater one, and in this way he will come to it involuntarily. For it is impossible that one should turn to evil through wishing to possess it as such, without being actuated by the hope of some good or the fear of some greater evil.

2. All the actions of the wicked man, then, are involuntary actions; 10 for if injustice is involuntary, then by so much the more will any unjust action by him be involuntary, even as it is a greater evil for him to activate his injustice than it would be for him simply to possess it unactivated. However, even if unjust acts are involuntary, one should none the less punish doers of injustice, and the punishments should vary in degree; for the injuries committed are various, and the 15 involuntariness may arise either from ignorance or from the onset of some passion, and all such latter states can be got rid of by reasoning and good habituation and care.

3. Injustice is such an evil that one should strive even more to avoid committing it than suffering it; for the former is the act of a wicked man, while being wronged is (merely) the misfortune of a 20 weak man. Both are shameful, but committing injustice is worse, in proportion as it is the more shameful. It is advantageous for the wrongdoer to undergo punishment, even as it is for a sick man to submit his body to a doctor for treatment; for all punishment is a kind of cure for the soul that has sinned.

32. The Emotions

25 1. Since most of the virtues operate in relation to the emotions, it is incumbent on us now to define what an emotion is. An emotion is an irrational motion of the soul, in response either to something bad or to something good. It is called an irrational motion because emotions are neither judgements nor opinions, but rather motions of the irrational parts of the soul; for they come about in the affective part 30 of the soul, and they are ⟨not⟩ really *our* actions, nor under our con-

trol. At any rate, they often come about without our wishing, and indeed despite our resistance. There are times, after all, even when we recognize that the sensations presented to us are neither unpleasant, not pleasant, nor yet worthy of fear, when we are nevertheless driven by them, which would not be the case had they been of the same nature as judgements; for judgements, when once we have condemned them (whether rightly or wrongly), we reject. We say 'in response either to something bad or something good', because the presentation of a thing of indifferent value does not provoke an emotion; all emotions arise as a result of the presentation of either something good or something bad. For if we suppose that something good is present to us, we feel pleasure; in the imminence of such a thing, desire; while if we suppose that something bad is present, we feel distress, and if imminent, fear.

2. There are just two simple and basic emotions, pleasure and distress; the others are compounds of these. For one should not count fear and desire in with these as being equally basic and simple. He who is in a state of fear, after all, is not entirely deprived of pleasure; for one could not even survive for any appreciable length of time, if one were devoid of all hope of relief from, or at least mitigation of, evil. Nevertheless, he suffers from a predominance of distress and trouble, and in this way he is involved with distress. Again, he who is possessed by desire, to the extent that he remains in a state of anticipation of attaining (what he hopes for), enjoys pleasure, but inasmuch as he does not have complete confidence or certain hope, suffers anxiety.

3. Since desire and fear are not primary emotions, it will be granted without hesitation that none of the other emotions is, either— I mean, for example, anger, and longing, and regret, and suchlike; for in these pleasure and pain can be seen, as if they were compounds of these.

4. Of emotions, some are 'wild', others 'tame'. 'Tame' are such as belong naturally to man, being necessary and proper to him. They remain in this state as long as they preserve moderation; if they come to exhibit lack of moderation, they become bad. Such are pleasure, distress, anger, pity, shame. It is proper, after all, to feel pleasure when things are in accordance with nature, and to feel distress at the opposite situation. Anger, for instance, is necessary for repelling and taking vengeance on enemies; pity is properly linked to regard for one's fellow man; and shame serves to keep us from disgraceful acts.

35

40

186

5

10

15

20

25 Other emotions are 'savage', such as are contrary to nature, arising as
they do from perversity and bad habits. Such are mockery, joy at the
misfortunes of others, and hatred of one's fellow men, which are
wrong irrespective of their degree of intensity or anything else, since
they do not admit of a 'mean'.

30 5. On the subject of pleasure and distress, Plato declares that these
emotions are produced by what are in a way natural motions originating from within us, distress and grief supervening upon motions that
are contrary to nature, while pleasure arises from tendencies to restore
the natural state. The natural state he considers to be that between
35 distress and pleasure, being the same as neither of them, and it is the
state in which we spend most of our time.

6. He teaches, furthermore, that there are many sorts of pleasure,
some relating to the body, others to the soul; and that of pleasures,
some mix with their opposites, while others remain pure and uncon-
40 taminated; some involve memory, while others arise from hopes; and
some are shameful, such as are intemperate and involve wrongdoing,
while others are moderate and to a certain degree participate in good-
187 ness, such as joy at good deeds and pleasures derived from the exercise of the virtues.

7. Since there are many pleasures that are disreputable, there is no
point in enquiring whether pleasure can be counted among the
absolute goods. It seems, in fact, to be precarious and without value,
being by its nature supervenient, and containing nothing proper to
5 true being or primary, and coexisting with its opposite. For pleasure
and distress are intermingled, which would not have been the case,
had the one been purely good and the other evil.

33. Friendship and Love

1. That friendship which most properly deserves the name is no
10 other than that which arises from reciprocal goodwill. This is manifested when either one wishes his neighbour to flourish equally with
himself. This sort of equality, furthermore, cannot be maintained
except among those of like character; for 'like exhibits friendship for
like when it is ruled by measure, but the unmeasured cannot be har-
15 monized either with each other or with the measured' (*Lg.* 4. 716c).

2. There are other relationships also that are accounted friendships, but they are not such, since they have merely a superficial colouring of virtue. These are the natural affection of parents for their children and of kinsfolk for one another, as well as so-called political and club friendships. These, however, do not always have the characteristic of 20 reciprocity of goodwill.

3. Erotic love is also in its way a form of friendship. There is an honourable form of love, which is that of a noble soul, there is a base form, which is that of a bad soul, and there is a median form, which is that of a soul in a median state. Therefore, even as there are three states of the soul of a rational being, the one good, the other bad, and a third which is median, so it would follow that there are three forms 25 of erotic love, differing from each other in form. That there are three is indicated particularly by the fact that they have aims which differ from one another. The one that is base is directed only at the body, dominated by pleasure and in this respect taking on a bestial charac-ter; the noble one is directed only at the soul, which demonstrates its 30 suitability for promoting virtue; and the median one is directed at the combination of body and soul, being attracted to the body, but direct-ing itself also towards the beauty of the soul.

4. The person who is a suitable object of love, also, occupies a median position, being neither bad nor good. For this reason the personification of Love should be identified, not as a god, but rather 35 as a daemon—never entering into an earthy body, however, but 'transmitting to men what comes from the gods' (*Smp.* 202e), and vice versa. Generally speaking, given that love is distinguished into these three aforementioned species, the love of the good lover, being free from passion, can be regarded as an art, and hence has its place 40 in the rational part of the soul. Its aims are to discern the worthy object of love, to gain possession of it, and to make use of it. One selects such a one on the basis of whether his aims and impulses are 188 noble, are directed towards Beauty, and are strong and ardent. He who sets out to gain such an object of love will not gain it by spoiling or heaping praises on his beloved, but rather by restraining him, and demonstrating to him that life in his present state is not worth living. When he captures the affections of his beloved, he will make use of 5 this position by passing on to him the means by which he may become perfectly exercised in virtue; and the aim for this pair is to progress from being lover and beloved to becoming friends.

34. Politics: The Various Types of State and Constitution

1. Among constitutions, Plato declares that some are non-hypothetical, and these he has described in the *Republic*. In this work he first sketched out the state free from war, and secondly that which is 'fevered' and involved in war, in the course of his enquiry into which are the best of these, and how they might be established. On the analogy of the division of the soul, the state is also divided into three elements, the guardians, the auxiliaries, and the artisans. To the first of these groups he allots the role of deliberation and administration; to the second that of such military and police action as may be necessary (these are to be regarded as the spirited element of the state, since they come to the aid of the rational element); and to the third he allots the exercise of the arts and crafts and other such activities. The rulers he considers should be philosophers and contemplators of the primary Good; for only in this way will they be capable of administering everything properly.

2. For human affairs, he says, will never have relief from evils, until either philosophers become kings or those who are called kings, by virtue of some divine dispensation, become true philosophers. States will not be administered to the best effect and with (true) justice until the position is reached where each part fulfils its proper role, so that the rulers take counsel on behalf of the people, the auxiliaries put themselves at the disposal of the rulers and do battle for them, and the remainder of the people freely obey both of these.

3. He says that there are five types of constitution: first, the aristocratic, when the best men rule; secondly, the timocratic, when the rulers are devoted to the acquisition of honours; thirdly, the democratic, and after this the oligarchic, and lastly, tyranny, which is the worst.

4. He describes other constitutions which are based on the presence of certain conditions, such as that in the *Laws* and the emended one in the *Letters*. This kind he employs for the 'diseased' states in the *Laws*, which already have a definite territory set apart for them and a picked selection of men of all ages, so that they require education, organization, and armament in accordance with the particular characteristics of their natures and territories. Those, for instance, which are by the sea will be involved in maritime commerce and naval warfare, while those which are situated inland will be suited to land warfare,

of the light-armed variety if their territory is mountainous, heavy-armed if they occupy level or gently rolling country; and some of these latter might also develop cavalry forces. In this kind of city he does not institute community of wives.

5. Politics, then, is a virtue which is both theoretical and practical, the aim of which is to render a state good, happy, harmonious, and concordant. It exercises a directive role, and has as subordinate to it the sciences of war and generalship and the administration of justice. Politics concerns itself with a vast array of subjects, but above all the question of whether or not one should make war.

35. The Difference between the Philosopher and the Sophist

1. Now that we have described the characteristics of the philosopher, we may observe how the sophist differs from him. First of all, in his manner, in that he makes himself available for hire by young men, and that he prefers to *seem* than to *be* noble. Then in his subject-matter, since the philosopher concerns himself with what exists always in the same state and in relation to the same things, whereas the sophist is concerned with non-being, retreating into an area which is so dark that it is difficult to discern anything clearly.

2. Non-being is not, after all, the contrary of being; for that is non-existent and uncognizable and without any substance, such that if one were forced to express it or to think it, one would be forced into circularity by reason of its inherent contradiction. Non-being, to the extent that one can attribute a sense to it, is not a pure negation of being, but expresses a secondary relation to another thing which follows upon being in the primary sense, in such a way that, if things did not participate in non-being, they could not be distinguished from each other. As things are, the varieties of non-being are as extensive as the things that are; for anything that is not a particular thing is to that extent a non-being.

36. Conclusion

So much, then, will suffice as an introduction to the study of the doctrines of Plato. Some of what has been said has been presented in

30 proper order; other parts, perhaps, somewhat randomly and out of
    order. But at any rate what has been expounded here gives one the
    capability to examine and discover subsequently all the remainder of
    his doctrines.

COMMENTARY

Introductory Note: Some sections of the commentary, which deal with textual or linguistic details, are enclosed in square brackets. This indicates that they will be of little or no interest to purely philosophical readers.

TITLE

The title of the work on the *pinax*, and at the beginning, of *Parisinus graecus* 1962 (**P**), which is the oldest and best manuscript (see Intro. 5.1), is *Alkinoou didaskalikos tōn Platonos dogmatōn*, while at the end of the same MS we find *Alkinoou epitomē tōn Platonos dogmatōn*. In the only other independent testimony to the text, *Vindobonensis philosophicus graecus* 314 (**V**), the title is lacking, but the subscription is identical with that of P, and there is every reason to suppose that the title was also. We may also note the complete unanimity of the MSS as to the name of the author—Alcinous.

CHAPTER 1

1. On the general conception of Plato's works as comprising a body of *dogmata*, see Introduction, Sect. 3. The expression *kyriōtata dogmata*, 'principal doctrines', is reflected in Clement of Alexandria, *Stromateis*, 5. 1. 10. 1 (*ta kyriōtata tōn dogmatōn*, with reference to the Greek philosophers having stolen them from Moses), and more remotely, in the title of Epicurus' *Kyriai Doxai*.

The initial definition of philosophy, as *orexis sophias*, 'striving' or 'desire for wisdom', seems to be just a watered-down version of that in the Platonic *Definitions* (414b), where philosophy is defined as 'the striving for knowledge of the eternally existent' (*tēs tōn ontōn aei epistēmēs orexis*), but ultimately it derives from *Republic* 5. 475b, where the *philosophos* is stated to be an enthusiast (*epithymētēs*) for *all* wisdom. The noun *orexis* is not in fact used by Plato (though frequently by Aristotle). As a philosophical term implying *rational* desire (as opposed to *epithymia*), however, it has a distinctively Stoic ring (cf. *SVF* 3. 442). Certainly, after the Stoics had made this distinction, *epithymia* would no longer have been felt suitable as part of a definition of philosophy.

This definition of philosophy is found also in Nicomachus of

Gerasa (*Ar.* 1. 2. 5 Hoche), and, slightly elaborated ('a striving for *divine* wisdom') in Diogenes Laertius' summary of Platonic doctrine, *Lives of the Philosophers* 3. 63. Later, Iamblichus (*VP* 159 Nauck), characteristically attributes it to Pythagoras. It is clearly basic in the tradition.

The second definition clearly derives from a combination of *Phaedo* 67d ('a freeing and separation [*lysis kai chōrismos*] of soul from body'—referring to *death*—and *Republic* 7. 521c, where 'true philosophy' is described as a 'freeing and turning away (*periagōgē*) of the soul'—although Plato does not say 'from the body', but rather from the night-time day of the Cave to the 'true daylight'. Alcinous has simply de-mythologized this latter, and hitched it up with the *Phaedo* passage. It is interesting that a similar definition occurs in Iamblichus (*Protr.* 70. 9–13 Pistelli).

The definition of wisdom given here (152. 5) is Stoic in its inspiration, cf. *Stoicorum Veterum Fragmenta* 2. 35 (= 26a Long–Sedley, from Aëtius): 'Wisdom is the science of the divine and the human', but long since, no doubt, accepted as common philosophic currency (cf. Cic. *Tusc.* 4. 26. 57; *Off.* 2. 5; Philo, *Congr.* 79; Apul. *de Plat.* 2. 6. 228).

2–3. These two sections are based closely on *Republic* 6. 485b–487a, where Socrates is setting out the requirements for the philosophic nature. Only certain details of terminology (*prosoikeioun* meaning 'fit', 'accommodate', *rheustē*, 'flowing', 'dissolute', as an epithet of material substance, *katestalmenos* meaning 'calm', 'restrained', *eidopoiein*, 'characterize') are non-Platonic, but even in these cases the thoughts being expressed are in no way un-Platonic. What is interesting is to see how a set of scholastic principles is extracted from Socrates' remarks. This, as we shall see, is a paradigm of how later Platonist scholasticism is created, by leaching out from the dialogues all that is literary, or tentative, or contradictory with any other passage, in order to produce a coherent body of doctrine.

The requisites for successful philosophizing in later Greek philosophy are often presented as a triad, an idea that goes back primarily to Aristotle, who enunciates it first at the beginning of the *Eudemian Ethics* (1216ᵃ15 ff.), though the substance of it can be extracted from the whole above-mentioned passage of the *Republic*, especially the final section. The attainment of happiness, Aristotle suggests, is the product of a combination of *physis* (natural aptitude), *mathēsis* (study), and *askēsis* (practice). That this formulation had become something of a commonplace by the Middle-Platonic period is indicated by its use in such sources as Pseudo-Archytas, *On Education* 3. 41. 20 ff. Thesleff), and Philo of Alexandria, *Life of Abraham* 52–4. A. doubtless knew of this formula, but he prefers to base himself more directly on the text of Plato. Plato returns to this topic in book 7. 535a–c, where his summary of the necessary qualities of the philosophic nature arranges itself more neatly into a triad of 'aptitude for study', 'willingness to study', and *philoponia*, which could be understood as love of practice.

4. This section sums up the doctrine of the previous two, but adds a warning about the dangers of failing to give proper education to the natures properly suited for it, that is, those endowed with the proper *euphyiai*, or 'good natural qualities'. This latter is an Aristotelian and Stoic, not a Platonic, conception (e.g. Arist. *EN* 3. 7. 1114^{b}12; *Rh.* 1. 6. 1362^{b}34; and *SVF* 3. 366—it appears also in the Platonic *Definitions*, 413d, but that document dates to a period later, at least, than the older Stoa), but here Plato is presumed to be aware of it, and his references to 'justice', 'courage', and 'self-control' at *Republic* 6. 487a (characteristically listed in reverse order here by A.) are taken as referring to their homonymous *euphyiai*. The term also occurs, we may note, in the Anonymous *Theaetetus* Commentary, 4. 46–5. 3, where it is combined with *askēsis* (with reference to Theaetetus himself, who is probably to be regarded as an *exemplum* of the ideal student in later Platonism).

CHAPTER 2

The distinction between the theoretical and the practical life, in its explicit form, at least, is Aristotelian, not Platonic (cf. e.g. *EN* 10. 7; *Metaph.* 6. 1), though Plato could be seen as prefiguring it in such passages as *Gorgias*, 500c–d, where Socrates makes the contrast between the 'political' life, as advocated by Callicles, and the philosophical life; *Republic* 7. 540b, where the contrast is made between the Guardians' pure philosophizing and their period of practical service to the state; and *Politicus* 258d, where the distinction is made between arithmetic and sciences akin to it which are 'unconcerned with *praxeis*', and skills such as carpentry and manufacture in general, which are intimately involved with *praxeis*. The distinction is explicitly attributed to Xenocrates by Clement of Alexandria (*Strom.* 2. 5 =

Fr. 6 Heinze), and was already accepted as Platonic, or at least as common philosophical currency, by Antiochus of Ascalon (*ap.* Cic. *Fin.* 5. 58; Aug. *CD* 19. 3), Eudorus of Alexandria (who throws in *hormē* ('impulse') for good measure, as a third division between the other two, cf. Stob. *Ecl.* 2. 42. 7 ff. Wachsmuth), and Philo of Alexandria, who, for instance, makes it the basis of his distinction between the Essenes, who follow the *bios praktikos*, and the Therapeutae, who, observe the *bios theorētikos* (*Vit. Cont.* 1). On the general topic of the classification of *bioi* in antiquity, see R. Joly (1956).

The superiority of the theoretical life to the practical, and the involvement of the practical life with *anankē*, which we might render 'constraining factors' (e.g. the general needs a war, the doctor a disease), is derivable from *EN* 10. 7–8, esp. 1177^{b}7 ff. (but for *timios*, which I have rendered 'of (primary) value', cf. particularly 1178^{b}31), though *anankaios* here may, as Whittaker suggests (n. 20 ad loc.), owe something to Socrates' remark in *Republic* (7. 521^{b}7), that 'you will *compel* (*anankaseis*) the Guardians to undertake the wardenship of the city'.

The Peripatetic commentator Aspasius, at the beginning of his commentary on the *Nicomachean Ethics* (*in EN* 1. 1–3 Heylbut), makes this contrast most succinctly: 'The treatment of ethics and politics, in respect of its necessity (*kata to anankaion*), is prior to theoretical philosophy, but in respect of dignity (*kata to timion*) it is inferior'. This is obviously a generally agreed-upon commonplace in Platonic and Peripatetic circles. Aspasius, however, means here, by *anankaios*, rather, 'necessary to life', whereas I am taking A. to imply something more negative, 'bound up with the necessities of life'. I may be wrong here, but it seems to me that A., by the way in which he has constructed the contrast (linking *anankaios* with *hepomenos*, 'secondary'), has given a different slant to the adjective. This interpretation is supported also by his remarks later in the chapter.

2. A good parallel to the distinction made in this section may be found in Plutarch (*An. Proc.* 1025d–e), where he says that 'the soul is at once contemplative (*theōretikē*) and practical, and contemplates the universals but acts on the particulars, and seems to cognize (*noein*) the former but perceive (*aisthanesthai*) the latter', in a context where he is discussing the composition of the soul.

As regards the terminology here, *energeia* is of course a distinctively

Aristotelian term, with the sense not just of activity, but of actualization. *Nous*, 'intellect', may here be taken as the technical term for the faculty of intuitive, or non-propositional, as opposed to discursive, cognition. It is actualized in the contemplation of God and the Ideas, presented here as the thoughts (*noēseis*) of God (as in ch. 9. 1 below; see note there, where the background to this concept will be discussed). The verb *eupathein* is a reference to *Phaedrus* 247d, where the soul 'gazing upon (*theōrousa*) truth is nourished and made happy (*eupathei*)', though it has also no doubt acquired the overtones of the Stoic conception of *eupatheia*, that is, the rational equivalent of passion.

That this highest mental state is described here, not as *sophia* (the Aristotelian term for it, cf. *EN* 6. 7. 114ᵃ9 ff.), but *phronēsis* (the Aristotelian term for *practical* wisdom) shows the influence of *Phaedo* 79d, of which the phrase 'this state of the soul is called wisdom (*phronēsis*)' is a virtual quotation (just a change of *keklētai* to *ōnomastai*—either a result of the fact that A. is quoting from memory, or a deliberate *variatio*); and that this in turn is identified with 'likeness to God' (*homoiōsis theōi*) is due to the influence of the famous passage *Theaetetus* 176b (but cf. also *R.* 6. 500c), which is the agreed characterization of the *telos*, or end of human life, for all Platonists from at least Eudorus on (cf. ch. 28 below).

The string of epithets describing the contemplative life (153. 9–11) is notable. The adjectives have a predominantly Stoic coloration: *prohēgoumenon* ('primary') and *oikeiotaton* ('most proper to us') certainly so; *euktaiotaton* ('most desirable') is not so readily identifiable (the sole Platonic usage, at *Laws*, 10. 906b7, has a different meaning), but from its use by Plutarch in a distinctly Stoic context (*Comm. Not.* 1070b, as one of a distinctly Stoic-sounding series of adjectives) one might adjudge it to be favoured by Stoics (it is also favoured by Philo, but this proves nothing definite); as for *timios* ('valuable'), though Platonic, it is employed frequently (as Whittaker, 1990: 78 n. 24 notes) by Marcus Aurelius, which is significant.

Why precisely A. should produce this string of epithets is not clear, but we can reasonably assume, I think, that he is not indulging in empty pleonasm. On other occasions when he produces strings of epithets, such as 10. 164. 30–4, or 27. 180. 7–9, he is intending to evoke definite Platonic or other contexts (see Comm. ad loc.). It seems likely here that, if indeed he is employing a string of identifiably Stoic epithets, he is seeking to co-opt them into

Platonism. We will see this process at work in respect of both Peripateticism and Stoicism throughout the treatise.

The description of *praxis* and the practical life (153. 12–15), though owing something, I think, to Aristotle, *Nicomachean Ethics* 10. 7, embodies a verbal echo of *Republic* 6. 500d, where 'compulsion is laid upon the philosopher to practise imposing upon human affairs both in public and in private the patterns that he sees there (sc. in the intelligible world)'.

3. This section continues the exposition of doctrine of *Republic*, book 7 (esp. 520a–521b), though it seems to take its start from Socrates' remark back in book 1. 347c–d, that the good man will only enter upon government reluctantly, through fear of being ruled by someone worse. The *spoudaios* (a perfectly Platonic term, but also, of course, a Stoic term for the wise man), like the Platonic Guardian, will 'descend' to the level of the *bios praktikos* to avoid the worse situation of having the affairs of state in the hands of inferior people, but he will never regard such activity as more than *peristatikos*, 'dependent on circumstances' (153. 17). This adjective is, once again, like the noun *peristasis*, distinctively Stoic (cf. *SVF* 3. 114. 496)—though the noun, at least, is employed by various Middle Platonists (e.g. Maximus of Tyre, *Diss.* 36. 6; anon. in *Tht.* 6. 17–29; Albinus, *Isagoge* 149. 31 and 35 Hermann)—denoting actions worthy in themselves (*kathēkonta*), but necessitated by circumstances which one would rather be free of.

It is fair to note here that A. differs significantly from Antiochus of Ascalon (and from Arius Didymus in his account of Peripatetic ethics, *ap.* Stob. *Ecl.* 2. 143. 24 ff.) in his attitude to the *bios praktikos*. Antiochus (cf. Cic. *Fin.* 5. 58; Aug. *CD* 19. 3) declared in favour of the 'mixed' life (i.e. one in which *theoria* and *praxis* were blended), claiming that at least such activities as the drafting of constitutions and legislation in general are to be chosen for their own sake, while A. would accord them only the highest rank among the *peristatika*. Arius, similarly, declares that the *spoudaios* will choose 'both to do and to contemplate *ta kala*', and this will include, if circumstances allow, 'consorting with (*sumbioun*) kings or legislation or other political activity'. This he will do by preference, not just in response to circumstances (*prohēgoumenōs, mē kata peristasin*, Stob. *Ecl.* 2. 144. 19–20). He too recognizes the 'mixed' *bios* as an ideal.

These are hardly major differences of opinion (Witt (1937: 44), indeed, tries to dismiss them altogether), but they are of interest, especially in the context of the interaction between philosophy and politics (both Antiochus and Arius practised what they preached, the former consorting with Roman statesmen, and advising Cicero to return to public affairs, the latter acting as an adviser to Augustus). A.'s position, however, is undeniably the one truer to the principles of Plato.

The conjunction of verbs 'foster and develop' (*trephein kai auxein*, 153. 22) is, we may note, a reminiscence of *Phaedrus* 246e2, where the context is the 'fostering and developing' of the wings of the soul by contact with the divine, which is 'beauty, wisdom, and goodness', a context which is intended to be evoked here.

CHAPTER 3

1. The triple division of philosophy into physics, ethics, and logic is attributed by Posidonius (*Fr.* 88 Edelstein–Kidd), in its explicit form, at least, to Xenocrates (= *Fr.* 1 Heinze), but he also, in the same passage, speaks of Plato as the *de facto* (*dynamei*) originator of it. In saying this, he probably does not have in mind any single passage, but rather a series of them, where Plato seems to refer to one or other of these divisions, such as *Republic* 7. 525a and 9. 582c, or perhaps *Phaedrus* 248b (for 'physics', i.e. 'the contemplation of what exists'), *Politicus* 259c–d ('theoretical' and 'practical' philosophy = physics and ethics), and *Sophist*, 253d (dialectic = logic). The attribution to Plato of the tripartite division seems to be accepted without qualification by Antiochus of Ascalon (Cic. *Acad.* 1. 19), and is taken up by such contemporaries of A. as Apuleius (*de Plat.* 1. 3. 187) and Atticus (*Fr.* 1. 19 ff. Des Places), both of whom give an account of the previous philosophers from whom he derived each part of philosophy—from the Pythagoreans first principles and ethics, from the Milesians physics, from the Eleatics logic and dialectic. This view of Plato as 'he who first gathered the scattered parts of philosophy into one', in the words of Atticus, is obviously accepted by A. as non-controversial.

A. here avoids the Xenocratean (and later) terms *phusikon*, *ēthikon*, and *logikon* (*meros*) in favour of the more Platonically justifiable *theōrētikē*, *praktikē*, and *dialektikē*, the first two of which terms he has just introduced in the previous chapter. He is thus able to grant a position of primary dignity to physics in the guise of *theoria*. There is, I think, an element of conscious correction of the tradition in A.'s use of this terminology (which is itself, however, chiefly Aristotelian rather than Platonic). 'Physics' becomes just one subdivision of 'theoretic', just below, along with theology and mathematics, even as 'ethics' is only one branch of 'practic', along with economics and politics, and 'logic' only one of the two branches of 'dialectic', the other being rhetoric (though logic itself undergoes a four-fold subdivision in sect. 2, which complicates the situation). There is no other example in the philosophical tradition of this terminology being used instead of the normal one, which is attested in a multitude of sources. There is considerable variation, however, in the order in which the three parts are presented. A. follows Xenocrates (at least as reported by Posidonius) in his exposition of them here (cf. also Apuleius, *de Plat.* I. 3. 187; Atticus, *Fr.* I. 19 ff. Des Places; Hippolytus, *Ref.* I. 18. 2; DL 3. 56), where he is listing them in order of dignity. When he sets out to discuss them in turn, however, he follows the order logic–physics–ethics, the more usual Peripatetic and Stoic order (cf. DL 7. 39–41; Cic. *Acad.* I. 5–7; and the order of Aristotle's works followed by Andronicus in his edition), since logic is agreed to be preliminary, as being a 'tool' (*organon*) for the rest of philosophy, and one's ethics depends on one's view of the world, so that it should follow physics. Some Platonists, however, among them Antiochus (*ap.* Cic. *Acad.* I. 19), Eudorus (*ap.* Stob. *Anth.* 2. 42. 11–13 Wachsmuth–Hense), and Atticus (*Fr.* I Des Places) did favour the order ethics–physics–logic, an order which Antiochus certainly attributed to Plato and the Old Academy.

Two details of A.'s characterization of the logical part of philosophy are worth noting, as indicating a degree of syncretism of the tradition of which he is a part. First of all, in dividing 'dialectic' into logic and rhetoric, he is subtly adapting the standard Stoic division (cf. DL 7. 41 = 31a LS), but with 'logic' and 'dialectic' changing places. Secondly, although the system of logic he presents is Peripatetic rather than Stoic, he ignores the well-known Peripatetic characterization of logic as *not* a 'part' of philosophy, but rather an instrument or tool *preparatory* to it (cf. Alexander, *in APr.* I. I. 3–4. 29).

2. The fourfold division of 'dialectic' given here in the MSS is paralleled by Sextus Empiricus in *Pyrrhoneiae Hypotyposeis* 2. 213 (though in the reverse order), who presents it as being that of 'some of the dogmatists', but it constitutes a problem. It should probably be aug-

mented, as suggested by Carl Prantl (1855–70: i. 610–11 n. 72), by the addition of *analutikon* after *horistikon*, since this quartet of procedures, division, definition, analysis, and induction is standard in later philosophy (e.g. Plot. *Enn.* 1. 3. 4; Ammonius, *in Porph.* 34. 17 ff. Busse; Proclus, *in Crat.* 2. 5 Pasquali), and A. in fact discusses all four just below, in chapter 5. 1. Syllogistic is not really to be grouped closely with these four. They are preliminary to it, and it has its own subdivisions. Prantl's emendation may be accepted, then, I think, despite the parallel with Sextus—*and* despite the circumstance that Aristotle's own account of syllogistic is in fact entitled 'Analytics', which might lead to the two terms being conflated in some accounts (such as that of Sextus mentioned above). The fact, however, that A. deals with them all in chapter 5 would seem to settle the matter.

A more detailed discussion of these divisions may be postponed to chapter 5, but the subdivisions of syllogistic other than the apodictic or 'necessary' may be noticed now, as they will not be mentioned again (except briefly at 6. 4, where Plato's use of *endoxoi* and *eristikoi* syllogisms is referred to).

Epicheirematic syllogisms, based on *endoxa* (denoting whatever you can get your opponent to agree to, i.e. based on reputable opinions, which he might be expected to accept), are generally referred to by Aristotle as 'dialectical' (e.g. *Top.* 9. 11. 162^{a}16), though Aristotle does use the term 'epicheirematic' at *de Memoria* 2. 451^{a}19. For *endoxon*, cf. Aristotle, *Sophistici Elenchi* 9. 170^{a}40, and *Topica* 1. 1. 100^{a}30, where it is identified with the dialectical syllogism. For a definition of the enthymeme, see Aristotle, *Analytica Priora* 2. 27. 70^{a}10 ff. and *Rhetorica* 1. 1. 1355^{a}4 ff., where the difference between dialectical and rhetorical syllogisms is set out. Aristotle nowhere describes the enthymeme as an 'incomplete syllogism', however, though this description of it is to be found in Demetrius, *Eloc.* 32, so it may go back quite far in the Peripatetic tradition.

We may note, once again, as at the end of chapter 2, 'necessity' being brought in as a description of the 'lower' activities, such as practical politics or forensic rhetoric, in which a philosopher may have to indulge in order to survive.

3. The tripartite division of 'practic' seems to go back in substance to the end of book 1 of Aristotle's *Eudemian Ethics* (1. 8. 1218^{b}8 ff.), where he is concerned with the proper end, or *telos*, of practical philosophy. This, he declares, is that which falls under the supreme among all the practical sciences, to which he gives the title of *politikē*

kai oikonomikē kai phronēsis, 'politics and household management, and practical wisdom'. These, however, are intended by Aristotle here as just three names for one thing, whereas the scholastic mind (no doubt looking also to *EN* 6. 8. 1141ᵇ23 ff., where Aristotle does distinguish politics from the rest of *phronēsis*) takes these as three names for three distinct subdivisions, understanding *phronēsis* as the name for ethics proper. This division is to be found in Arius Didymus' account of Peripatetic ethics (*ap*. Stob. 2. 147. 26 ff.), and later in Calcidius' *Commentary on the Timaeus*, chapter 265 (where it forms part of an exegesis of *Tim*. 47b6–c1, indicating a Middle-Platonic attempt to appropriate the tripartite division for Plato.

We may note the use of the un-Platonic (and indeed post-Classical) term *prostasia*, 'administration' (153. 40). It occurs, interestingly enough, three times in Philo (*Spec. Leg.* 1. 16; *Virt.* 58; and *Flacc.* 105), in all of which places Philo combines it with *epimeleia*, 'care', which A. has just used here in connection with morals. This is hardly coincidence. We seem here to have a snippet of Hellenistic scholastic terminology—though it is notable that both terms are common in the administrative language of Roman Egypt and elsewhere, so that the influence may come rather from that quarter (*sōtēria*, 'preservation', of the state being proper to the Emperor himself).

4. The tripartite division of 'theoretic' is also of Aristotelian inspiration, deriving specifically from *Metaphysica* 6. 1. 1026ᵃ6 ff., where Aristotle identifies physics, mathematics, and 'first philosophy' or theology as the three divisions of theoretical science. The description of theology as being concerned with 'the motionless and primary causes' is borrowed directly from this passage, though A. does not go on to characterize the other two, as does Aristotle, as 'movable and dependent' (physics) and 'motionless but dependent' (mathematics). Instead, to characterize 'physics', he borrows phrases from Plato, 'the motion of the heavenly bodies', probably, from *Republic* 7. 530a (though cf. also *Grg.* 451c8, *Smp.* 188b5, and *Lg.* 12. 966e2–3); and 'the constitution of this world' from *Timaeus* 32c.

On a further point of detail, the use of the term *apokatastasis* (154. 3) to denote the return of a planet to its former position after a periodic circuit is not Platonic or Aristotelian, but taken from Hellenistic astronomy. It is first attested in Diodorus Siculus (2. 47; 12. 36), but is probably to be seen behind Cicero's Latin in *Laws* 1. 24, where it is linked with *periodos*, also used here by A. (*perpetui cursus* (*periodoi*) *conversionesque caelestes* (*apokatastaseis*).

CHAPTER 4

1. A. now turns to the first of his divisions of philosophy, Dialectic, and takes his start from an exposition of the *kritērion*, or the mechanics of making a judgement. This topic, which falls under what we should now regard as epistemology, became in Stoic philosophy, and then, as a result of Sceptical attacks on the Stoic position, in Hellenistic philosophy generally, the accepted preliminary to any systematic exposition of logical theory. The term occurs in Plato at *Republic* 9. 582a (though cf. also *Tht.* 178b–c), a passage which was probably taken by later Platonists as proof that the Master was familiar with the concept (he also seems to refer to the *kritērion di' hou*, or *organon* of judgement just below, in 582d).

In later times, in fact, the *Theaetetus*, as we are informed by the Anonymous *Theaetetus* Commentator (2. 11 ff.), was declared by some Platonists to be concerned with the *kritērion* (though he himself—in agreement with Thrasyllus in his edition—considers it to be about knowledge). Interestingly enough, when explaining what he means by the *kritērion*, he uses the terminology of *Republic* 582d, 'that by means of which we judge as an instrument' (*to di' hou krinomen hōs organou*). The *Theaetetus* may, however, have been produced as a properly *sceptical* discussion of the *kritērion* already by the New Academy. Indeed, the passage 184c makes a distinction between the instrument (*di' hou*) and the means (*hōi*) of sense-perception which could hardly escape the notice of the scholastic mind.

The most comprehensive discussion of the *kritērion*, though from the sceptical perspective, is to be found in Sextus Empiricus, *adversus Mathematicos* 7 (cf. also *P.* 2. 14–79), and it can be used to elucidate the doctrines presented rather summarily here. A. begins by distinguishing three elements, *to krinon*, 'the judging element', *to krinomenon*, 'the object of judgement', and the *krisis*, the judgement itself, resulting from the conjunction of the first two. Properly speaking, he says, the act of judgement itself would be the criterion. What does he mean here by the *krisis*, or 'act of judgement'? If we turn for enlightenment to Sextus (*M.* 7. 34 ff.; *P.* 2. 70 ff.), we may conclude that, in Stoic terms, it is the *katalēptikē phantasia*, or 'cognitive impression' (cf. *SVF* 2. 105 = 40a LS), though A. will not use this terminology, and rather dismisses the actual act of judgement as a candidate, while granting that it is the criterion *kuriōs*, 'properly speaking'.

For Sextus, the *phantasia* is the criterion *kath' ho*, 'according to which'. To characterize it, he utilizes what was nicknamed by Willy Theiler (1930: 20 ff.) 'the metaphysic of prepositions'—by which he meant the expression of metaphysical relationships by means of prepositional phrases—which we see A. employing to distinguish two senses of *to krinon*, 'the judging element', *to huph' hou*, 'that by which', or the agent, and *to di' hou*, 'that through which', or the instrument. This means of distinguishing causes may indeed go back to Antiochus of Ascalon, as Theiler would argue (1930: 55 n. 1)—it was certainly utilized by his follower Varro (*ap.* Aug. *CD* 7. 28), as well as by the 'eclectic' philosopher of the first century BC, Potamon of Alexandria (DL, *Proem.* 21)—but it is at any rate common philosophical currency by A.'s time. Sextus uses the same prepositional descriptions for the agent (*M.* 7. 22) and the instrument (*M.* 7. 48) of judgement, in the process of disposing of each of them as reliable criteria. For A., we may note, there is no problem any longer about the *existence* of a criterion. The sceptical challenge has long since receded, as far as Platonist circles are concerned.

A discussion of the *kritērion* also occurs in a little work of the second-century astronomer Ptolemy, *On the Kriterion and the Commanding Faculty* (on which see the most useful discussion by Long (1989: ch. 10), followed by a text and translation of the work). Like A., Ptolemy gives no indication that there is any problem about the existence of a *kritērion*. In chapter 2 of his work, he distinguishes (1) the agent of judgement, which he identifies as the intellect (*nous*), the instrument of judgement, which he identifies as sense-perception (*aisthēsis*), and the means, identified as the *logos*, all of which accords fairly well with the distinctions made by A.

2. Having made these distinctions, A. turns to an examination of levels of *logos*, or reasoning, which he has identified as the *di' hou* of judgement. The highest level is that attributable only to divine intelligences, since it is unattainable by the human intellect. If we ask what the nature of this could be, a suggestion is perhaps provided by the analysis given later by Plotinus (e.g. in *Enn.* 5. 3) of the peculiar nature of the cognition of *nous*. It possesses its objects *immediately*, not being dependent on any sort of image or efflux between which and the object itself a sceptical wedge could be driven. This sort of cognition is thus absolutely immune to error, while the level of *logos* to which we can attain is variable in its grasp of its objects. Only when it is directed towards the knowledge of

realities (*hē tōn pragmatōn gnōsis*) can human *logos* aspire to freedom
from error.

We may note in this connection some interesting terminology.
What, first of all, does it mean to describe divine reasoning as *aleptos*
(154. 22), which I have translated, perforce, as 'ungraspable'? One
would have expected an adjective expressing freedom from error, to
go with *atrekēs*, 'unerring'. Some light may be thrown on this, however, as Whittaker points out, by comparison with Sextus Empiricus
(*M.* 7. 122), where Sextus attributes to Empedocles the doctrine that
there is one sort of 'right reason' (*orthos logos*) which is divine, the
other human, and that the divine level of *logos* is 'inexpressible' (*anex-
oistos*), while the human is expressible. Sextus actually uses the adjective *aleptōs* just below (124), when giving Empedocles' view that the
truth is not entirely ungraspable by men. It sounds as if A. is rather
elliptically combining two different aspects of divine intellection, its
incomprehensibility by us and its accuracy.

As for *atrekēs*, it is not a Platonic adjective—indeed, it is very
largely poetical—but it is notable that Plutarch introduces it *three
times* into a quotation of *Timaeus* 40b8–c2, at *de Facie in Orbe Lunae*
937e, 938e, and *Quaestiones Platonicae* 1006e, so that it seems to have
been introduced into the scholastic tradition, possibly from (at least
one reading of) Parmenides (Fr. 1. 29 Diels–Kranz).

3. Human reasoning is now in turn divided into two, according as it
is directed towards objects of intellection (*noēta*) or objects of sense-
perception (*aisthēta*), and is characterized accordingly as *epistēmonikos*
or *doxastikos*. The distinction between *epistēmē* and *doxa*, of course, is
thoroughly Platonic (*R.* 5. 476c ff.; 6. 511d; 7. 534a), but the adjectival forms linked with *logos* are not (though Plato does use *doxastikos*
in other contexts, e.g. *Tht.* 207c2; *Sph.* 233c10). The terminology
does go back to the Old Academy, however, as we can see from
Sextus' account of Speusippus' epistemology at *adversus Mathematicos*, 7. 145–6. There, however, Speusippus is presented as making
a distinction between *epistēmonikos logos* and *epistēmonikē aisthēsis*,
which is a rather more subtle one than that being made here, so it
would not be apposite to relate A. too closely with Speusippus himself. Again, it would seem from Sextus' account of Xenocrates just
below (*M.* 147–9) that he used *doxastikos* as well as *epistēmonikos* with
logos, but this is in the context of a triadic division of reality into
objects of *epistēmē*, *doxa*, and *aisthēsis*, so that no close connection can
be made with Xenocrates either. What we have here, rather, is a sort

of boiled-down basic Platonism, owing nothing specific to any individual Platonist. Plutarch, in an exegesis of *Timaeus* 37b–c (*An. Proc.* 1023f–1024a), makes a distinction between the opinionative (*doxastikē*) and intellective (*noētikē*) motion of the soul, which is similar to this, without being identical.

The collocation of terms *bebaion kai monimon* (154. 29–30) is Platonic, borrowed from *Timaeus* 29b (*monimou kai bebaiou*), but with the characteristic Alcinoan inversion (see Intro., Sect. 3).

4. A. next turns to the definitions, in turn, of sense-perception, memory, opinion, and intellection, which occupy the rest of the chapter, and exhibit various interesting features. Some introductory remarks on the whole exposition may be in order. A. is here constructing an epistemology (or, more probably, presenting one which has been previously constructed) on the basis of certain key passages of Plato (*Ti.* 43c; *Phb.* 33c–34a; *Tht.* 191b–192a), though borrowing formulations and concepts from both Aristotle (e.g. opinion as a *symplokē*) and the Stoics (e.g. *physikē ennoia*). This may be usefully compared with other Platonist epistemologies, notably that of Antiochus of Ascalon, found in Cicero's *Academica Priora* 19–21 and 30, and that attributed to the Peripatetics in Sextus Empiricus (*M.* 7. 217–26). Sextus credits 'the Peripatetics' with distinguishing two classes of things, the intelligible and the sensible, and positing two criteria to correspond with them, intellect and sense, 'while common to both, as Theophrastus used to say, is the evident (*to enarges*)'. On sense, however, there supervenes impression (*phantasia*) and memory, the former being 'of the sense-object which produced the affection (*pathos*) in the sense', while the latter is 'of the *pathos* arising in the sense', and thus at one remove from the external stimulus. As we shall see, while A. envisages more or less the same role as here for memory, he has very little use for *phantasia*.

The definition of sense-perception (*aisthēsis*) given here plainly owes much to *Timaeus* 43c, where Plato talks of sensations as 'motions caused by all these (sc. affections (*pathēmata*) of colliding bodies) being borne through the body and falling upon the soul', as well as to *Philebus* 33c–34a, where the process of acquiring impressions through sense-perception is similarly described. Even his definition of *aisthēsis* as an affection (*pathos*) rather than a motion of the soul (as e.g. in the Platonic *Definitions*, 414c), which has been claimed as a Stoicism by Witt (1937: 54 n. 1) and Invernizzi (1976: 91), is derivable from the mention of *pathēmata* in the *Timaeus* passage, and of both *pathēmata* and *pathos* in the *Philebus* passage (33d2; 34a2), as well as figuring in the account of Peripatetic epistemology in Sextus (*M.* 7. 219). The possibility of Stoic influence need not be excluded, I suppose, as long as it is recognized that the Stoics themselves may have been influenced by the Platonic passages. The description of *aisthēsis* as an 'impression' (*typos*) in the soul might more plausibly be claimed as Stoic (though the Chrysippan term seems rather to have been *typōsis* (*SVF* 2. 55 = 39a LS, but cf. *typos* in *SVF* 2. 58); one might, however, adduce the use of *typos* in *Theaetetus* 192a4, in a context involving sense-perception and memory, a passage which may itself have influenced the Stoics.

Similarly, the definition of memory as a 'preservation' (*sōtēria*, 154. 39) of sense-perception is derivable directly from *Philebus* 34a10, though the possibility of later intermediaries, once again, need not be excluded. The description of it as 'remaining' (*emmonos*) is probably borrowed from Critias' description in *Timaeus* 26c of how he remembers the story of Solon's *Atlantis* poem as told to him by his grandfather. The phrase 'through passage of time' (*dia khronou plēthos*, 154. 38), in turn, is probably borrowed from *Politicus* 269b5, as is 'fading away' (*exitēlos*) from *Critias* 121a10, though these borrowings would be purely verbal.

5. The definition of opinion (*doxa*) as a combination (*symplokē*, 154. 40) of memory and sensation is derived from *Philebus* 39a, but seems to owe its formal structure, at least, to Aristotle's definition of 'impression' (*phantasia*) in *de Anima* 3. 3. 428ᵃ25 (where, however, Aristotle is concerned to specify, *contra* Plato in *Sophist* 264a, what *phantasia* is *not*, sc. not a *symplokē* of opinion and sense-perception). In this connection, it is interesting to observe the rather minimal role of *phantasia* in A.'s scheme, as opposed, for instance, to Sextus' account of the Peripatetics (*M.* 7. 221–2), where *phantasia* is the motion that immediately arises in the soul consequent on the onset of a sensation (Sextus actually identifies it with memory, which cannot be quite right, surely—though *phantasiai* in turn immediately become memories). It is precisely this use of *phantasia*, however, that corresponds to A.'s use of *aisthēsis* here. This presumably reflects Plato's own relatively sparing use of the term (only *Tht.* 152c, 161e; *Sph.* 264a—*R.* 2. 382e hardly counts), but it results in the term *aisthēsis* having to do duty (as so often elsewhere in Greek) for both 'sensation' and 'perception', i.e. both the mere reception of sense-data, and the initial processing of these, making translation difficult.

Phantasia is finally brought in at the end of the section as an alternative term for the 'painter' of *Philebus* 39b, which is a reasonably accurate equivalence, though in the *Philebus* the work of the 'painter' supervenes upon that of the 'scribe', which is the conjunction of memory, sensation, and the *pathēmata* consequent upon memory. This is a rather more elaborate picture than that presented in *Sophist* 264a, for example, where *phantasia* is presented merely as the *pathos* which results from a judgement (*doxa*) based on a sensation.

The latter part of the section is substantially based on *Theaetetus* 191d–194b, where Socrates is describing how a false judgement can arise, though with some input also from *Philebus* 38b–39c and *Sophist* 263d–e, as noted in the text. The term *anazōgraphēsis*, 'delineation' (155. 16), however, though derivable in substance from *Philebus* 39d–40a, is not to be found in Plato, but occurs first in Stoic sources (e.g. in the title of a book by Chrysippus, *SVF* 2. 9. 23).

A comparable, but significantly different, Platonist account of concept formation is to be found in Cicero's *Academica Priora* 19–21, adapted from Antiochus of Ascalon, who presents a far more Stoicized theory than the present one, but similarly traces the process of knowledge-acquisition up from simple sense-data ('White!' 'Sweet!'), through complex ones ('Horse there!', 'Dog there!'), to propositions ('If it is a human being, it is a rational mortal animal'). Witt is once again misguided in juxtaposing them too closely (1937: 53–5), despite the reservations he allows himself.

One difficulty in the last part of the section (155. 15–16) is the reference of the expression 'those things from which they derive' as opposed to the opinions (*ta doxasthenta*) which the soul looks upon. I presume this refers to the sensible objects which will have produced the memory-images which it possesses, and which it is now perceiving again.

6. The next section concerns intellection (*noēsis*). A.'s definition of it recalls verbally his definition of *theōria* in chapter 2, except that here he specifies 'the *primary* objects of intellection (*noēta*)', a specification he will elaborate on in a moment. As in the first section of the chapter, he distinguishes the activity of pure, disembodied minds (pure souls, daemons, gods) from that of the mind in the human body. The 'primary intelligibles', as becomes plain in the next section, are the Forms in their transcendent state. Here arises the question of the origin of A.'s view of the Forms as 'thoughts of God', about which much discus-

sion has taken place (cf. e.g. Rich (1954: 123–33). That the concept goes back as far as Antiochus of Ascalon is not, I think, in much doubt, though it is only attested for Antiochus' pupil Varro (*ap.* Aug. *CD* 7. 28). For a Stoicizing Platonist like Antiochus, the concept fits comfortably with the Stoic Logos-doctrine, and we can see him giving a suitable Stoicizing interpretation of Plato's doctrine in the *Timaeus* in such a passage as Cicero, *Academica Posteriora* 27. But it seems to me extremely probable, if not inevitable, that this doctrine was already developed in the Old Academy, and specifically by Xenocrates—if not already in Plato's lifetime. After all, constructive meditation on such a passage as the Sun Simile of *Republic* 6 should lead one to conclude that the Forms, dependent as they are on the Good for their existence as well as their knowability, are only fully actualized when cognized by a mind. This is not a conclusion emphasized by Plato himself, admittedly, but it does none the less seem to follow, at least as soon as the Good comes to be taken as the supreme god. Similarly, if one demythologizes the *Timaeus*, as Speusippus and Xenocrates certainly did (rightly, in my view), then inevitably the Demiurge becomes merged with the Essential Living Being, the sumtotal of the Forms, as simply the active principle of the intelligible world. Indeed, Plato seems to hint at this when, having asserted that the Demiurge is contemplating an eternal model in his fashioning of the physical world (*Ti.* 29a), he then declares that he wished everything to be as like as possible to *himself* (*Ti.* 29e). In any event, whether or not Plato intended such deductions to be made, it seems very likely that Xenocrates, at least, made them, if one may conclude that from his declaring his first principle to be Mind (Frs. 15–16 Heinze). A mind must think, and its contents can only be the Forms, in whatever guise Xenocrates understood them. The problem of the origin of this doctrine, therefore, seems to me not a great one.

Pure intellection, then, is the immediate cognition of the Forms by a disembodied mind. When the mind is 'installed' in a body, on the other hand—A. borrows the verb *embibasthēnai* from *Timaeus* 41e1— its activity is to be termed rather *physikē ennoia*, 'natural concept', or, better perhaps, 'natural concept-formation'. This is a distinctively Stoic term, adopted by A. to express a Platonist concept. A good account of the Stoic theory is given at *Stoicorum Veterum Fragmenta* 2. 83 (from Aetius). For the Stoics, a *physikē ennoia*, also termed a *prolēpsis*, or 'preconception', is a concept that arises naturally in the soul of man as a result of repeated similar sense-perceptions, in contrast to concepts which we acquire by a conscious process of learning and attention. A Platonist such as A. can accept this formulation, with the qualification that what the repeated sense-perceptions are doing is stirring up in our minds a recollection (*anamnēsis*) of a Form, which we are then enabled to discern as immanent in sensible particulars. A. sees Plato as alluding poetically to this concept at *Phaedrus* 246e, where he declares the 'wing' of the soul to be its capacity to be 'carried upward' to a knowledge of the Forms by contemplating instances of beauty and goodness in the physical realm. It is worth noting that the concept of *physikē ennoia* is employed also by Albinus in the *Isagoge* (6. 150. 22 and 33 Hermann), and in Anon. *in Tht.* 46. 43 and 47. 44, apropos *Theaetetus* 148d–149a, and in both cases the connection with *anamnēsis* is explicit.

It is interesting also that A. credits Plato with using the expression 'simple item of knowledge' (*epistēmē haplē*, 155. 33), which he does not in fact use. Aristotle talks of *epistasthai haplōs* and *haplōs epistēmē* in *Analytica Posteriora* A 2. 71^{b}9–16, but he is referring there to 'absolute knowledge' in the sense of knowing 'both that the explanation because of which the object is is its explanation, and that it is not possible for it to be otherwise' (trans. Barnes), whereas A.'s use of the expression here seems to refer merely to basic items of knowledge, out of which the sciences, or 'natural and scientific reasoning' are built up, as we learn at the beginning of sect. 7. However, it could be argued that such items of knowledge, to qualify as such, would have to meet the conditions propounded by Aristotle in *Analytica Posteriora* 1. 2., so it may be that A. is taking the expression from that passage.

The image of the 'wing of the soul', as referring to the rational part, was, not unnaturally, popular in later Platonist circles, e.g. Philo, *de Plantatione* 22; *Heres* 126; Plutarch, *Quaestiones Platonicae* 1004c–d.

As regards memory, it is notable that back in sect. 4 (154. 39), it is presented as simply the result of the preservation of sense-impressions, whereas here it is given as a synonym for *physikē ennoia*. There is no real contradiction here, however. For A., memory's activity in preserving and 'collating' sense-impressions also serves to give us an intuition of the forms as they are manifested in matter. It does serve to remind us, however, of the ambiguous status of memory (and imagination) in late Platonist epistemology.

7. In the next section, A. moves on to consider the proper objects of both intellection and sense-perception (or 'opinion'), in a passage which is to a large extent an exegesis of *Timaeus* 28a1–4, and in the

process makes an interesting distinction between 'primary' and 'secondary' objects of each. Primary objects of intellection are the transcendent Forms (*ideai*), which are cognized properly by *noēsis*, direct intuition (it is also described below, at 156. 6, as 'a kind of comprehension'—*perilēpsis tis*, the noun being derived from *perilēpton*, *Ti*. 28a2—as opposed to *diexodos*, 'discursive reasoning'), while its secondary objects are the 'forms in matter" (*eidē epi tēi hulēi*—elsewhere, *enula eidē*), of which the relevant organ of knowledge is rather *epistēmonikos logos*, 'scientific reasoning'. In each case we get the interesting qualification, which is not entirely easy to interpret, that whichever of these two activities of the mind is seen as being primary is exercised with some sort of back-up from the other ('not without', *ouk aneu*, is the formula used). Presumably this means that, for example, when one discerns the 'form' of beauty or justice in a particular physical object or action, it is one's *logos epistēmonikos* that comes into play first, but *noēsis* is brought in to confirm its findings, whereas in pure contemplation one first intuits a given Form, and only then turns to reasoning about it.

The term 'forms in matter' is not Platonic, but can be derived from the works of Aristotle. Indeed, the terminology used here by A. is very close to that appearing in such a passage as Aristotle, *de Caelo*, 1. 9. 278ᵃ9, where Aristotle, however, is contrasting the form (*eidos*) of, for example, a circle considered *in itself*, and the form of the circle thought of in conjunction with its matter (*en tēi hulēi*), though without, of course, any implication of transcendence on the part of the form. The form in matter, then, is substantially the Aristotelian form, regarded as the Platonic form in its 'participated' aspect.

The separate status of 'forms in matter' in the philosophy of Plato himself is very doubtful, though later Platonists had no doubts on the question. Plato could be seen as employing the concept in the last argument of the *Phaedo*, while the entities which pass into and out of the Receptacle in *Timaeus* 50c could hardly, it was thought, be anything else. The contrast between *idea*, for the transcendent form, and *eidos*, for the immanent, seems to occur first in an interesting passage of Seneca (*Letter* 58, sects. 16–22), where Seneca is following a Platonist source, possibly Eudorus (not, I think, Posidonius, cf. Dillon 1977: 136–7). It is plainly by his time an established feature of Middle-Platonist scholasticism. Calcidius, we may note, in chapter 337 of his *Commentary on the Timaeus*, discussing *Timaeus* 51b7, speaks of two levels of form in the following terms:

In the same way (sc. as there are two levels, or aspects, of matter) a duality of form can be observed on the paradigmatic side of reality: the form by which matter is adorned, and, alongside it, that form after the image of which the form conferred upon matter is made. The form impressed in matter is the second form; the first is the one after the image of which the second has been made.

This has an interesting resemblance to A.'s distinction between primary and secondary intelligibles.

In the case of sense-objects, the situation is more complicated again, since we are presented with not two but three types, or levels, of object, bearing only a superficial resemblance to the objects of intellection. Indeed, the formal parallelism set up between the two classes of object is quite illusory. First we have, as 'primary sense-objects', qualities as distinct from qualified objects, such as 'whiteness', or 'sweetness', or 'heat'. 'Whiteness', for instance, we may note, is to be viewed as not inhering in any particular white object, but, as perceived by 'primary' sense-perception, it is not the *form* of whiteness, since that would be an intelligible object. It must rather be the basic apprehension of the sense-datum 'white', as opposed to the perception of the whiteness in a particular object. Plainly the ultimate source, at least, of this distinction is the passage *Theaetetus* 182a, where Plato introduces to philosophical discourse the term 'quality' (*poiotēs*), and makes a distinction between 'whiteness' (*leukotēs*) and 'white (thing)' (*leukon*). But Plato's 'whiteness' there is rather the whiteness in the object *before* it is perceived, as opposed to the white sense-datum, and that can hardly be described as a primary object of perception, one would think. In fact, the distinction which A. is making seems to owe more to that made by Aristotle in *Metaphysics* 5. 7. 1017^{a}7 ff., between being 'accidentally' (*kata sumbebēkos*) and 'essentially' (*kath' hauto*), since Aristotle gives as an example 'the just man being cultured' (*mousikos*) or 'man' being white *accidentally*. A. describes his 'white' as *kata sumbebēkos*, which seems to be the result of grafting an Aristotelian distinction onto a theory of perception which he attributes to Plato on the basis of the *Theaetetus* passage.

However that may be, both 'primary' and 'accidental' sense-objects are opposed to what he terms the 'aggregate' (*athroisma*), that is to say, the physical object seen as a bundle of instantiated qualities (the whole physical world, we may note, is described as an *athroisma* just below, at 156. 10). This term is, once again, derived ultimately from the *Theaetetus*, this time from 157b10–c2, where Socrates first unveils the theory of perception recapitulated in 182a ff., though it also seems to have become a technical term in Hellenistic philosophy, if we may judge from Epicurus' use of it in Plato's sense in the *Letter to Herodotus* (DL 10. 62), and Chrysippus' use of it in a rather different connection ('an *athroisma* of concepts and preconceptions') in his treatise *On the Passions* (*ap.* Galen, *Hipp. et Plat.* 5. 3 = *SVF* 3. 841). For A. it is plainly a technical term, its Platonic credentials assured by the *Theaetetus* reference.

The distinction, then, at the level of sense-perception, turns out to be between qualities and *qualia*, on the one hand, perceived, or rather *sensed*, by *aisthēsis* (though *doxa* is brought to bear on them, in order to make the raw sensation a *perception*), and physical objects, perceived by *doxa*, which, however, bases its conclusions on *aisthēsis*.

It can be seen that quite an elaborate theory of knowledge is being adumbrated here, the nature of which is somewhat obscured by the efforts which A. makes to establish a formal parallelism between the processes of intellection and sense-perception. How much of it is original to A. is obscure, but I would guess not much, except perhaps the effort at parallelism, its least fortunate aspect. The most obscure aspect of the theory, I find, is the concept of quality as a primary perceptible, particularly as, in chapter 11 below, A. is going to argue for the incorporeality of qualities, with the implication that they are forms of some sort, which they surely cannot be here. But this question can be discussed further at that point.

8. The final section of the chapter constitutes a summing-up of the theory, and an application of it to the traditional dichotomy of *theōria* and *praxis*, discussed by A. above in chapter 2. The two types of *logos* distinguished earlier in the chapter are now subsumed into a unified 'right reason' (*orthos logos*, cf. the *physikos logos* at the beginning of the chapter, 154. 18), which provides a standard both for questions of truth and falsehood, and of right and wrong action (the influence of Aristotle's discussion in *EN* 6 is discernible here). Since this unified *orthos logos* is in possession of 'natural concepts' (*physikai ennoiai*), which are, as we have seen, the forms as manifested in the physical world and cognized by the embodied intellect, we may take it that it is the agent of intellect, and that the human agent has now, at the end of the chapter, been reintegrated.

The final sentence of the chapter, we may note, seems to contain a reference to *Phaedo* 76d–e, where Socrates says:

Then is our position as follows, Simmias? If the objects we're always harping on exist, a beautiful and a good and all such Being, and if we refer all the things from our sense-perception to that Being, finding again what was formerly ours, and if we compare these things with that, then just as surely as these objects exist, so also must our soul exist before we are born. (trans. Gallop)

CHAPTER 5

1. A. turns now, in this chapter and the next, from epistemology to logic proper—although he has made it clear that for him investigation of the *kritērion* is part, and indeed the primary part, of *logikē*. The topic of Logic as such not being recognized by Plato, A. uses the 'approved' term 'Dialectic', which, however, is made to serve for the whole field of logic. Throughout these chapters, in fact, he will be found quite unhesitatingly claiming Aristotelian and even Stoic logical discoveries for Plato—as, indeed, would his Platonist predecessors at least from Antiochus on, including his own near contemporaries, Apuleius (if the *de Interpretatione* is indeed his) and Galen, in his *Institutio Logica*.

He begins, however, with an attempt to claim Platonic ancestry for the whole topic. His first sentence is presumably a reference to *Republic* 7. 534b, where Socrates says: 'And do you not also give the name 'dialectician' to the man who is able to exact an account (*logos*) of the essence of each thing?' (the amplification about accidents (*symbebēkota*) is Aristotelian, though implicit, it could be argued, in the *Republic* passage). The two modes of enquiry which he distinguishes, that 'from above' (*anōthen*)—division, leading to definition—and that 'from below' (*katōthen*)—analysis, are Platonic enough, being introduced at *Phaedrus* 266b (though the Platonic term used there for the activity of *analysis*—a term which Plato does not use—is *synagōgē*, 'collection'), and are much utilized thereafter, particularly in the *Sophist* (cf. esp. 218d–231b; 264c ff.) and *Politicus*. Significantly, A. has no problem about using the distinctively Aristotelian term. All the other terms in the section, induction (*epagōgē*), syllogism, and the expressions which I have translated 'restricted' and 'more general' (in fact the passive and active participles respectively of *periechō*, in its logical sense of 'include', cf. Arist., *APr.* 1. 27, 43^{b}22–30; *Metaph.* 5. 26, 1023^{b}26–32) are unequivocally Aristotelian in origin. It may be, however, that an acceptance of, in particular, Aristotle's *Topica* as essentially a formalization of the rules of procedure for the dialectic of the Academy made A.'s procedure (and that of Apuleius and Galen) more reasonable than it seems to us. In one important respect, though, A.'s concept of dialectic remains Platonic, as opposed to Aristotelian: it is not presented as an abstract, logical enquiry; for A. (as we see particularly in the exposition of analysis, below), it is still intimately involved with ontology.

The description of dialectic as dealing with the essences of things and their accidents finds a parallel in Pseudo-Galen's *History of Philosophy*, 6 (603. 9–11 Diels *DG*), where logic is defined as 'that (part of philosophy) through which we learn what each thing is, both as regards its essence and as regards its accidents.' It is a fairly obvious definition, justification for which could be seen, as Whittaker suggests, in such a passage as *Sophist* 255c12–13, where things are distinguished into those that 'are what they are in themselves' (*auta kath' hauta*) and 'what they are with reference to other things' (*pros alla*), though Plato's distinction between 'absolute' and 'relative' being in that passage is not in fact the same as that between substance, or essence, and accidents.

2. A. now proceeds to deal in turn with the parts of dialectic which he has distinguished. The distinction of types of *diairesis* is doubtless not original to A. (reasonably close parallels occur in Ps.-Galen, *Hist. Phil.* 14 (607 Diels *DG*), and Clement, *Strom.* 8. 19. 3). Division of a genus into species is thoroughly Platonic (cf. e.g. *Sph.* 267d), and very popular in the Old Academy, especially with Speusippus, as we know (cf. e.g. Arist. *APo.* 2. 97ᵃ6–22 = Fr. 63 Tarán).

Division of a whole into parts, on the other hand, is not presented as such in the dialogues, although the first example of it that A. gives—the division of the soul—is Platonic enough in principle (the actual double division, however, first into 'rational–irrational' and then of 'irrational' into 'spirited' and 'passionate', is a later Platonist attempt to reconcile the tripartition of the *Republic* with the virtual bipartition presented in the *Phaedrus* and the *Timaeus*, such as we find in many other sources (cf. Aëtius, *Plac.* 4. 4. 1 (389a10–390a4 Diels *DG*); Plu. *Virt. Mor.* 442a; Galen, *Hipp. et Plat.* 9. 6. 584. 28–30 De Lacy). In this connection we may note that A. (like Aëtius) avoids the Platonic term *thymoeides* for 'spirited' in favour of the Aristotelian *thymikon* (e.g. in *de An.* 3. 9. 432ᵃ24–6, which is a key passage for later doxography); it only occurs once (178. 45–6), as against seven instances of *thymikos*.

The next example, again, that of the division of speech into meanings, with the distinguishing of homonyms given as an instance, is not
attested in the dialogues, but Speusippus (Fr. 68a–c Tarán) is known
to have made an exhaustive classification of words, employing *diairesis*,
and distinguishing *homōnyma* and *synōnyma* (though with meanings
different from those of Aristotle), so that we need not take this as distinctively Aristotelian. An example for what A. has in mind would be
kuōn, used to mean terrestrial dog, dog-fish, or the dog-star, an example alluded to by Aristotle in the *Sophistici Elenchi* 166ᵃ16, and much
beloved by the commentators (e.g. Simp. *in Cat.* 24. 12. Kalbfleisch).

The last two types of division, that of accidents (*symbebēkota*)
according to subjects (*hypokeimena*), and that of *hypokeimena* according to their *symbebēkota*, are not attested for Plato either, though the
example of the first type is taken, ultimately at least, from Plato, *Laws*
3. 697b (cf. also Arist. *EN* 1. 8. 1098ᵇ12–15), while the second type
could be derived, remotely, from *Lysis* 220c–d, though it doubtless
owes more to Peripatetic polemic against the absolute Stoic division
of men into good and bad.

3. The next section deals in more detail with the most important type
of division, that of genera into species. The connection between division and definition is already made, implicitly at least, in *Politicus*
262a–c (cf. esp. 262b5–c1: 'but it is not safe, my dear fellow, to chop
off little bits (*leptourgein*); it is safer to go down the middle in one's
cutting, since you are more likely to hit upon forms in that way. And
this is of the highest importance in investigations [sc. about
definitions]'), though a more explicit connection is made by Aristotle
in *Analytica Posteriora* 2. 13. 96ᵇ15 ff. and *Metaphysica* 7. 12, especially 1037ᵇ32 ff. However, A., though he uses the same example
('man') as does Aristotle, selects more 'Platonist' differentiae ('rational', 'mortal'), as opposed to Aristotle's 'tame', 'two-footed'. In fact,
the Old Academic definition seems to have been 'wingless (broad-
nailed) biped', as in the Platonic *Definitions* (415a), but 'rational
mortal animal' is well established in the later Platonist tradition (cf.
Philo. *Vit. Abr.* 32; Sext. Emp. *M.* 7. 277; Simpl. *in Cat.* 104. 20).
Also, A. uses the expression '*proximate* differentiae' (*prosekheis
diaphorai*), which is not used by either Plato or Aristotle (Aristotle
uses *prōtai*, 'primary', *Metaphysica* 7. 12. 1037ᵇ32 ff.).

4. A. turns next to the process which he terms *analysis*. This, as has
been noted above, is an Aristotelian, not a Platonic, term, but it cov-

ers a number of procedures which are certainly Platonic, and indeed
A. supplies examples from the Platonic corpus for each of the three
procedures which he identifies. For Aristotle, the term has various
senses, but all involve logical rather than metaphysical operations, e.g.
analysing syllogisms into their proper premisses (*APr.* 1. 49^{a}19; 50^{a}8);
analysing an object into differentiae or qualities and substrata
(*Metaph.* 5. 1024^{b}12); solving a problem by analysing it into its component parts (*EN* 3. 1112^{b}20–4). In this last passage, however,
Aristotle makes a remark which can be given metaphysical or ontological implications: 'That which is the final product in the analysis is
primary in point of generation.' This seems to provide a guiding
thread to A.'s use of the term. In each case we are involved in an
'ascent' (*anodos*) from the physical to the intelligible level of being,
though his two latter procedures have a logical aspect as well.

The terminology of the section is largely Platonic. The *anodos* in
the first type of *analysis* is derived from *Republic* 7. 517b5, where the
progress out of the cave is explained as the soul's *anodos* to the intelligible region (*noētos topos*), while the third embodies a direct reference
to the description of the highest segment of the Line in *Republic* 6.
510b6–7. Only the second type employs Aristotelian terminology, cf.
Analytica Posteriora 1. 3. 72^{b}18–22, where Aristotle declares that 'not
all knowledge is demonstrative; the knowledge of immediate premisses
(*amesa*) is not by demonstration (*anapodeiktos*)'.

5. The first procedure is that employed by Plato, through the mouth
of Diotima, in the *Symposium* (210a ff.), a sort of 'resolution' of the
concept of beauty by studying, first, what it is that makes an individual physical person or thing beautiful, and then proceeding 'upwards',
through the consideration of what it is for entities of ever greater
degrees of abstraction to be beautiful, until one reaches an intuition of
beauty in the absolute.

The second procedure could be seen to be based on Plato's
description of what occurs in the highest segment of the Line, at
Republic 6. 510b and 511b, where the soul 'advances from a hypothesis to a first principle which transcends hypothesis', and then (511d)
'after attaining that, takes hold of whatever follows immediately from
it, so as to proceed downwards to the conclusion'. However, A. over-
lays this with a certain amount of distinctively Aristotelian terminology, as we have seen.

He now produces as an example of this procedure the proof of
the immortality of the soul from *Phaedrus* 245c–e. Apart from the

obviously Aristotelian terms mentioned above, A. uses certain terms, such as 'what is being sought' (*to zētoumenon*) and 'evident' (*enarges*) in a rather more technical sense than is attested in Plato, but one cannot, I think (as Witt (1937: 63) seeks to do) build very much on this in the identification of intermediate sources.

6. As an interpretation of the procedure envisaged by Plato in the top segment of the Line, A.'s formulation here may seem pretty tendentious, but we ourselves cannot, after all, be sure what Plato had in mind there, and in any case, A. is not tying himself too closely to that passage. Nevertheless, it remains problematical as to what distinction he himself is drawing between his second and third types of analysis. The second is described initially (in sect. 4) as ascending from demonstrable to indemonstrable propositions, and the third as ascending from hypotheses to non-hypothetical first principles. However, it becomes clear from his fuller explanation that, whatever may be the real distinction between the procedures, A. himself, at least, has in mind, in connection with this third type, primarily the passages at *Phaedo* 100a and 101d, where Socrates speaks of

assuming in each case some hypothesis which I consider strongest, and whatever seems to me to agree with this, whether relating to cause or anything else, I regard as true, and whatever disagrees with it, as untrue

and then (101d) specifying

if anyone attacks the hypothesis, one pays him no attention and does not reply to him until one has examined the consequences to see whether they agreed with one another or not; and when one has to give an explanation of the hypothesis, one gives it in the same way by assuming some other hypothesis which seems to one the best of the higher ones, and so on until one reaches one which is adequate (*hikanon*).

This 'adequate' principle is widely taken (as it is here by A.) to be identical with the *archē anhypothetos* of *Republic* 510b, so the two passages are after all connected closely in his mind. What, then, is the distinction between them?

On this question, the comments of Invernizzi are useful (1976: ii. 103):

This third type of analysis differs from the second type by the manner in which it arrives at the non-hypothetical. Whereas in the second type the ascent takes place by means of demonstrations, and so according to the model of Aristotelian science, in this third type the ascent to unconditional principles takes place through the verification of the consequences deriving from the principles as they are postulated.

There is, then, some difference in procedure, but it seems to me nevertheless likely that the primary reason for postulating the two types is the (presumably false) belief that the *Phaedo* and *Republic* passages are describing different procedures. It is unfortunate, but interesting, that A. provides no example to illustrate his third type. Plato in fact employs it to 'hypothesize' that the beautiful, the good, the large, and other forms exist (100b5–7), and then postulating that individual things are beautiful, good, or large because they participate in the corresponding forms. But he does not show how one proceeds if one's initial hypothesis is challenged.

7. The chapter closes with a brief mention of induction (*epagōgē*). The term itself is Aristotelian (though the use of the verb *epagein* at *Plt.* 278a should be noted), and indeed A. plainly has such a passage as *Topica* I. 12. 105ᵃ10 ff. in mind, where Aristotle is contrasting induction and syllogistic reasoning, and defines induction as 'the progression from the particular to the general'. A. quotes this, but he prefixes it to 'passage from like to like', which may probably be derived ultimately from the passage of the *Statesman* mentioned above (278b), where mention is made of comparing letters and syllables one knows with other similar ones which one does not know, and pointing out the similarity (*homoiotēs*) between them.

The mention at the end of 'activating (*anakinein*) the natural concepts' is inspired by *Meno* 85b, where the notions (*doxai*) of the slaveboy are said to have been 'activated' (*anakekinēntai*) by the dialectic. A. merely substitutes for this the more 'modern' (Stoic-inspired) term *physikai ennoiai*, which, as we have seen, is his preferred term for the forms as perceived·by the embodied intellect immanent in matter.

CHAPTER 6

1. A. prefaces his discussion of formal logic, and of the syllogism in particular, with an exposition of the various types of proposition, affirmative, negative, universal, and particular, taken ultimately from Aristotle, *de Interpretatione*, chapters 6–8. It is true that Plato uses *phasis* (though not *kataphasis*—that only occurs in *Def.* 413c) and *apophasis* for 'affirmation' and 'negation' in such a passage as *Sophist*,

263e, and this would have reassured a later Platonist that the whole system was basically Platonic, but the technical use of all these terms is Aristotelian (cf. also the beginning of *APr.* 24ᵃ18 ff.). A.'s account here is extremely summary, and he omits the third class of proposition distinguished by Aristotle in *Analytica Priora* 1. 1, the indefinite (*adioriston*), for example, 'contraries are studied by the same science' or 'pleasure is not a good', presumably because they are regarded by Aristotle, and by all later commentators, as equivalent to the particulars.

In *de Interpretatione* 7. 17ᵇ1–3, we may note, Aristotle uses the terms *katholou* and *kath' hekaston* for 'universal' and 'particular', whereas A. uses *epi merous* here for 'particular', but this latter term occurs elsewhere in Aristotle, e.g. *Nicomachean Ethics* 2. 7. 29–31; *Meteorologica* 2. 4. 359ᵇ31, so it is not un-Aristotelian.

Note further that A.'s examples are not those of Aristotle, but have a 'Platonic' flavour.'Socrates walks' is not a Platonist example, but becomes normative in later Platonist and Aristotelian commentary, for example, Simplicius, *in Aristotelis Categorias commentarium* 54. 12; for the propositions 'some pleasure is good' and 'some pleasure is not good' we may refer to *Gorgias* 495a and 499c; for 'all that is base is evil' to *Alcibiades* 1. 116a.

2. The distinction A. now makes between categorical and hypothetical propositions is neither Platonic nor Aristotelian, but it may be attributable to Theophrastus, who certainly dealt with hypothetical syllogisms (cf. Graeser (1973: 92 ff.), and Frs. 29–30 of his collection). Theophrastus' influence in this chapter will be discussed below, but any such influence will have been overlaid in the tradition by that of the Stoics. The terms used here for consequentiality and incompatibility, *akolouthia* and *machē*, were certainly employed by the Stoics (cf. Epict. *Ench.* 52. 1; Sext. Emp. *M.* 7. 392), though one cannot be sure that they do not go back to Theophrastus as well.

The expression *haplē*, 'simple', as applied to *protaseis*, is not found in Aristotle, but does occur in the commentators (e.g. Ammonius, *in Int.* 161. 5–9; Philp. *in APr.* 371. 4 ff.).

3. A. now turns to a discussion of the syllogism itself. The statement that Plato uses syllogism both for refutation (*elenchōn*) and demonstration (*apodeiknyōn*) finds quite a close parallel in chapter 3 of Albinus' *Isagoge* (148. 26 ff. Hermann), where Albinus distinguishes between two main types of dialogue, the 'instructional' (*hyphēgētikos*)—a term

A. uses just below, in section 4—which is concerned with demonstration (*apodeixis*) of the truth through exposition (*didaskalia*), and the 'investigative' (*zētētikos*), the purpose of which is the refutation (*elenchos*) of error, but this cannot be used, I think, to argue for identity of authorship, since both terms are thoroughly Aristotelian. *Apodeixis* and *elenchos* are linked and contrasted, for instance, at *Sophistici Elenchi* 9. 170ª24 ff. and *Metaphysica* 4. 4. 1006ª16 ff., and are both discussed extensively in the *Analytica Priora* (*elenchos* particularly at 2. 20. 66ᵇ11 ff.).

A. follows this with the basic Aristotelian definition of the syllogism (*APr.* 1. 1. 24ᵇ18; *Top.* 1. 1. 100ª25–7—actually adopting the exact phraseology of the latter passage), with the addition of the phrase 'from those very assumptions', but that is just an amplification of Aristotle's phrase *tōi tauta einai*, 'from the fact that they are such', such as Aristotle himself provides in the next sentence. As Witt (1937: 65) points out, A. (and his predecessors) may have been encouraged in crediting Plato with syllogistic reasoning by Aristotle's remark at the beginning of the *Analytica Priora* (24ª24 ff.) to the effect that both demonstration (*apodeixis*) and dialectic may produce a syllogism: 'for both the demonstrator and the interrogator (i.e. the dialectitian) draw a syllogistic conclusion by first assuming that some predicate applies or does not apply to a subject' (A.'s use of the phrase *erōtāi logous* (158. 38) in reference to Plato may embody a reference to *erōtāi* in this passage, but the verb is common enough in logical contexts, cf. also *APr.* 2. 19. 66ª26).

The enumeration of three types of syllogism is not Aristotelian (Aristotle just mentions hypothetical syllogisms at *APr.* 50ª39 ff., but never gets around to discussing them), but may go back to Theophrastus or Eudemus. The pure hypotheticals listed here are credited to Theophrastus by Alexander, *in APr.* 326. 8 ff. (= Fr. 30 Graeser), who gives details of them, which will be discussed below. The 'mixed' (sc. hypothetical premisses, categorical conclusion) are in effect the Stoic 'indemonstrables', as we shall see. These are also attributed to Theophrastus by Prantl (1855–70: 1. 385 and 473 ff.), but the evidence is simply not there (Philoponus, *in APr.* 242. 14 ff., conflates the contributions of Theophrastus and the Stoics, and cannot be given the weight which Prantl puts upon him). In any case, Theophrastus and Eudemus will still have been operating with a logic of terms, rather than of propositions, as do the Stoics, and the example which A, produces conforms to the Stoic format. Who first called this type 'mixed' is obscure; A. is the only surviving Platonist authority to do so (Apuleius, Galen, and Boethius simply present Aristotelian categoricals and Stoic hypotheticals), but Alexander (*in APr.* 262. 28 ff.) attributes this term for Stoic-type hypotheticals to 'the ancients', indicating, perhaps, early Peripatetic discussion of them (Eudemus?).

4. The three types of syllogism distinguished here pick up the distinction made back in chapter 3 (153. 27 ff. Hermann), where the terms used are 'demonstrative', 'epicheirematic', and 'rhetorical' to which 'sophisms' are tacked on as a fourth. Here, however, the rhetorical syllogism, or 'enthymeme' is left out of account, since what are used against people like Euthydemus or Hippias are sophisms. The epicheirematic are here described as *endoxoi*.

5. We turn now to a survey of the three Aristotelian figures, depending ultimately, if not immediately, on *Analytica Priora* 1. 4–7. The only thing remarkable here is the form in which the syllogisms are presented, which is not that of Aristotle himself, but of the later Peripatetic tradition, the so-called 'Classical' form (cf. Jan Łukasiewicz, (1951: chs. 1 and 2)), perhaps developed first by Ariston, but of which A., Apuleius, and Galen are the earliest surviving exponents. We may note also that the middle term, called by Aristotle the *meson* (cf. *APr.* 1. 4. 25^{b}35–6), is called by these three the 'common term' (*koinos horos*), since the term *meson* only seemed to hold good for the first figure.

A. now proceeds to the production of examples from the dialogues. An example of the first figure is discerned in the *Greater Alcibiades*, 115a–116e. We may note here that, although Plato himself gives the first premiss in properly universal form: 'All just things are noble'— the other premiss and the conclusion are only implied in the dialogue—A. omits the universal quantifier (he may have felt that the definite article served adequately to convey universality). It is interesting that he should select the *Alcibiades* when seeking an example, since we learn from Proclus, in his *Commentary on the Alcibiades* (12. 17 ff.), that certain commentators prior to Iamblichus (and thus probably Middle Platonists) divided the dialogue into ten syllogisms, of which the one selected by A. is in fact the fifth combined with the sixth (13. 2–6)—two conclusions are actually reached in this passage: (1) that all just things are advantageous, and (2) that all noble things are good; A. has conflated them. This same argument, we may note, is produced by Sextus Empiricus (*P.* 2. 163), as an example of a Peripatetic syllogism, so it must be firmly established in the scholastic tradition, both Platonist and Aristotelian.

Examples of the second and third categorical figures are derived from the *Parmenides* (as indeed are examples of all but one of the hypothetical and mixed figures), of the second in *Parmenides* 137e4–138a1 ('So if the One had either straight or curved shape, it would have parts and so be many. Therefore, since it has no parts, it is neither straight nor curved'), whereas the third is derived, rather optimistically, from the preceding passage, 137d6–9 ('Further, the beginning and end of a thing are its limits. Therefore, if the One has neither beginning nor end, it is without limits'). The notion of being qualified (*poion*) is deemed to be implied in the passage.

The *Parmenides*, particularly its second part, plainly lends itself to being analysed into syllogisms. Proclus, in his *Commentary*, instances a good many, including that at 137d9–e1 (1125. 1 ff. Cousin). He confines himself, however, to categorical syllogisms, except in the case of 137c9–d4 where, besides discerning a categorical syllogism in the second figure, he constructs a Stoic hypothetical (in A.'s terms, a 'mixed') as well (1104. 23 ff.).

6. We pass now to examples of Theophrastean hypotheticals (also known as 'analogical' or 'total' (*di' holon*) hypotheticals), of which three figures (or rather, three *moods* representing each one of the three figures) are distinguished by Alexander in his report of Theophrastus' doctrine, *in APr.* 326. 20–328. 5 Wallies (= Fr. 30 Graeser):

1. If A, then B, and if B, then C; so if A, then C
2. If A, then B, and if not A, then C; so if not B, then C
3. If A, then C, and if B, then not C; so if A, then not B

(Alexander also distinguishes two by-forms of 1 and 2 which need not concern us, as A. is not concerned with them). A., for a reason which will become plain, I think, in a moment, proposes to switch the second and third figures. He also complicates things a little by choosing as examples propositions containing negatives, which result in different moods for each figure from those set out by Alexander, but this should not distract us too much. The fact, also, that he appears to be using propositions here rather than terms in presenting 'Theophrastean' hypotheticals (we should really use *p*, *q*, *r* rather than *A*, *B*, *C*) is interesting, and bears out the acute observation of Michael

Frede (1956 and 1987: ch. 7), that the distinction between a logic of terms and a logic of propositions is more apparent to us than it was to the ancient logicians.

Of the examples he comes up with from the dialogues, two are from the same passage of the *Parmenides* which he has already mined for categorical syllogisms, and the third is extracted from the *Phaedo*. For Figure 1, he comes up with 137d4–9, which he organizes without too much difficulty into suitable form (the passage involves four propositions rather than three, but that is no matter). For Figure 2 (3), he takes the immediately following passage, 137e1–138a1, which has already served to illustrate *Darapti*, and derives from it (if we discount the negatives), 'If A, then C, and if B, then not C, then, if A, then not B'. Finally, for Figure 3 (2), A. turns to the *Phaedo*, and derives from 74a9–75e7 an argument of the pattern: 'If not A, then B, and if A, then C; so, if not B (assuming the conversion 'if not B, then A'), then C', which is certainly derivable from the text of Plato (one must supply the conclusion, which has dropped out of A.'s text as we have it).

Precisely the fact that it is possible to use the second *Parmenides* passage to illustrate the second categorical figure may have prompted someone (this is hardly an innovation of A. himself) to place Theophrastus' third hypothetical second, in order to achieve symmetry.

It is curious, I think, that, after having boldly claimed that Plato uses these syllogisms 'in many of his works', A. should confine himself very largely to this one section of the *Parmenides*, but it may have pleased him to demonstrate that Plato's arguments could be expressed in various different forms. Certainly Proclus, much later, likes to put Platonic arguments first into Peripatetic and then into Stoic logical form. At *in Platonis Parmenidem commentarii* 1104. 23 ff., for instance, as we have seen above, he works out Plato's argument at 137c9–d3 in both forms, while at *in Platonis Timaeum commentarii* i. 259. 2, he commends Iamblichus for expressing *Timaeus* 28a in terms of a first figure categorical instead of a hypothetical, as do 'certain others' (presumably Middle Platonists, rather than just Porphyry). One would have thought that this procedure in fact constituted a tacit admission that the Master himself was employing neither of these modes, but plainly faithful Platonists took this rather as implying that he was the father of both equally (though A.'s qualification 'in effect' (*dunamei*) before his *Phaedo* example constitutes a sort of admission of the former alternative). Whether this tradition goes back to Antiochus of

Ascalon, as Witt would have it (1937: 66), is uncertain, but not improbable. It is possible also that Ariston of Alexandria (first century BC), a pupil of Antiochus' who turned to Peripateticism, and Boethus of Sidon, are of some importance in this connection, as we know from Apuleius, *peri Hermeneias* (ch. 13), that Ariston took an interest in syllogisms, and from Galen, *Institutio Logica* (ch. 7), that Boethus did. Boethus was a rather idiosyncratic Peripatetic, who was sympathetic to Stoicism, so he may be a better candidate. See on both these men the relevant sections of Paul Moraux's *Der Aristotelismus bei den Griechen* i. 181–92 and 147–70.

It is notable that neither Apuleius nor Galen pays any attention to Theophrastean hypotheticals, though Galen treats of Stoic hypotheticals (chs. 3–5), while Apuleius confines himself to Aristotelian assertoric syllogisms.

7. A. now turns to the consideration of what he calls 'mixed' syllogisms, but what we know as Stoic hypotheticals, or Chrysippean indemonstrables. Once again for an illustration he turns to the *Parmenides*, this time to the section of the Second Hypothesis (145a5–b5) corresponding to that part of the First which he used above for the other two types of syllogism. This he can turn, without too much trouble, into Chrysippus' first indemonstrable argument: 'If *p*, then *q*; but the first, so the second.'

A.'s survey of Stoic hypotheticals in the dialogues seems very perfunctory, but it may be that there is in fact a lacuna after *houtō*, 159. 29. The syntax of the sentence as it stands is very peculiar (one would have to assume *theōreisthai* to be an imperatival infinitive— unless, as is suggested to me by Matthias Baltes, one reads *dei* before it—and *kata touto* seems redundant after *houtō pōs*), and the meaning is hardly satisfactory. In that case, A. will have given us, first, an example of a 'consequentially refutative' (*ex akolouthias anaskeuastikos*) syllogism, Chrysippus' second indemonstrable being of this type (we find an example, in fact, in Galen's *Inst. Log.* 15. 10, taken from *Alc.* 106d—if *p*, then *q* or *r*; but not *q* or *r*; so not *p*); and then, perhaps, examples of the third and fourth indemonstrables, which are actually 'refutative on the basis of conflict' (*ek machēs anaskeuastikos*). He may not, however, have entered into these latter complexities. At any rate, I do not think that he can have ended his survey of 'mixed' syllogisms as abruptly as he appears to here. I wish to take the latter part of the sentence as in fact constituting the conclusion of a different sentence, following a lacuna of indeterminate length, and I translate it accordingly.

The terminology used here by A.—*ex akolouthias katasakeuastikos, anaskeuastikos*—to describe the Stoic indemonstrables is not, so far as we can see, Stoic, but is used by later Peripatetic commentators such as Alexander, *in Aristotelis Topica* 165. 6 ff. Wallies). The adjectives (or rather, the adverbs from them) are used by Aristotle himself, for example in *Analytica Priora* 52ᵃ31 ff., to describe methods of proof, which is where the commentators will probably have derived them from (he also speaks of *kataskeuastikoi* and *anaskeuastikoi topoi* in *Top.* 7. 2. 152ᵇ36 ff.). A. is our earliest source for these terms, but they are plainly, from the way in which he introduces them, not original to him.

8. A.'s summing up here owes a good deal to Plato's account of true oratory in *Phaedrus*, 271a–272b, though with very little exact verbal reminiscence ('perceives with precision (*oxeōs*)', however, seems to be a reminiscence of *Phdr.* 263c4, and the reference to the 'complete (*teleos*) orator' and his art picks up 272a7–8). The actual definition of rhetoric, however, is one that is employed by the Stoics (cf. *SVF* 2. 293), though Sextus attributes it to Xenocrates as well (*M.* 2.6 = *SVF* 2. 294).

9. The basic text for the study of sophistic reasoning is presented here as the *Euthydemus*, but the reference to sophisms 'dependent upon words' (*para tēn phōnēn*) as opposed to those 'dependent on facts' (*para ta pragmata*)—found also in Diogenes Laertius, 7. 43—is a fairly clear reference to the division made near the beginning of Aristotle's *Sophistici Elenchi* (ch. 4, 165ᵇ23–4) between refutations dependent on language (*para tēn lexin*) and those independent of language (*exō tēs lexeōs*), thus claiming the *Sophistici Elenchi* as an exposition of Academic techniques (which it may very well be). If we turn to the *Euthydemus* in search of examples of either kind of sophism, we might take the first two puzzles (275d–277c) as examples of refutation dependent on language ('ambiguity', *amphibolia*), while the second group of six (283b–288a) could be seen as examples of the second kind, concerned as they are with problems of being.

10–11. Next, A. claims the system of categories for Plato (though the use of the verb *hupedeixen* indicates a realization that the Master is less than explicit in his use of them). He is extremely cursory and vague here, speaking merely of 'the *Parmenides* and elsewhere'. If one looks closely at the *Parmenides*, one might discern the following 'categories', some in the First Hypothesis (137c–142a), being denied of the One, others in the Second (142a–155e), being asserted of it; Quantity (150b); Quality (137b, 144b); Relation (146b); Place (138a, 145e); Time (141a); Position (149a); State (139b); Activity and Passivity (139b)—I give them in the normal Aristotelian order, but we may note that in fact Quantity is dealt with last of all. That it is the categories that are being denied of the One in the First Hypothesis (and asserted in the Second) is presented by Proclus (*in Prm.* 1083. 37 ff.) as being the view of some earlier (probably Middle-Platonic) commentators, a view which he rejects himself. Other Platonists saw the categories being employed elsewhere in the Platonic corpus, Plutarch finding them in the *Timaeus*, 37a–b (*An. Proc.* 1023e), the Anonymous *Theaetetus* Commentator (at least some) at *Theaetetus*, 152d (68. 1 ff. Diels–Schubart).

A. now addresses Plato's theory of language (we may note that the actual term *etymologia* is not Platonic, but probably Stoic—Chrysippus, at any rate, wrote a work entitled *Etymologika*, DL 7. 189), with reference primarily to the *Cratylus*. Whatever we may consider the true subject of the *Cratylus*, by the ancients it was seen as a serious contribution to the theory of language. Before entering on a summary of the doctrine of the dialogue, however, A. directs a few words of praise to Plato as a consummate master of every aspect of dialectic, probably drawing on the passage of the *Phaedrus* (266b) where Socrates avows himself 'a lover of these processes of division and collection, as aids to speech and thought', though without any verbatim borrowing. It seems necessary to add, with Whittaker, a third noun after 'division' (*analytikē* seems the best bet), in order to justify the 'all' (*pasai*) in the next clause. For the 'power of dialectic', cf. *Republic* 6. 511b, 7. 537d, *Parmenides* 135c, and *Philebus* 57e–58a.

He now runs through the subject-matter of the *Cratylus*. That the correctness of names was a matter of convention (*thesis*), but convention based on nature (*physis*), is proposed at 422d, 428e, and 435b–c. The example of attaching the name 'horse' to man is taken from 385a. The view that speaking is a kind of action is taken from the passage 387b–d, as is the whole sentence following. The description of the best name-giver (*onomatothetēs*—a term not in fact used by Plato, though it appears in some MSS of the *Charmides*, 175b4, and A. may have read it at *Cra.* 389d9 as well) and of the name as an instrument (*organon*) is dependent on 389d–390a, and the final remarks about using names for teaching each other things come from 388b–c. The remarks about the role of the dialectician, too, in section 11 are derived from 390b–d. It is the section 385–90 of the dialogue, then, that provides A. with the essentials of his doctrine of language.

A notable feature of A.'s treatment of dialectic is the emphasis placed on etymology, which is treated at far greater length than is, for example, syllogistic—an indication, surely, that A. is not much interested in logic as an autonomous discipline, but only as a tool for clarifying questions of physics and ethics.

CHAPTER 7

1. A. now turns from the subject of logic to that of theoretical philosophy, the first of the three basic divisions of philosophy which he distinguished back in chapter 3. As we have seen, he declines to use the commoner term for this, 'physics', preferring to confine that title to the study of the physical world proper, and basing himself instead on the Aristotelian distinction (which he may have felt he could trace back to *Plt.* 259c–d) between *theoria* and *praxis*. The area of theoretical philosophy which he chooses to discuss first, by reason of its introductory nature, is that which he listed last in chapter 3, mathematics. His treatment of it is heavily dependent on *Republic* 7. 524d–533d, as we shall see, and betrays no independent interest in mathematics on the part of A.

The descriptions of the divisions of philosophy largely repeat those of chapter 3 (on which see Commentary ad loc.), though the subject-matter of physics is here given in more detail—the study of man, and of God's providence, being added to, simply, 'the constitution of this world'. All these subjects will be discussed in the following chapters, up to chapter 26.

The subdivisions of theoretical philosophy, as noted above (3. 4), are probably taken from Aristotle, *Metaphysics* 6. 1. 1026ª19, though (characteristically for A.) listed in reverse order.

2. The stated purpose of mathematics as 'the sharpening of the intellect' is plainly based on *Republic* 525d, where Socrates talks of mathematics 'directing the soul upward, and compelling it to discourse about pure numbers' (cf. also 526b), but the actual expression *oxytēs dianoias* is perhaps borrowed from *Charmides* 160a, where 'readiness of mind' (*anchinoia*) is defined as 'sharpness of soul' (*oxytēs tēs*

psychēs)—a definition picked up by the Platonic *Definitions* (412e), where *anchinoia* is defined as *oxytēs nou*. That A. should use *dianoia* here, rather than *nous*, is no doubt prompted by the fact that it is precisely *dianoia* ('discursive reason') that is the faculty which apprehends mathematical reality (cf. *R.* 6. 511e, and sect. 5 below).

The expression 'sharpening' or 'honing (*thēgein*) the soul' is not used by Plato, though it is by Xenophon, albeit in military contexts (*Cyr.* 2. 1. 20; *Mem.* 3. 3. 7), and it is employed in similar contexts by later authors (such as Philo, *de Gig.* 60; *Ebr.* 159 (*parathēgōn*), and Galen, *Script. min.* 1. 49. 25 ff.). The phrase 'ascent to Being' is taken from *Republic* 521c. The word *planē*, 'error', has of course distinct Platonist connotations (cf. e.g. *Phaed.* 81a; *R.* 4. 444b; 6. 505c). Everything else in the section is derivable from *Republic* 525d–527c, including the remarks about the usefulness of geometry for warfare (526d).

[At 161. 21, it is interesting that the archetype MS, P, reads *praseōs heneka*, 'for buying (and selling)', instead of the *praxeōs heneka* of the Platonic text of *Republic* 527a7. Whittaker adopts this, and he may be right, since Plato actually uses the phrase *praseōs kharin* a little earlier, at 525c3, to describe the vulgar uses of arithmetic. However, A. is speaking of geometry here, which is the context being discussed in 527a, so I am inclined to retain *praxeōs*. *Praseōs*, though, is certainly the *lecto difficilior*, and there remains the intriguing possibility that either A., or, less probably, an 'intelligent' scribe, has the earlier passage in mind.]

The general theme of the propaedeutic value of mathematics is quite widespread, not surprisingly, in later Platonist authorities; cf. Nicomachus, *Arithmetica Introductio* 1. 3. 6–7; Theon Smyrnaeus, *Expositio* 1. 1–2. 2 Hiller; Plutarch, *Quaestiones Conviviales* 718e.

3. A. turns next to stereometry and astronomy, drawing heavily on *Republic* 527d–530c, but ignoring, naturally enough, the by-play in the dialogue about the proper place of stereometry, and the true purpose of astronomy. The actual term *stereometria*, we may note—which is actually here a (necessary) emendation of Marsilio Ficino for the *geōmetria* of the MSS)—is not used by Plato in the *Republic*, though it occurs in a similar passage of the *Epinomis* (990d).

While there is nothing here that is not derivable from the *Republic* passage, it is notable that A. considerably tones down Plato's attack on 'vulgar' astronomy as the study of the heavenly bodies as such (529d–e); indeed, he almost seems to reinstate it, relying rather on 530a, only suggesting at the end of the section that its real purpose is to lead us up to the contemplation of 'the creator of all things'. This may indicate a later Platonist modification of Plato's rather extreme position in this passage.

There is also a slight, though interesting, development in the meaning accorded to the phrase Plato uses at 530a7, 'the creator (*dēmiourgos*) of the heaven'. It is not quite clear to whom or what Plato is referring here (it may simply be a quasi-poetical flourish), but A. seems to interpret it definitely (in the process of making a fascinating conflation of it with Plato's phrase at *Ti.* 40c1–2, 'creator of night and day', referring to the *earth*!) as denoting an entity which can be distinguished from a higher entity, termed 'the creator of all things'. The creator of 'night and day, the months and the years' (the latter two introduced from *Ti.* 37e1) cannot, I think, be simply identified with the sun, as Whittaker (1990: 94 n. 124) suggests, since, though the sun is responsible, no doubt, for night and day, it is rather the moon which is responsible for the months, while they might be said to co-operate to produce the years. It seems, in fact, as though this entity is best seen as the 'intellect of the whole heaven', which we hear of below in chapter 10 (see Commentary ad loc.), in which case the 'creator of all things' will be the supreme God of that chapter. If we can assume this, it will have the important consequence that A.'s theological system involving a primary and a secondary god is not something that simply appears in chapter 10 (as has been sometimes suspected), but rather a principle which underlies his whole work (as one should expect). If he introduces it here without fanfare, it is no doubt because he himself saw it as Platonic, the *dēmiourgos* of 530a standing in contrast and subordination to the Good of 509b. On this question see the excellent discussion of Donini (1988: 128–30).

[An alternative solution to the problem, suggested to me by Matthias Baltes, is to read *dēmiourgous*, 'creators', for *dēmiourgon*, which would then refer clearly to both sun and moon, and dispose of the difficulty, though at the cost of emendation.]

The word *hupobathra*, 'foundation', is notable as not Platonic, and indeed not attested before the second century AD. Plotinus uses it on a number of occasions to describe matter as a base for forms (*Enn.* 6. 1. 28. 17; 6. 3.`4. 2–5). The idea, however, of the preliminary disciplines as 'stepping–stones' to the knowledge of true being doubtless owes something to the description of the lower stages of beauty as stepping-stones to the intuition of the beautiful itself in *Symposium* 211c (where Plato uses the word *epanabasmoi*).

4. The treatment of music, in turn, is based on *Republic* 530d–531c, without notable development (though the phrase 'only by the reflective activity of the soul', *monōi tōi tēs psychēs logismōi*, is actually an interesting conflation of two key passages, *Phd.* 79a3 and *Phdr.* 247c7–8). The emphasis on the importance of studying all these disciplines in the proper way and in the proper order is taken from the immediately following passage, 531d, as is the reference to the preliminary studies as a prelude (*prooimion*) to the study of true being, while the contrast between dreaming and waking is taken virtually verbatim from 533b–c, Plato's point being that the preliminary studies base themselves on hypotheses which they leave undisturbed, and thus never attain knowledge of first principles (*archai*).

5. The chapter ends with a resumé of the contents of the passage 533d–535a, including the reason given for denying the preliminary studies the title of 'sciences' (*epistēmai*), the specification of the level of cognition proper to them as *dianoia* ('discursive reason'), and the recapitulation of the four levels of cognition from the Line Simile, repeated by Plato here. It is noteworthy that A. makes no attempt to reconcile this purely Platonic schema with the rather more sophisticated epistemological system propounded in chapter 4.

The final sentence, describing dialectic as a 'coping-stone' (*thrinkos*), set 'above' all the other disciplines, is taken from 534e2, while 'guard' (*phylakē*) may well embody a reference to the later passage 8. 560b, where *mathēmata kala* are said to be 'the best watchmen and guardians (*phylakes*) in the minds of men who are dear to the gods (sc. against the assaults of the passions)'.

CHAPTER 8

1. A. now turns to what may properly be termed metaphysics, or the study of first principles, and it is only here for the first time that we can establish parallels with the similar handbook of Platonism of the second-century AD Roman rhetorician Apuleius of Madaura. The problem of the relationship of these two handbooks has been discussed in the Introduction, Sect. 3. After a recapitulation of the two remaining divisions of 'theoretical' philosophy which he had listed in 3. 4 (mathematics was the first), A. takes in turn, in the next three chapters 8–10, the three traditional Platonist principles, God, Forms, and Matter, in reverse order, that is, ascending order of dignity

(Apuleius, we may note, treats of them in the order God–Matter–Forms, *de Plat.* 190–3). He then adds a curious little appendix on the incorporeality of qualities (11). It is fair to say, I think, that the discussion of first principles, especially that of God in chapter 10, is the most original and interesting section of A.'s handbook.

In formulating his proposed procedure here ('examine, first, the nature of the world, and finally the origin and nature of man'), A. borrows his language from the similarly programmatic passage in the *Timaeus*, 27a5-6—an advance signal of how central a place the *Timaeus* will occupy in his exposition of physics.

2. In expounding the Platonist doctrine of matter, A. sticks pretty closely to Plato's account in the *Timaeus*, particularly 49a–52d. The term 'matter' (*hyle*) itself, of course, is not used by Plato, being employed first as a technical term by Aristotle (though Old Academics such as Speusippus may have adopted it, if we accept on other grounds that ch. 4 of Iamblichus' *Comm. Math.* is essentially Speusippus, since the term occurs there; cf. Dillon (1984: 325 ff.)), and Aristotle's doctrine differs significantly from that of Plato, though the differences were generally obscured by later Platonists (and even by Aristotle himself, cf. *Ph.* 1. 9. 192^{a}10 ff.). For a comprehensive account of Greek theories of Matter, see Clemens Bäumker (1890).

A. proceeds to quote all the terms which Plato uses in this section of the *Timaeus* to characterize the 'receptacle'. Only the term 'substratum' (*hypokeimenon*) is not Platonic, but Aristotelian (e.g. *Cael.* 3. 8. 306^{b}17) and Stoic, but that is significant, as reinforcing the equivalence which A. plainly recognizes between the Platonic and Aristotelian doctrines. The term is used already, we may note, along with *hylē*, by Timaeus Locrus (97e: 'The first principles of generated things are, as substratum, matter (*hōs men hypokeimenon, ha hyla*)', and later by Calcidius (*in Tim.* ch. 316: 'matter is . . . the basic material and primary substratum (*silvam . . . materiam principalem et corporis primam subiectionem*)'). A good discussion of the Middle-Platonist doctrine on matter is to be found in van Winden (1965).

At 162. 32, A. separates by 'and' the phrases 'perceptible by non-sensation' and 'by a bastard reasoning', which Plato links in a single phrase. This would not be of much significance, except that Calcidius (*in Tim.* 346. Wasz. 338. 6–7) seems to do the same, which points to a common tradition of interpretation.

[At 162. 34 the MSS have *pherein autas*, 'to bear them' which does not fit the context. H. Strache (1909: 122–3), proposes emending to *trephein autēn*, to fit in with the mention of 'nurse' just previously, and I have accepted this, despite the suggestion of Whittaker (1990: ad loc.) that this could be just an inconsequentiality of A.'s, resulting from his careless summarizing of a source work. If Strache is right, it is admittedly a rather curious error palaeographically.]

The sequence of three adjectives used to describe matter at 162. 36, *amorphos, apoios*, and *aneideos*, here translated 'without shape, or quality, or form', is of interest, since only the first is Platonic (cf. *Ti.* 50d7), *apoios* being characteristically Stoic (attested first by DL 7. 134 for Zeno in his *peri Ousias = SVF* 1. 85, but often elsewhere), while *aneideos* is attested first in Philo (e.g. *Mut.* 135, in conjunction with *apoios*). It is notable, however, that Aristotle, in his characterization of Plato's 'receptacle' in the *de Caelo* passage mentioned above, uses *aeides* (*kai amorphon*), so the third epithet might be claimed as Peripatetic, giving a comprehensively eclectic impression. Calcidius (*in Tim*, 310. 310. 13 Wasz.), produces the same sequence of epithets, *silvam sine qualitate esse ac sine figura et sine specie*, where the phrases with *sine*, 'without', very probably represent the Greek negative adjectives. In fact, the bestowing of these three epithets on matter is also to be found in Aëtius' *Placita* (308. 5 ff. Diels), so it is not original to A. (cf. also Antiochus of Ascalon, in Cic. *Acad. Post.* 29). Aëtius, however, also describes the matter 'of Aristotle and Plato' as 'corporeal' (*sōmatoeides*), a characterization which, as we shall see below, A. rejects.

[Note further that, of the two verbs 'moulded and imprinted' (*anamattomenēn kai ektupoumenēn*) used of matter at 162. 36–7, only the second occurs in Plato (*Ti.* 50d6—though *apomattein* occurs at 50e8), while the first is found only in the parallel passage of Timaeus Locrus, 94a (*anamaxamenan*). The position here is complicated, though, since this is the reading only of *most* MSS, while the best reads *enapomaxamenan*, a compound form that is attested for the early Stoics (Zeno uses it in connection with *kataleptikē phantasia, SVF* 1. 59) and for Philo of Alexandria (e.g. *Opif.* 151; *Leg. All.* 1. 79), while Plotinus uses *anamattesthai, Enn.* 4. 3. 26. 26. It looks, then, as if A. (and perhaps Plotinus) had a copy of Ti. Locr. with this reading.]

The latter part of the section, with the comparison of matter to odourless oil used by perfume-makers, depends heavily on *Timaeus* 50d–e. The term *ektypōsis*, 'imprint' (162. 40), while not being Platonic, recalls the rare Platonic term *ektypōma* of *Timaeus* 50d4; and the adjective *aosmotatos* (163. 1) reflects Plato's *aōdēs* at 50e7. It is notable that in 50e Plato does not actually identify the base for perfumes as *oil* (though he doubtless means that). A. shares with Plutarch (*An. Proc.* 1014f) the specification of this (162. 43). Again, A. makes more specific Plato's mention of moulding figures 'in any soft material' (50e8) by producing that of a man modelling in clay or wax (cf. Apuleius, *de Plat.* 1. 6. 193, and Calcidius, *in Tim.* 309, for the image of wax, at least). These are simply scholastic amplifications, and we cannot know who initiated them.

3. This passage is dependent upon *Timaeus*, 51a, but the characterization of matter as 'neither body nor incorporeal, but *potentially* body (*dunamei sōma*)' seems to have been developed at some later stage of the Platonist tradition. It is found in Apuleius (*de Plat.* 5. 192: 'neither corporeal nor yet incorporeal, but potentially and theoretically incorporeal' (*neque corpoream nec sane incorpoream . . . sed vi et ratione corpoream*)) and Calcidius (*in Tim.* 319: 'neither body nor something incorporeal . . . but potentially both body and corporeal' (*neque corpus neque incorporeum quiddam . . . sed tam corpus quam incorporeum possibilitate*)) in very much the same terms. As well as this, the concept of matter as 'potentially body' (which can be traced ultimately to Aristotle, cf. *GC* 2. 1. 329ᵃ32–3; *Metaph.* 12. 5. 1071ᵃ10) occurs in the account of Platonism by Hippolytus (*Ref.* 1. 19. 3, Diels 567), and before that (earlier than Philo, indeed, since he refers to it, *Aet.* 12) in the treatise *On the Nature of the Universe*, by the Neopythagorean 'Ocellus Lucanus' (ch. 24); and that of it as being neither body nor incorporeal occurs in Hermogenes (*ap.* Tertull, *Adv. Herm.* 35. 2). All this is derivable, no doubt, from Aristotle's discussions of matter, and even from Plato's presentation of the 'receptacle' or 'space' (*chōra*) as neither sense-perceptible nor intelligible, but cognizable only by 'a sort of bastard reasoning' (*Tim.* 52b2), but who first devised the scholastic formulation is not clear, except that he is later than the tradition represented by Aëtius (see above, sect. 2). As for Arius Didymus, his formulation that matter is not body, but *bodily* (*sōmatikē*), *Fr. Phys.* 2. 448 Diels *DG*, seems to go at least part of the way towards the formula that we have in A. and other second-century sources.

The example of the bronze and the statue is, of course, Aristotelian; compare, for example, *Physica* 2. 3. 194ᵇ24 ff.; 3. 1. 201ᵃ29 ff.; *Metaphysica* 5. 2. 1013ᵇ6–8.

CHAPTER 9

1. After a brief characterization of the three Platonist causal principles, the material, the paradigmatic (or formal), and the efficient, A. turns to a description of the formal cause, here named by him (as often in the doxographers, e.g. Aët. 1. 10. 308 Diels *DG*; Plut. *QC* 8. 2. 720b; Calc. *in Tim.* 307) in the singular, *Idea*. The adoption of this curious collective noun is presumably influenced by the presentation of the world of forms as a coherent whole, the 'Essential Living Being', in the *Timaeus*, but also by the Stoic concept of Logos, of which 'Idea' in the singular thus becomes a re-Platonization—if we can take the Stoic doctrine to be itself influenced to some extent by an interpretation of Plato's doctrine in the *Timaeus*. This can be seen most clearly, I think, in the reported allegorization by M. Terentius Varro (who was in philosophy a disciple of Antiochus of Ascalon) of God, Idea, and Matter as Jupiter, Minerva, and Juno (*ap.* Aug. *CD* 7. 8).

The system of three principles is, of course, not the only such system traditional in Platonism. In fact, it is arguable that the system really favoured by Plato himself, and by the Old Academy, was a two-principle system of monad and indefinite dyad derived from Pythagoreanism, such as is attested for Plato by Aristotle, and even hinted at obscurely in the *Timaeus* itself, at 48c ('We shall not now expound the principle of all things—or their principles, or whatever term we use concerning them; and that solely for this reason, that it is difficult for us to explain our views while keeping to our present method of exposition'). Indeed, the system of three 'principles' commonly extracted from the dialogue is somewhat shaky, especially as regards the Demiurge, who, if taken literally, cannot be regarded as a supreme deity, and can only serve as such if assimilated to such entities as the Good of the *Republic*, the One of the *Parmenides*, and the 'cause of the mixture' of the *Philebus* (30b).

The precise origins of the three-principle system in Platonism are actually somewhat obscure. It is possible that it was only formulated in response to criticisms by Aristotle, in such passages as *Metaphysica* 1. 992^{a}25–9 and *de Generatione et Corruptione* 2. 9. 335^{a}24 ff., to the effect that Plato ignores the efficient cause, and appears to think that the forms can do the job by themselves. The strange thing here is that Aristotle concentrates his fire on the *Phaedo* (96a–99c), and takes no account of the Demiurge of the *Timaeus*, which leads to the suspicion that, despite his claim to take the *Timaeus* literally when attacking Plato in *de Caelo* (1. 10. 279^{b}33 ff.; 1. 12. 263^{a}4 ff.), he accepted the Old Academic position that the Demiurge is a fiction, and that all one is presented with in the *Timaeus* is (in his terms) a final cause. However that may be, it would seem that the formulation God–Forms–Matter constitutes a sort of response to such a criticism as Aristotle's of the more original, two-principle system. When it arose is obscure, since it must really be later than Xenocrates, who maintains the Monad and Dyad as supreme principles. If in fact the Stoic system of God, Logos, and Matter is an influence here, then the system can really be no older than Antiochus of Ascalon.

A. launches now into an elaborate scholastic listing of the points of view from which the system of forms may be considered, a feature which occurs in almost the same words in Calcidius, *in Timaeum* 339 (332. 5–10 Wasz.), strongly suggesting a common source. Five relationships are listed, to God, to humanity ('us'), to Matter, to the sense-world, and to the Form itself. Let us take these in turn.

The first relationship is perhaps the most interesting, as it presents the forms as 'thoughts' (*noēseis*, *noēmata*) of God. This relationship is notoriously not present, or at least not spelled out, in Plato (though it could be seen as implied in a non-literal interpretation of the *Timaeus*, and in particular in the passage *Tim.* 39e). It seems to me, however, that more mystery is made of the provenance of this idea than is necessary. At least once Xenocrates declared that the supreme god was an intellect (Fr. 15 Heinze/213 Isnardi Parente), it seems necessarily to follow that the system of forms becomes the contents of that intellect. That this was the popular view, at least, of Plato's doctrine is indicated by the account presented by the patriotic, fourth-century BC, Sicilian Greek writer, Alcimus, who, in the course of his efforts to show how much Plato had borrowed from Epicharmus, declares (*ap.* DL 3. 13): 'Each one of the ideas is eternal, a thought (*noēma*), and moreover impervious to change.' Alcimus may well be drawing on the systematization of Platonic doctrine provided by Xenocrates, but at least he attests the existence of such a concept from the period of the Old Academy. As for the later period, the evidence of Varro (*ap.* Aug. *CD* 7. 28) indicates that it was accepted, albeit in a Stoicized form, by Antiochus, and it is certainly firmly established in the thought of Philo of Alexandria (*Opif.* 17–18). Indeed, Philo in this passage, by using the terms *demiourgos* and *paradeigma*, indicates that he interprets the myth of the *Timaeus* in this light. Certainly, for both Antiochus and Philo, the Stoic concept of *Logos* is influential, but the Stoic concept itself, as I have suggested above, may owe something, at least, to an interpretation of the *Timaeus* current already in the Old Academy.

The characterization of form as the 'primary object of thought' (*prōton noēton*) simply picks up the doctrine of chapter 4. 6–7, where the distinction between primary and secondary objects of intellection is made. That of form as the 'measure' (*metron*) of matter is not Platonic as such, but the idea is derivable from such a passage as *Timaeus* 53b, where the Demiurge is described as 'marking (the disorderly trace-elements of fire, earth, air, and water) out into shapes by means of forms and numbers'. Who first used the expression *metron* in connection with form's acting on matter is not clear, but we can see Plutarch using it in his paraphrase of the above passage of the *Timaeus* at *Quaestiones Conviviales* 8. 2. 720b: 'Now God's intention was to leave nothing unused or unformed, but to reduce nature to a cosmos by the use of proportion (*logos*), and measure, and number.' The description of form as the model (*paradeigma*) of the sense-world, on the other hand, is quite straightforwardly derivable from the *Timaeus* (e.g. 29b, 48e). As for the final characterization, of form in relation to itself as *ousia*, that can be derived from a famous passage of the *Phaedrus* (247c), where the realm of true being, home of the forms, is described as 'the colourless, shapeless, and intangible truly existing essence (*ousia*)'. The Aristotelian commentator Asclepius, we may note (*in Metaph.* 377. 32 Hayduck), refers the identification of forms as *ousiai* to the well-known passage of the *Timaeus*, 27d, not unreasonably.

The expression 'as a result of reflection' (*kat' epinoian*, 163. 18) is notable, as being Stoic (cf. *SVF* 2. 88–9) rather than Platonic (though Proclus, at least, at *in Tim.* 3. 18. 12–17, is prepared to attribute the noun to Plato on the basis of the verb *epenoei* at *Timaeus*, 37d5) or Aristotelian. The thought, however, seems to owe a good deal to Aristotle, particularly *Metaphysica*, 7. 7. 1032a28 ff., where Aristotle first declares that 'all productions proceed from either art (*technē*), or potency (*dynamis*), or thought (*dianoia*)', and then goes on to say: 'things are generated by art whose form (*eidos*) is contained in the soul'—though by 'form', he says, he means simply each thing's essence (*ti ēn einai*) and primary substance (*prōtē ousia*). A. gives a Platonist twist to this, though, allowing that the artist (*technitēs*) may have a *paradeigma* within himself that does not exist externally. This seems an irrelevant remark in the circumstances, but it may well be provoked by his reading of this passage of the *Metaphysics* (Invernizzi's assumption (1976: 118 n. 6) that A. means, by the *technitēs*, God himself, seems improbable, since A. here talks, not of 'the artist', but of *every* artist). The image of the artist, we may note, turns up in Seneca's description of the Platonic forms in *Letter* 65. 7 (cf. Theiler (1930), 15–18).

2. We now come to the definition of form. Here A. adopts the definition that seems, on the evidence of Proclus, *in Platonis Parmenidem commentarii* 888. 18–19, to go back to Xenocrates (= Fr. 30 Heinze): 'the paradigmatic cause of whatever is at any time composed according to nature (*aitia paradeigmatikē tōn kata phusin aei sunestōtōn*)'. To that A. merely adds 'eternal' (*aiōnion*), which is certainly implied in the Xenocratean definition. There is actually much that is peculiar about this definition, at least in the way that A. interprets it, that is, as excluding ideas not only of things 'contrary to nature' (*para phusin*)—freaks of nature and evils—but also products of art (*technē*). Harold Cherniss (1944: 257 n. 167) has a valuable discussion of this question, arguing that Xenocrates need only have meant by *ta kata phusin sunestōta* 'things properly formed', as opposed to mistakes of one sort or another, and would thus not necessarily be rejecting Plato's broad definition in *Republic* 10. 596a: 'We are accustomed, are we not, to posit a single form for each of the various multiplicities to which we give the same name', and his entertaining of the possibility of an Ideal Bed or Shuttle. Furthermore, it is not quite clear where Xenocrates' definition, thus interpreted, would leave forms of abstractions, which are more or less Plato's favourite type of form. Diogenes Laertius, we may note, produces a version of the same definition (3. 77: 'The Forms are causes and principles in virtue of which the world of natural objects (*ta phusei kathestōta*) is as it is'), but without expounding what he understands by this. Nor yet does Seneca, our earliest testimony for this definition, in *Letter* 58. 16–22 (probably dependent on Eudorus, via Arius Didymus). Seneca does, however, give as examples of a form only natural objects (man, fish, tree), which would seem to indicate that he understands it in the same way as A. As for A.'s contemporary Apuleius, he does not give the definition as such (*de Plat.* 6. 192–3), but he makes the remark that 'everything that comes to be (*gignentium omnium*) has, like wax, its form and its shape marked out by the imprint of these models',

which is sufficiently imprecise to allow of either a broad or a narrow interpretation, but cannot be used, I think, in support of Cherniss's proposal, in default of anything more definite. Certainly for A., as for Proclus after him (*in Prm.* 827. 26 ff.), this definition rules out forms of artificial objects. It seems, indeed, to be the case that even Aristotle felt that the Platonists did not accept forms of artificial objects (*Metaph.* 991^{b}6–7; 1080^{a}5–6; 1084^{a}27–9), which would tell against Cherniss's interpretation.

However, the truth may be on Cherniss's lines, as is suggested by Heinrich Dörrie (though without reference to Cherniss). He proposes (1987: i. 314), basing himself on the evidence of the rhetorician Alcimus (mentioned above), that *phusis* in Xenocrates' formulation, as in Alcimus' critique (*ap.* DL 3. 13), has a broad reference to the physical realm in general, which was not intended by Xenocrates to exclude any properly formed physical object, artificial or otherwise, nor yet physical instantiations of forms such as Justice or Beauty. In that case, the scope of the definition will have become restricted in the course of later Platonist discussions about the nature of forms, when Xenocrates' definition became separated from whatever arguments he advanced in its support.

This definition, at any rate, leads A. to a survey of the next topic which arises in Platonist discussions of the forms. 'Of what things there are forms.' We find the fullest discussion of this only much later, in Proclus' *Parmenides Commentary* 815. 15 ff. Cousin). Since at least the substance of this must go back into the Middle-Platonic period, it is worth quoting Proclus' introductory list of questions:

What things have forms and what things do not? We ought to consider this question first, so as to have a general theory of forms from which to follow Plato's thought in this passage (sc. *Prm.* 130c–d). And it is no slight matter to deal with these 'hackneyed topics', as they have been called (*Phlb.* 14d), especially if one does so in the following way: (1) Is there a paradigm of intelligent being in the Demiurge? (2) Is there a form of soul, and are they one or many? Are there paradigms of irrational life, and if so, how? (3) And of natural objects (*physeis*), and how many? (4) And of body, *qua* body, and if so, is it one or many? (5) And of matter? And if so, is it of the matter of perishable things only, or of the heavenly bodies as well? (6) If there are forms of animals, are they generic only, or do they include the individual species? And of plants likewise? (7) Are there forms of individuals along with these? (8) Or forms of the parts of animals, such as the eye, the finger, or suchlike? (9) and forms of attributes, or of some and not of others? (10) Are there also forms of the products of art and of the arts themselves? (11) And finally, forms of evil things? If we take each of these questions in turn, we shall be enabled thus to discover Plato's thought.

He then proceeds to do that, at considerable length, adding, as something of an afterthought (832. 2 ff.) that there are of course no forms of such things as hair, mud, or dirt (A.'s 'trivial things'), such as are mentioned in *Prm.* 130c. It can be seen that the dimensions of the topic as it reached Proclus are much more comprehensive than what we have in A., but many of the same categories are present in both. A.'s first category, artificial objects, is Proclus' tenth, while his second, things *para physin*, 'contrary to nature', will come under the heading of 'evils'—though the connection is not actually made, I think, before Syrianus, *in Metaph.* 107. 8–9; forms of individuals (on which Plotinus has interesting ideas, cf. *Enn.* 5. 7, though the Platonic tradition in general rejected them) corresponds to Proclus' seventh, but relative terms (*ta pros ti*) are not covered by Proclus.

A.'s only attempt at a rationale for these exclusions comes in the last sentence of the section, and it does not explain much. Presumably what he means is that none of the aforementioned categories of entity would be suitable for inclusion among the 'eternal and perfect' thoughts of God, individuals and relative terms not being eternal, and dependent relative terms not being perfect.

The word he uses for 'perfect', *autotelēs*, is mildly notable, as being, not Platonic, but Aristotelian (e.g. *Pol.* 7. 3. 1325^{b}21–2). It is also used by the Stoics, mainly in grammatical contexts, to designate a 'perfect' or 'complete' utterance (*autotelēs lekton*). A. uses it again in the next chapter, as we shall see, as an epithet of God (164. 32).

3. In this section and the next, A. produces four arguments for the existence of forms, a topic which one might expect logically to precede the question of what things there are forms of (as it does in Proclus' *Parmenides* Commentary, 783. 10–807. 23, where Proclus presents six arguments, only one of which, interestingly, concords with any of A.'s four—Proclus' third with A.'s third). All of these could well go back to the Old Academy, but A. is our first testimony for them. It is interesting that he uses the plural ('*they* argue'), meaning 'the Platonists'; he is not asserting that these arguments go back to Plato himself.

The first argument is just the one that I would put forward in support of the thesis that, once Xenocrates had declared the first principle to be an Intellect, he had to make the forms his thoughts. It is notable also that Alcimus, in the passage mentioned above (DL 3. 13), describes each of the forms as 'eternal and *a thought* (*noēma*) and impassible (*apathes*)', more or less answering to the epithets presented by A. here (if 'unchanging' [*atrepta*] can be seen as answering to 'impassible'). Alcimus does not specify *whose* thought, but, in conjunction with the epithets 'eternal' and 'impassible', it would be hard to imagine that he means that they are merely the objects of *human* thought.

It is worth speculating, perhaps, as to what distinction A. intends by speaking of God as *either* an intellect (*nous*) or 'possessed of intellect' (*noeron*). Whittaker (1990: 99 n. 163) wishes to make much of this, as 'd'une importance capitale pour le développement de la structure métaphysique néoplatonicienne'. This seems to me a little optimistic. All A. need mean, I think, is something rather vague—God either *is* intellect, or at least is an entity possessing intellect. But then one might ask, of what nature would that entity be? In view of the distinction between a primary and secondary God developed in the next chapter, there may be something interesting being suggested here, but I am not clear as to what it is.

The second argument, from the intrinsic unmeasuredness of matter, can be seen as based on such a passage as *Timaeus*, 53a–54d, where the receptacle is first presented as 'in a state devoid of reason or measure' (*echein alogōs kai ametrōs*), and then receives the forms through the medium of the basic triangles, which are themselves immaterial. The fact that A. uses a singular here in referring to the agency which imposes measure, if pressed, might suggest that A. is here assimilating the Demiurge to the Paradigm, and combining the efficient with the formal cause, but since he specifies the forms in the plural in the next sentence, we may conclude that the singular here is just a vague generic neuter. The characteristically Stoic phraseology of the conclusion may be noted (cf. above, ch. 6. 159. 28).

The third argument, broadly an argument from design, introduces both the Aristotelian distinction, found in *Metaph.* 7. 7. 1032^{a}12 ff., between things generated naturally (*physei*), artificially (*technēi*), and spontaneously (*apo t' automatou*). Since the cosmos is not of the last type (and certainly not of the second), it must fulfil the conditions which Aristotle identifies for the first, which are that it must have something *in accordance with which* (*kath' ho*) it is generated, something *from which* (*ex hou*), and something *by which* (*huph' hou*). For Aristotle's *kath' ho*, A. substitutes *pros ho*, and makes that form, whereas Aristotle had identified the cause *kath' ho* as nature, and the agent (*huph' hou*) as form, but Aristotle is here thinking primarily of the male parent as the bearer of form. The agent for A. will be God (cf. above, 163. 14), the subject of the next chapter.

We may note here the use once again of the so-called 'metaphysic of prepositions', discussed comprehensively by Theiler in 1930: part 1, which A. has employed already at the beginning of chapter 4, in connection with the criterion of knowledge. Theiler has shown that the use of these prepositional formulae, originally developed by Aristotle (in such a passage as that just quoted) for metaphysical purposes, goes back at least to Antiochus. A good passage to compare with A.'s usage here occurs in Philo, *de Cherubim* 125, where Philo, in his typically verbose way, exercises all the prepositional phrases to describe the various types of cause, though employing *di' ho* for A.'s *pros ho*, and including the instrumental cause, *di' hou* (the *Logos*), which A. has no use for here.

We may note once again, in conclusion, the Stoic format of all these arguments. They are all couched in the form of Chrysippean First Indemonstrables.

4. The fourth argument is based on the Platonic distinction between knowledge (*episteme*) and opinion (*doxa*), as set out in *Timaeus* 51d–52a. This argument, we may note, is more or less the converse of the first argument for the existence of God presented at the beginning of the next chapter, which moves from the existence of objects of intellection to the postulation of 'primary, simple' objects of intellection. The introduction of 'the primary object of sense-perception' here (and again in the next chapter) recalls the distinction made back in chapter 4. 155. 42 ff., but the assertion of their existence here does not seem to *prove* the existence of primary intelligibles, since, as we saw in the Commentary, ibid., they are very different sorts of thing, and not mutually implied. A. is here relying on a sense of parallelism between the intelligible and sensible worlds to carry his point.

CHAPTER 10

We come now to perhaps the most interesting and original chapter of the work, in which A. treats of the third (or first) of his first principles, God. It is usefully commented upon (with a French translation) by

A. J. Festugière (1954: iv. 95–102), and has attracted much other scholarly attention.

1–2. After beginning with a reference to the famous passage of the *Timaeus*, 28c, A. presents first, in the first two sections, two proofs of the existence of God. Note his use here of the Aristotelian technical term *epagein* (164. 9), which can be used for proceeding in argument from the known to the unknown, cf. *Topica* 8. 1. 156ᵃ4.

The characterization 'more or less beyond description (*mikrou dein kai arrhēton*)' seems to have misled some commentators into assuming that A. declares his primary divinity to be quite simply ineffable, but this is precisely what he does *not* do, by his careful qualification. As it stands, what A. says concords with *Timaeus* 28c: 'To discover the maker and father of this universe is no light task; and having discovered him, to declare him to all men is impossible' (the term *arrhētos* in this sense, though not occurring in the *Timaeus*, is at least minimally Platonic, occurring at *Sophist* 238c to describe the Parmenidean 'that which is not'). Plato's remark here might be taken to mean either that it is impossible to communicate the nature of the deity to *everyone*, that is, it is possible only to a few; or it could be understood more comprehensively, as asserting that the true nature of the 'maker and father' is quite simply indescribable in words. Plato almost certainly meant the former, but the phrase is interpretable in the latter sense also (cf. Wlosok (1960: 252–6)), and it may be that A. is so interpreting it here—though Apuleius, who actually quotes it, just after declaring that God is ineffable and unnameable (*indictus, innominabilis, de Plat.* 1. 5), plainly interprets it in the former sense. Certainly, the concept of the ineffability of God, at least as regards his essence, became widespread in later Platonism, taking its start, perhaps, from such a passage as *Republic* 6. 506e, where Socrates declines to describe the nature of the Good itself (*auto ti pot' esti t' agathon*), but undertakes to represent it by means of the Sun Simile. The fact that Philo of Alexandria is the first surviving author actually to describe God as *arrhētos* (e.g. *Somn.* 1. 67, where God is described as not only *arrhētos*, but 'unnameable' and 'utterly incomprehensible') is interesting, but cannot, I think, confer on Philo the importance which Wolfson (1952) would claim for him. Passages in the Platonic Epistles, beginning with the philosophical digression of *Ep.* 7. (343d–344d), and continuing with the mystifications of *Ep.* 2. 312e–313a, are surely manifestations of this view, though they do not use the key words.

To turn to the arguments, the first is presented rather elliptically, but ultimately clearly enough. It is, as noted above, the converse of that presented for the existence of forms in the last section of chapter 9: if there are objects of intellection at all (and we accept that there are), there must be *primary* objects of intellection (and therefore an intellect to cognize them). But this intellect cannot be a human intellect, since all human consciousness is inescapably contaminated with sensible images; so it must be a divine intellect. In fact, A. only mentions the existence of 'gods', in the plural, and it is not clear what status he intends these to have; but his argument serves to establish the existence of a divine principle in general.

The second argument might be termed that from a hierarchy of value. Since we observe an ascending sequence of dignity between soul and intellect, and even within intellect, between potential intellect and intellect in actuality (*energeiāi*), there must be something which is superior to this latter also, and that would be the supreme principle. This argument is problematical. It only makes sense, it seems to me, if we take it that the *potential* intellect is, as in Aristotle (cf. *de An.* 3. 5. 430ª10 ff.), the intellect in the human being (the initial statement, after all, that intellect is superior to soul, is quite vague as between individual and cosmos, and intentionally so, I think), while the *active* intellect is presented as being the intellect of the cosmos as a whole. Both of these intellects are immanent in something, and related to that thing, but there must logically be prior even to this eternally active intellect of the cosmos some intellect which transcends any substratum whatever, and this would be the first principle. Otherwise, it is not obvious why there should be anything prior to the intellect *in act*. It is, indeed, precisely this entity which A.'s approximate contemporary, the Aristotelian Alexander of Aphrodisias, makes the supreme principle, equating it with the unmoved mover of *Metaphysica* 12 (*de An.* 87–91; *Mant.* 106–110).

There is a further problem which has exercised many commentators on this page (Loenen (1956–7), Dörrie (1954; 1960; 1970), Merlan (1970: 62–71), Invernizzi (1976: i. chs. 5–7), Mansfeld (1972: 61–7), Donini (1988: 118–31), and that is the purport of the phrase, 'and whatever it is that would have its existence still prior to these'. How many entities, or levels of being, is A. proposing here? It seems to me that this phrase need only be taken as parallel to 'the cause of this', and thus as being merely a further description of the primary, transcendent intellect, but it still has to be admitted that A. has phrased this ambiguously (the *eti* ('still') in particular is bothersome). It seems best, however, in view of what A. says later in this chapter, and elsewhere in the work (cf. in particular ch. 7. 161. 30 ff., and Comm. ad loc.), to postulate simply, on the cosmic level, a world-soul, an intellect *of this world-soul* (otherwise described as 'intellect of the whole heaven (*tou sumpantos ouranou*)')—which, however, is to be reckoned as a distinct entity—and a First Cause, which is also still an intellect, to which A. grants here the salient features of Aristotle's Unmoved Mover—it is 'unmoved (*akinētos*), and 'an object of desire (*orekton*, cf. *Metaph*. 12. 7. 1072^{b}3 ff.), while he also makes reference to the Sun Simile of *Republic* 6, in describing it as acting on the cosmic intellect in the way that the sun acts on the faculty of vision.

3. A. begins this section with what constitutes the clearest statement of the doctrine of the forms as thoughts of God, the possible origins of which we have discussed already (above, 9. 1). The connection of the doctrine with Aristotle's characterization of the Unmoved Mover in *Metaphysica* 12 is particularly clear here (cf. 1074^{b}33 ff.: 'Accordingly, a divine mind knows itself, since it is the supreme excellence; and its intellection is the intellection of intellection'), except that for the formulation 'intellection of intellection' (*noesis noeseos*) A. substitutes, Platonically, 'form' (idea).

There now follows a most interesting sequence of epithets of the supreme god. The nature of these attributes has caused problems for commentators (e.g. Freudenthal (1879: 286 f.); Festugière (1954: iv. 137 f.); Wolfson (1952: 115–30), Invernizzi (1976: i. ch. 8), because they seem to conflict with A.'s repeated assertion (164. 7. 28; 165. 4) that God is 'ineffable' (*arrhētos*). The attributes cannot, therefore, it is argued, be describing his essence, but only serve to characterize his relations to his creation. However, it is not clear to me that that is a distinction that A. would make. Indeed, if one accepts that these epithets are taken from *Philebus* 65a (see below), then the first two in that passage are precisely characterizing the essence of the Good, which is the first principle.

At any rate, let us consider them in turn. We have first two epithets derived from the early part of the *Timaeus*. The connection of 'ineffable' (*arrhētos*) (with its important initial qualification 'all but') with *Timaeus* 28c, has been already noted above. The first epithet, 'eternal' (*aidios*) is also readily derivable from the passage just following (29a), where the Demiurge is said to contemplate the Eternal (*to aidion*). Especially if one interprets the *Timaeus* account of the Demiurge figuratively (but even if one does not), this inevitably involves the Demiurge himself in being eternal (assuming, of course, that A. is identifying the Demiurge-figure of the *Timaeus* with the supreme god).

On these two basic attributes, however, there follows a rather curious triad of epithets, all ending in -*telēs*: *autotelēs*, *aeitelēs*, *pantelēs* ('self-perfect', 'ever-perfect', 'all-perfect'), and each accompanied by a sort of 'translation' or interpretation, as if A. himself had found these epithets in some rather high-flown or poetic source, and felt the need to gloss them. I have suggested (1977: 283) that this string of rhyming epithets is reminiscent of the sort of litany one might expect to find at the end of an Hermetic tractate, but we do not in fact find these epithets conjoined in any surviving text. The middle one, *aeitelēs*, is found nowhere else at all, but *autotelēs* (used in logical contexts by Aristotle and the Stoics), is a Neopythagorean epithet of the monad (Nicomachus, *ap. Theol. Ar.* 3. 18 De Falco); and *pantelēs* (which, admittedly, occurs at *Ti.* 31b2 as an epithet of the Essential Living Being) is used by Philolaus (Fr. 44b11 Diels–Kranz) as an epithet of the decad, so a Pythagorean background might be conjectured for this threesome.

The glossing of 'self-perfect', *autotelēs*, by 'non-deficient', *aprosdeēs*, may be influenced by Plato's language at *Timaeus* 33d2–3 and 394b7–8 (describing the physical cosmos), where he described it as 'self-sufficing rather than in need of other things', and 'consorting with itself and needing nothing besides', but finds a verbal analogy in Plutarch, *de Tuenda Sanitate* 122e, and very probably a more substantial one in Calcidius, *in Timaeum* 186. 204. 8–9 (speaking of the 'highest god', *summus deus*): 'since he is a being of complete perfection, and in need of no companionship (*cum ipse sit plenae perfectionis et nullius societatis indiguus*)'. Apuleius also (*de Plat.* 1. 5. 190), again speaking of God, is quite close: 'in need of nothing, himself bestowing all things (*nihil indigens, ipse conferens cuncta*)'.

These adjectival epithets are followed by five substantival ones. The first two, 'divinity', 'essentiality' (*theiotēs*, *ousiotēs*) go together, and are thoroughly peculiar. It is not possible to parallel the use of either of these abstract nouns, as used in precisely this sense (which I take to be 'form' or 'principle' of God and substance), in normal Greek usage, though *theiotēs* is common enough among the Church Fathers. It is used in the LXX (Wisdom 18: 9) and by St Paul (Rom.

1: 20), and also in Plutarch (*QC* 4. 2. 665a), but not in quite the sense in which it appears here; the usage most closely approaching the present one occurs in a Hermetic tractate (9. 1), where intellection is declared to have the same relation to intellect as 'divinity' (*theiotēs*) does to God. As for *ousiotēs*, it is not found before Damascius—except, once again, in the Hermetic Corpus. There, however, the word occurs four times. One interesting passage occurs at the beginning of Tractate 12. 1, where Intellect is declared to be 'not cut off from the essentiality of God'. Since I am unwilling to postulate any direct dependence of A. on the Hermetists, I am driven to suggest, once again, some Neopythagorean (of mildly dithyrambic tendencies) as a common source for them both.

Truth, Commensurability, and Good are less troublesome. They seem, in fact, to derive from *Philebus* 65a, a passage popular at least in Neoplatonic times (Proclus wrote a monograph on it, which is lost, and discusses it also at *Theol. Plat.* 3. 11 Saffrey–Westerink): 'Then if we cannot use just one category to catch the Good, let us take this trio, Beauty, Commensurability, and Truth, and treating them as a single unit say that this is the element in the mixture that we should most correctly hold responsible, that it is because of this as something good that such a mixture becomes good.' Why A. should omit Beauty (*kallos*) from this enumeration is not clear. I would actually propose that he did *not* omit it, but that it has simply dropped out of the text. After all, when he is explicating these epithets just below, he brings in beauty along with symmetry, just as if he *had* mentioned it. We would thereby also observe another instance of A.'s curious habit of 'mirror quotation', which I have mentioned in the Introduction (end of Sect. 3), since he produces these epithets in exactly the reverse order to Plato (though admittedly Plato does vary the order in the passage immediately following). The specification at 164. 34–6, that he is not intending these three (or four) terms to be distinct, is probably just echoing Plato's language in 65a ('treating them as a single unit'), but it is of interest none the less, as indicating A.'s concern not to impute a series of discrete qualities to God.

After specifying in what mode he is employing these epithets, A. goes on to explain in what sense he means the last three (or four), and an additional one, 'father', derived from *Timaeus* 28a. It could be said that three of the four explanations do involve the relations of God with the world, but it is more to the point, perhaps, that he is declared to be Good and Truth *causally*, in the sense that he is productive of goodness and truth in other things (he is Beauty, however, not as causing beauty in others, but by reason of his own perfection and symmetry), and Father as being the cause of existence and order for all things.

What we see here is a conflation of the Good of *Republic* 6–7 (and *Phlb.* 65a–66b), with the Demiurge of the *Timaeus*, indicating that, for A., the latter is identical with the supreme principle. The characterization of God as *agathon* ('the Good', as a neuter) on the grounds that 'he benefits all things according to their capacities' is a significant blending of *Republic* 6. 509b, with *Timaeus* 29e ('He was good (*agathos*, masc.), and in him that is good no envy arises ever about anything; and being devoid of envy, he wished that all things should be as far as possible like himself'). It is significant because precisely this distinction between the neuter and the masculine of the adjective gives A.'s Neopythagorean contemporary Numenius the excuse for making a distinction between the Good of the *Republic* and the Demiurge of the *Timaeus* (Fr. 16 Des Places): the supreme principle is *agathon*; the secondary god, the Demiurge, only *participates in* the Good, and is thus *agathos* (Numenius also makes a contrast (Fr. 21) between the 'father' and 'creator' of *Tim.* 28a!). A. in fact expressly denies, just below (165. 7–8), that God is good by reason of participating in goodness; he is only Good, therefore, by being the cause of goodness in everything else.

The description of the relations of the Father to the heavenly intellect and the soul of the world is interesting. The intellect is presented, not as a really distinct entity, but rather as the intellect *of* the world-soul, which the Father brings into being by bringing the soul into contact with his own thoughts (sc. the forms). If we assume the *Timaeus* as the background to all this, it can be seen that what we have is a world-soul in itself essentially irrational, which is given intellect, and thus 'roused up' by the Father (himself a supreme intellect), and which then in turn, as intellect, confers order on the whole physical world. See Loenen (1956–7) on this question.

The Platonic verb *diakosmeō* used here (165. 4) embodies a reference, not to any passage in the *Timaeus*, but rather to *Cratylus*, 400a8–10, where intellect and soul are described as imposing order on all bodily nature. We find that passage explicitly referred to by Atticus (Fr. 8. 3–4 Des Places), and the verb is used in cosmological contexts fairly frequently by Philo (e.g. *Opif.* 20; 45; *Fug.* 10) and Plutarch (e.g. *An. Proc.* 1014c, 1016d; *de Prim. Frig.* 946f).

[It is to be noted that at 164. 33, the reading of the MSS is not *teleon*, 'perfect, complete', but *pleon*, 'full'; *teleon* is Hermann's emendation. One might be tempted to put in a plea for the MSS reading. It is a little strange, after all, to have the form *teleios* just above, at 164. 29, and *teleon* here, and *pleon* could be seen as a reference to Parmenides' description of Being in Fr. 8. 24 Diels–Kranz (and that of Melissus in Fr. 7. 11–14); but in fact *Philebus*, 66b1–3, provides a convincing source for the combination of *teleon* with *symmetron*, so Hermann is doubtless right.]

4. The next section is devoted to an exposition of the 'negative' method (*kat' aphairesin*) for attaining an understanding of the nature of God (in later scholasticism termed the *via negativa*). One arrives at this understanding by denying of God a series of qualities, or opposed pairs of qualities, in such a way as to suggest his superiority to both of them. A. begins this exposition by recalling God's ineffability (cf. 164. 8. 31), and adding to that the phrase 'graspable only by the intellect' (*nōi monōi lēptos*), which contains interesting echoes of both *Phaedrus* 247c (*monōi theatē nōi*) and *Timaeus*, 28a (*noēsei meta logou perilēpton*), though it is distinguished from the *Timaeus* passage precisely in that the *nous* with which the first principle is grasped is a sort of intuitive cognition which transcends *logos*, or discursive reasoning. A. begins, indeed, by denying of the first principle all the logical categories by means of which a definition (necessarily by genus, species, and differentia) could be given. The first principle has none of these, nor do any accidental attributes (*sumbebēkota*) apply to it; therefore it is not susceptible to definition. A. seems here to be making creative use of Aristotelian principles, as laid down in *Posterior Analytics* 2 (cf. esp. 13. 97^{a}23 ff.), culminating in the conclusion of *APo*. 2. 19, that there can be no 'scientific knowledge' (*epistēmē*) of first principles, only intuitive knowledge (*nous*), and applying them to God. Admittedly, as Jonathan Barnes (1975: 256–9) has argued, Aristotle probably does not mean 'intuitive knowledge' by *nous* in chapter 19, but rather something like 'comprehension', such as could arise from sense-perceptions, but a man like A. would naturally, I think, take him to be referring to a distinct faculty here, and one which would correspond with what Plato would have meant by *nous*.

    To this extent, then, none of the previous epithets constitutes a definition of God's nature; they are simply labels, indicating at the

most his powers, or his relations with the world, but otherwise just
serving to 'name' or identify him, e.g. 'there is one and only one
entity which is "self-perfect"', i.e. owes its perfection to nothing but
itself: this is not to be regarded as providing a differentia or an
attribute of God, in the sense of an intrinsic quality; it simply
describes his mode of relating to the world—he needs nothing from
it.

Having established this, he goes on to provide a series of basic
pairs of opposites, each of which the nature of God transcends
(though in the case of 'good' and 'bad' he feels the need, in deference
to the Stoics, to add 'indifferent'). As regards this first 'pair', the
denial of 'good' is maintained on the ground that this would involve
God participating in a form of goodness, which would then be
superior to him. This has an interesting connection with the distinction made by Numenius, mentioned above, according to which the
primal god is *agathon*, Goodness itself, while the second god is
agathos. We can see here that denying God the characteristic 'good'
does not conflict with naming him 'Good' just above.

The denial of the second pair, 'qualified–unqualified', only works
if, as A. does here, one restricts the meaning of the negative *apoios* to
'bereft of a characteristic which one might have had', as for example,
'sightless' or 'hornless'. An interesting parallel to this occurs in Philo,
Legum Allegoriae 3. 206, which says: 'Who can assert of the (first)
cause either that it is incorporeal or that it is a body, that it is qualified or unqualified, or in general make any firm assertion concerning
its essence or quality or state or movement?'—and this although he is
frequently prepared to describe God as *apoios* elsewhere (e.g. 1. 36.
51; 3. 36).

The last three sets of epithets, 'part–whole', 'same–different',
'motive–mobile' are taken directly from the first hypothesis of the
second part of the *Parmenides*—'part–whole' from 137c5–d3,
'same–different' from 139b4–e6, and 'motive–mobile' a slightly dis-
torted reflection of 138b7–139b3, where the true antithesis is 'at
rest—in motion'. This distortion, and the fact that the latter two are
transposed from the order in the *Parmenides*, may be due to A.'s concern to negate the characteristics of Aristotle's Unmoved Mover of
Metaphysica 12, but he is still unmistakably basing himself on the
negations of the first hypothesis, and this is of interest for the history
of the ontological interpretation of the second half of the *Parmenides*.
It is not quite clear, admittedly, that A. is basing himself directly on

the dialogue (he may be dependent on an intermediary), but he does provide evidence for the interpretation of the first hypothesis as a negative description of the first principle by his time. E. R. Dodds, in a famous article (1928), has shown, certainly, that at least the first three hypotheses of the *Parmenides* were being given an ontological interpretation in Neopythagorean circles (specifically, Moderatus of Gades) before the end of the first century AD, but Albinus, in his *Isagoge* (ch. 4), is still taking *Parmenides* as a logical exercise in the middle of the second century, so this evidence of A.'s is important for the 'mainline' Platonist tradition (the fact that he discerns syllogisms of various kinds in *Parm.* back in ch. 6 is no evidence one way or the other).

5–6. A. now presents a set of three ways to approach a conception of God, that of negation or abstraction (*aphairesis*), which he has just illustrated, that of analogy (*analogia*), and a third to which he does not give a clear title, but for which one may derive a title from his concluding characterization of it as having to do with pre-eminence (*hyperochē*). These are customarily given their later names in Latin scholasticism, the *via negationis*, the *via analogiae*, and the *via eminentiae*. That A. is not the first to make such a synthesis of 'ways' is indicated by the fact that a comparable trio turns up in the work of his approximate contemporary, the Platonist philosopher Celsus (*ap.* Origen, *contra Celsum*, 7. 42), in Celsus' case too following upon the quotation of *Timaeus* 28c:

You see how the way of truth is sought by seers and philosophers, and how Plato knew that it was impossible for all men to travel it. Since this is the reason why wise men have discovered it, that we might get some conception of the nameless and primary (*akatonomastos kai prōtos*) which manifests it either by composition (*synthesis*) with other things, or by analytical distinction from them, or by analogy, I would like to teach about that which is otherwise indescribable (*to allōs arrhēton*). (trans. Chadwick, slightly altered)

It seems to me possible that Platonist thinkers may have conceived the idea of transposing this doctrine from the realm of epistemology to that of theology. In particular, *sterēsis* may be seen as a possible antecedent of the *via negativa*, since it may be applied just as well to non-physical as to physical characteristics.

A. rounds off his description of *aphairesis*, in fact, with a mathematical example, the process of abstracting from a solid body to arrive at the concept of a mathematical point, the nature and origin of which is well discussed by Whittaker (1969). Various versions of this example are to be found in Middle-Platonist and Platonist-influenced sources, such as Plutarch (*Quaest. Plat.* 1001e–1002a) and Clement of Alexandria (*Strom.* 5. 11. 71. 2–3). It seems to be a standard example of the method of attaining to a concept of immaterial essence, which may go back even to the Old Academy. We may note that Plutarch uses the term *aphairesis*, favoured by A., while Clement talks of *analysis*, as does Celsus.

A. then goes on to illustrate the two other methods by examples from the dialogues, *analogia* from the Sun Simile of *Republic* 6 (508b–509b), and *hyperochē* from Diotima's account of the ascent to the vision of the Beautiful Itself in *Symposium* 210a ff. To the *Symposium* passage, however, A. links, first, a reference to the Aristotelian Unmoved Mover as 'object of striving' (*epheton*, cf. *Metaph.* 12. 7. 1072^{a}26; *Ph.* 1. 9. 192^{a}17 ff.), and then an allusion to the well-known passage of the *Seventh Letter* (341c–d), where understanding is described as 'brought to birth in the soul suddenly, like a light that is kindled by a leaping spark from a fire'.

7–8. He next embarks on a set of scholastic proofs that God is (1) partless, (2) motionless, and (3) incorporeal, which round off the chapter.

The argument that God is 'without parts', *amerēs*, owes something both to *Parmenides* 137c5 ff. and to *Sophist* 245a1 ff., but makes the rather different point that there would need to be something prior to that which had parts, whereas in both the above passages Plato is arguing from the *unity* of the One. A. in fact links this proof with his geometrical example of *aphairesis* above, in which the point is partless, and thus prior to line, surface, and solid, while nothing is prior to it.

The argument for God's motionlessness (*akinētos* covering both local and qualitative alteration) owes something to the argument for the One's freedom from rest or motion at *Parmenides* 138b7–139b3, but in respect of its main point, that whatever is altered must be so either by its own agency or that of another, and necessarily in the direction of the better or the worse, derives from *Republic* 2. 380d8 ff.

It has been noted by a number of scholars (Festugière (1954: iv. 101 n. 1); Invernizzi (1976: ii. 83–4)) that Aristotle also makes use of this argument (himself, admittedly, borrowing it from the *Republic*) in his *peri Philosophias* (Fr. 16 Walzer), and Untersteiner, in particular, argues that A. may be dependent for all his three arguments here on that work, rather than on Plato himself. That, it seems to me, is a possibility, but by no means a necessity. Certainly the point which A.

makes below about the form in material things being assimilated to and participating in the Forms 'in a manner difficult to express' (a direct reference to *Ti.* 50c6) is hardly to be attributed even to the Aristotle of the *peri Philosophias*.

At any rate, the third argument, in favour of God's immateriality, is presented as following from the first two (165. 37). It has two stages, or levels, linked by *kai autothen de*, which I have translated by 'and again'; admittedly, *autothen* generally seems to mean rather 'directly' or 'straightforwardly', but some such meaning as I have proposed seems needed here. It relies on the same argument as was employed in the first argument against God having parts, that God would then be composed of elements more primordial than himself; which is absurd. As a body, he would have to be composed of matter and form; and if of matter, then necessarily of some or all of the four elements, which in turn are merely modes of matter. It is interesting that Calcidius employs a version of this argument at *in Timaeum* 319, to prove the incorporeality of matter.

One may be moved to wonder why A. feels it necessary to append these rather banal proofs, following on his flights of negative theology, especially since they might seem to conflict to some extent with his doctrine in section 4 above, according to which God would transcend both sides of the opposed pairs 'partless–having parts, motionless–in motion, and corporeal–incorporeal'. But in fact the two modes of discourse are not in conflict so much as complementary (though these arguments might more logically precede the contents of sect. 4); they arrive at the doctrine of God's partlessness, motionlessness, and incorporeality by a different route.

[A philological detail: the word *sunduasma* (166. 3), which A. uses for the combination of matter and form, appears to be used nowhere else in extant Greek literature, and is not mentioned in LSJ.]

CHAPTER 11

1. This short chapter, which serves as a kind of appendix to the discussion of first principles, is not without a certain interest. It comprises a set of five formal arguments in favour of the position that qualities are incorporeal, directed by implication against the Stoics, for whom they were corporeal (*SVF* 2. 383; 389 = 28k, LS). For the Stoics, a quality (*poiotēs*) was *pneuma*, 'spirit', at a certain tension,

which was part of the active principle (*poioun*) of the universe (as opposed to the matter of the given individual, which was passive), but equally corporeal none the less. For Aristotle, as for the Platonists, qualities were incorporeal, but in a different sense, since he would recognize no separate status for them, or rather no transcendent form answering to them, of which they would be the immanent aspect.

Why does A. feel it desirable to discuss qualities at this point? Presumably in so far as they are forms in matter, and thus a topic relating to at least two of the three first principles, while constituting a good introduction to the next topic he will take up, which is the formation of the world.

This is the earliest connected discussion of quality from a Platonist perspective that we have (for a comprehensive survey of the history of the concept of quality from a Neoplatonic perspective, see Simplicius, *in Cat.* 208–19 Kalbfleisch), apart from an interesting document, a little treatise *On the Incorporeality of Qualities*, found among the works of Galen, but universally agreed not to be by him. Orth (1947) proposed that this might be attributed to Albinus, who was after all Galen's teacher (we know from a reference in Ephraim the Syrian that Albinus wrote a treatise with this title). This identification has been discounted, since its contents and its style do not accord at all closely with this chapter of the *Didaskalikos*, but if the *Didaskalikos* is not after all by Albinus, it seems to me that the identification may well stand. In any case, it is a useful document of Middle Platonism.

We have, admittedly, earlier than this, a very Stoicizing account of quality from the hand of Cicero, in *Academica* 1. 24–8, almost certainly deriving faithfully from Antiochus of Ascalon (his pupil Varro is the speaker). We can see from this how qualities come to be associated with the active principle in the universe, on the basis of the etymological connection (for which there may actually be some basis) between *to poioun*, the active principle, and *poios*, 'qualified'. For Antiochus, however, (though Varro is not explicit about this), qualities are still corporeal, being in effect spermatic *logoi*, and thus *pneumata*, inherent in individual things, so his account hardly counts as a Platonist exposition.

The structure of the arguments in the essay of pseudo-Galen is perhaps worth setting out here, in order to compare them with the present chapter:

   1. Definition of 'body', as 'three-dimensional substance resistant to the touch' (sect. 2).

2. Inapplicability of this definition to qualities (sects. 3–7).

3. Problems arising from the (Stoic) postulate that qualities are corporeal:

(a) In relation to the concept of an accident (*sumbebēkos*), sect. 8;
(b) in relation to the infinite divisibility of bodies, sects. 9–10;
(c) in relation to place (*topos*), sects. 11–12;
(d) in relation to time and change, sects. 13–16;
(e) in relation to the Stoic doctrine of primary substance and of Zeus as creator, sects. 17–20;
(f) in relation to motion and affection (*pathos*), sect. 21;
(g) in relation to Platonic and Aristotelian doctrines, sect. 22;
(h) in relation to the concepts of animal and 'animality' (*zōotēs*), sects. 23–4;
(i) in relation to our mode of knowledge of body, sect. 25.

4. Concluding argument, returning to the original definition, and challenging the Stoics to apply it to qualities.

It will be seen that the structure of the essay is not very close to the present chapter, any more than any two Platonist authorities might be who were concerned to refute the Stoic position. A. in fact makes more use of Aristotelian concepts and modes of argumentation than Ps.-Galen. His first three arguments are based on concepts and distinctions to be found in Aristotle's *Categories*, the distinction between subject (*hypokeimenon*) and accident (*symbebēkos*), the concept of 'being in a subject' (1^a20 ff.), and the observations that qualities, and not substances (i.e. bodies), have contraries (10^b12 ff.). Of these three, only the first has something to correspond with it in Ps.-Galen (sect. 8), but the analogy is not very close.

The next two arguments are of a rather different nature. In the fourth, A. bases himself on his own definition of matter, enunciated back in ch. 8 (162. 35 ff.), which involves matter being by nature devoid of quality (*apoios*); it follows from this that quality must be devoid of matter (*aülos*). The fifth is based on the denial of what the Stoics were forced to assert (*SVF* 2. 463–81; 48 LS), that two or more bodies can occupy the same space. Here also there is some degree of concordance with Ps.-Galen (sects. 11–12), but the mode of argument used, once again, is quite distinct.

On the other hand, if there are no very close connections with Ps.-Galen, one can observe quite close analogies with a section of the *Mantissa* of Alexander of Aphrodisias, entitled 'That Qualities are not

Bodies' (122. 16–125. 4 Bruns), where a number of the same arguments are produced, sc. (1) that all bodies are substances (*ousiai*), and no quality is a substance (*Mant.* 122. 16–25); (2) that one body does not differ from another *qua* body, but in virtue of quality, so that qualities cannot be bodies (124. 29–32); and (3) that if qualities were bodies, there would be a multiplicity of bodies in the same place (123. 12–13). Also, Alexander presents his arguments in the same formalized, staccato way as A. does here. It looks very much as if A. has taken some Peripatetic text very like that of Alexander, excerpted it, and given it a Platonist colouring. We may note, however, that the argument that one quality is contrary to another, while no body is, though derived from Aristotle's *Categories*, as noted above, is not to be found in Alexander.

2–3. It is in this second section that the point of this excursus on quality becomes apparent. A. is really concerned with the nature of the forms in matter. He does not speak of *eidē*, however, but uses the Stoicizing term 'the active principles' (*ta poiounta*), thus making explicit the etymological connection between *poion* and *poioun*), although he comes up with the significant Platonic phrase (used negatively of bodies): 'identical with themselves and in the same state (*aei kata ta auta kai hōsautōs echonta*)', to indicate that he is referring to the forms.

And with that he ends the section of the work on *theologia*, or first principles, which began with chapter 8.

CHAPTER 12

1. The 'physical' section of the *Didaskalikos*, it must be said, at least from chapter 12 to chapter 22 (the last four chapters, on the soul, immortality, and fate, are a little more interesting) is of much less interest than what went before it, mainly because it is very largely a paraphrase of the *Timaeus*, which by A.'s time, and indeed long before it, had become the accepted Platonic authority on the cosmos and its contents, including man from the physiological point of view. We cannot even assume that A. is making use of the *Timaeus* at first hand, though he doubtless was well acquainted with it. Much more probably, the selection and organization of relevant sections of the *Timaeus* had already been carried out generations before, at least by the time of Arius Didymus, Augustus' court philosopher, whom we must suspect

to have been A.'s major source in all of this section (see below). The sections of the *Timaeus* relevant to the account of the construction of the world and the world-soul will dominate the next three chapters, and may usefully be listed at the outset. They are: (*a*) 31b–34a, the creation of the world from the four elements; (*b*) 34a–37c, the soul of the world; (*c*) 48c–52a, matter; and (*d*) 52d–56c, the derivation of the four elements from matter. We can observe their use in more detail below. These sections, we may note, are also used in the same way by Apuleius in the *de Platone*, 1. 7–9. On this whole section of the *Didaskalikos*, see Spanier (1920) and Invernizzi (1976: i. ch. 11).

A. begins his exposition of physics with a reminder that the physical world is constructed on the model of an intelligible one, even as each individual natural object is constructed on the model of an eternal intelligible form. In this connection, he uses the traditional Platonic language of Demiurge and Paradigm, taken from the *Timaeus*, without specifying whether the model is within or without the mind of the Demiurge, or how this traditional scenario of temporal creation fits in with the theology of chapter 10. It is not even clear whether or not the Demiurge is envisaged here as a supreme god. An explanation for the traditional nature of the language used may be that this section can be seen to be taken virtually verbatim from a passage of the treatise *On the Doctrines of Plato* of Arius Didymus, quoted by Eusebius at *Praeparatio Evangelica* 11. 23. 3–6, and by Stobaeus (without attribution) at *Anthologia* 1. 12. 135. 20–136. 14 Wachsmuth–Hense.

Close examination of A.'s method of borrowing here gives an interesting result. He begins by copying virtually word for word (just a few minor changes: 'individual', *kata meros* for *kata genos* at 166. 35; the added flourish 'myriads upon myriads', *myriai epi myriais*—a Platonism, cf. e.g. *Theaet.* 155c4; *Soph.* 259b4—for Arius' 'many' (*sykhnas*) at 167. 4), but then progressively deviates into his own language, though keeping closely to the overall sense of his source. At the end of the first section, the quotation from Arius gives out, so the curtain is drawn on further comparison, but a large question arises from this fortuitous glimpse: is this an isolated case of borrowing, or is it rather the tip of an iceberg? It seems to me, on the basis of the very nature of A.'s work, that the latter alternative is the more likely, and that passages where A. is being original (such as, perhaps, ch. 10) are very much in the minority. I am on record (1977: 269) as describing A.'s work as 'essentially a "new edition" of Arius' *On the*

Doctrines of Plato, [but] how far this "new edition" is to be seen as a "new, *revised* edition" is not quite clear', and I have been mildly chided for this statement by Whittaker (1989: 68 n. 10), but I would stand by it, though not wishing to minimize the complexity of the relationship. Despite what I regard as this important insight into A.'s methods of composition, it would be extremely hazardous to claim any given section of the *Didaskalikos* either as unadulterated Arius, or as an original contribution by A. (not to mention the possible intervention of other intermediaries). I am in agreement here with virtually all commentators on the *Didaskalikos*, Freudenthal (1879: 297), Witt (1937: 77–8), and Giusta (1960–1: 187–90). The objections of Loenen (1957: 41 ff.), based on minor differences of style and emphasis between A. and Arius, are without much substance, and Invernizzi (1976: i. 222–3), while very probably correct in singling out chapter 14. 3 as original to A. (cf. Comm. ad loc.), is unjustified in making that the basis of an objection to his general dependence on Arius.

[Some linguistic details from the latter part of the section are worth noting. At 167. 8, A. uses the noun *kataskeuasma*, 'construction', which is not used by Plato (though the corresponding verb frequently is). The word is used, however, in a cosmic context, by Philo, *Legum Allegoriae* 3. 98, where he is comparing the universe to a vast *polis*, whose maker we are naturally led to seek, and also by the mysterious 'Athenian sage' Secundus (virtually a contemporary of A.'s, if he is the sophist who was the teacher of Herodes Atticus), in the first of his *Sententiae*, as an answer to the question 'What is the world?', where he describes it, remarkably, as a *theorētikon kataskeuasma*, 'a construction cognizable (only) by contemplation'.

Apeikonizō, 'copy from' (167. 11), is attested first only in Philo (*Opif.* 16 and 69)—in a similar cosmogonical context—and is then widely used in Neoplatonic texts, particularly in Proclus' commentaries. It may be taken as part of the technical vocabulary of the exegetical tradition of which Philo and A. are both members.

Then we may note the word *diaita*, at 167. 14, with the meaning 'administrative care' (the nearest analogy in LSJ is 'arbitration', in Athenian law). This so bothered Friedrich Solmsen, in his review of Louis' Budé edition (*CP* 45 (1950), 63–4) that he wished to emend to *di⟨kaiotatēn⟩ ait⟨i⟩an*, 'supremely just causation'. This is a rather desperate remedy, I think, although the word remains peculiar, and I can find no proper analogies for it (Plato, *R.* 407c8, offered by Invernizzi, is quite irrelevant). Another possibility, suggested to me by Matthias

Baltes, is *dianoian*, 'thought', but this does not seem to go well with *pronoian*, just before it.]

2–3. When A. is not quoting Arius directly, his exposition is shot through with reminiscences of the *Timaeus*, as one would expect. Section 1 ended with a direct reference to *Timaeus* 29e1, and the latter two sections are not much more than a close, though summary paraphrase of 30a–34a, combined with 52d–53c, to give a traditional, uncritical account of the creation of the world by the Demiurge.

Rather than pick out each of the *Timaeus* references, which are easily discernible if one reads the original passages, it seems more profitable to note the few deviations. First of all, as one would expect of a later Platonist, A. has no hesitation about referring at 167. 15 (cf. also 23) to *hylē*, 'matter', a term not used by Plato (whose concept of *chōra*, 'place', was, however, rightly or wrongly, very soon assimilated to Aristotle's concept of matter) whereas Arius, in the parallel passage (with which his extract ends) uses rather the Stoic term *ousia*.

The expression 'the mere capacity of receiving the potency of the elements' (*to dektikon tēs tōn stoicheiōn dynameōs*, 167. 22) contains various points of interest. First of all, the adjective *dektikos*, though Aristotelian, is not Platonic. It is found, however, in Philo (*Quod Det.* 99; *Mut.* 211; *Aet.* 22), in Plutarch (*de Is. et Os.* 367c; 372e; *de Fac.* 944a), and in Neoplatonic texts, so it is part of the scholastic vocabulary. Then, the equating of the 'traces' (*ichnē*) of the forms of the elements with their 'potency' is to be found spelled out in Calcidius, (*in Tim.* 354. 345. 1–5 Wasz.) (cf. esp. 'the trace signifies the potency of a thing, not the thing itself' (*vestigium quippe potentiam rei, non rem significat*)), making explicit a connection which A. simply assumes. It is indeed a problem to fathom what Plato had in mind by 'traces' of the elements, especially if one were to take the *Timaeus* account literally. Plutarch, who does, talks mysteriously in the *de Iside et Osiride*, 373c, of a 'first' or 'prior creation' (*prōtē genesis*) which is imperfect (*atelēs*), and in *de Animae Procreatione in Timaeo*, 1024c, of a *genesis* 'when the cosmos had not yet come to be'. To introduce the language of potency or potentiality here is to try to get round the problem by resorting to Aristotelian formulations. Werner Deuse has a good discussion of this question in an excursus to (1983), entitled 'Zur mittelplatonischen Interpretation der Elemente-Spuren und der vorkosmischen Beziehung zwischen Materie, Ideen und Demiurg' (pp. 236–44).

[We may also observe, as we can generally with A.'s quotations of Plato, and as has been well elucidated by Whittaker, both in (1989: 72–4) and the introduction to his edition, the curious habit of 'mirror quotation', where the two (or more) elements of a compound Platonic phrase are presented in reverse order. Good examples here are *ataktōs kai plēmmelōs* (167. 12) for Plato's *plēmmelōs kai ataktōs* of *Timaeus*, 30a4–5, and *anoson kai agērō* (167. 35), for Plato's *agērōn kai anoson* of 33a2. As Whittaker suggests, this quirk, and other little alterations, are better seen as deliberate *variatio* for stylistic reasons than as the product of carelessness (though the quotations *are* no doubt from memory). Cf. Intro. Sect. 3]

Near the beginning of section 3, at 167. 34, we find *idea* used in the singular, as it was back in chapter 10. 3 (164. 27), but here plainly referring to the Paradigm, which shows how the usage arose, the Paradigm or Essential Living Being being seen as the sum-total of the forms, and thus Form.

CHAPTER 13

A. turns now to the formation of the so-called 'elements' (*stoicheia*), drawing heavily on *Timaeus* 52d–56e, together with 58a–c. He points out quite forcefully (168. 14, 'by God', *ma Dia*, which I have rendered 'we must emphasize') that they are not yet properly elements at all, but apparently is not bothered, as modern commentators have been, by the contradictions involved in the literal interpretation of *Timaeus*, 53b. Once again, there is very little in this chapter which differs from the *Timaeus* account, comment on which is proper to a commentary on that dialogue, not on the *Didaskalikos*. I confine myself to the little that is distinctive.

We may note, first of all, that the opening phrase of the chapter is closely matched by Plutarch, *Quaestiones Platonicae* 2. 1001b: 'There being two components out of which the world is put together, body and soul . . .' This may be a coincidence, but it may betoken either dependence by A. on Plutarch, or, less improbably, the presence of a common source, such as Arius' handbook.

Note also that A. employs all the normal geometrical terms for the five basic solids, whereas Plato himself mentions by name only the pyramid (56b4), and otherwise prefers to use periphrases. We find all the usual terms also employed by Plutarch, at *Quaest. Plat.* 5. 1003b–1004a.

Most interesting is A.'s treatment of the dodecahedron, which, we recall, is artfully *not* named as such by Plato at 55b: 'And seeing that there still remained one other compound figure, the fifth, God used it up for the universe in his decoration thereof (*diazōgraphōn*).' The actual name first appears in the corresponding passage of Timaeus Locrus (98d), and the construction of it is first (in surviving literature) presented by Plutarch (*Quaest. Plat.* 5. 1003d). This latter passage is worth quoting:

Did he, as some surmise, associate the dodecahedron with what is spherical, since he said that God employed the former for the nature of the universe in his decoration thereof? For, being furthest removed from straightness by the multitude of its elements and the obtuseness of its angles, it is flexible and, like the balls that are made of twelve pieces of leather [cf. *Phd.* 110b6–7], by being distended becomes circular and all-embracing (*perilēptikon*), for it has twenty solid angles, each of which is contained by three plane angles that are obtuse, since each consists of a right angle and a fifth; and it has been assembled and constructed out of twelve equiangular and equilateral pentagons, each of which consists of thirty of the primary scalene triangles, and this is why it seems to represent at once the zodiac and the year in that the divisions into parts are equal in number.

If one compares this account (which is ultimately, I think, in view of *Def. Or.* 427a ff., to be credited to the rather mysterious Theodorus of Soli, who was a contemporary of the old Academy—Crantor, at any rate, is reported as criticizing a view of his on *Ti.* 35b, at Plut. *An. Proc.* 1029d) with that of A. given here (168. 40–169. 4), we see in both cases the ingenious working out of a mathematical way in which the dodecahedron can represent the heavens, the twelve pentagons representing the signs of the zodiac (to which Plato's own expression *diazōgraphōn* may well be a reference), and the thirty basic triangles in each adding up to the total of degrees. The evidence of Theodorus indicates that all this was worked out already in the Old Academy, and so is in no way original to A. What we do not find explicitly stated here, but do in at least some quarters of the Old Academy, is the doctrine that the dodecahedron constitutes a fifth element, none other than the Aristotelian ether (possibly a deduction from the *Phaedo* myth, where the upper or 'real' earth is (*a*) said to resemble in appearance a twelve-sided variegated leather ball (110b6), and (*b*) is said to have ether where we have air (111b1)). Xenocrates, at any rate (Fr. 53 Heinze/265 IP—a rare verbatim quotation, from his *Life of Plato*), maintains this, and Theodorus, as reported by Plutarch, certainly comes near to it (*Def. Or.* 427b). In fact, it would seem from chapter 15 below, where he is discussing daemons, that A. did accept the ether as a fifth element, though envisaging it in its Aristotelian position as the stuff of the heavenly bodies, rather than in the curious position in which it is found in the *Epinomis* (984b, cf. 981b–c Tarán). The author of the *Epinomis* (probably Philip of Opus, but certainly Old Academic) wants to have things both ways, implicitly identifying ether with the fifth regular solid, but nevertheless wanting to rank it next below fire, as the abode of the higher class of daemons (again, possibly influenced by the *Phaedo* myth). From the order of elements which A. gives at the beginning of chapter 15 ('ether, fire, air'), we might conclude that he is implicitly correcting the account given in the *Epinomis*.

[A small but interesting indication of the scholastic intermediaries between A. and the text of the *Timaeus* itself occurs in section 3, the doctrine of which is entirely taken from *Timaeus* 58a–c. At 169. 11–12, A. uses the terms *leptomerē* and *hadromerē*, 'fine-grained' and 'coarse-grained', to describe the various sizes of particles, where Plato himself in the relevant passage uses simply 'small' and 'large' (*smikra*, *megala*, 58b). Neither of these terms is found anywhere in Plato, but the first is found in Timaeus Locrus at 100e, though he uses *pachymerēs* (not Platonic either, but used by Aristotle, *Cael.* 304^{a}31) rather than *hadromerēs* for its opposite. This pair of opposites is also to be found in an interesting passage of Philo (*Heres* 134), in a very 'Timaean' context (Philo is describing God's initial demiurgic 'division' of opposites in the making of a cosmos), but Philo uses *hadromerēs* just a little later (*Heres* 142), still on the same subject. Philo, like A., is plainly dependent primarily on some handbook such as that of Arius Didymus rather than on the *Timaeus* itself, while the relationship of Timaeus Locrus to the handbook tradition remains obscure, by reason of the uncertainty of his date, but I am prepared to accept the arguments of Matthias Baltes, *Timaios Lokros* 20–6, for seeing him as dependent on Eudorus, and thus no earlier than the first century AD.]

CHAPTER 14

1. [The beginning of the chapter is corrupt in the MSS. I translate the emendation proposed by Louis (*sunistas* for *eis ta*, and *ek* inserted before *tōn emphainomenōn*), as it gives reasonable sense, but, as Cherniss (1949: 76 n. 5) pointed out in his review of Louis, it leaves an awkward *men* at the beginning without a balancing *de*, so that some further lacuna is to be suspected.]

At any rate, A. now turns from the analysis of the composition of bodies to an account, first, of the composition of the world-soul, based on *Timaeus* 34c–35a, and then of the world and the heavenly bodies, based respectively on 36b–e and 38b–39e. In the midst of this account, however, which is probably still based substantially on Arius Didymus, he inserts a section (3) which serves to correct the impression made by the hitherto uncritical summary of the *Timaeus* that has been given, that the world was created at a point in time. It is possible, of course, that even this comes from his source, but it sounds more like an editorial insertion by A. himself.

The introductory remarks in section 1 are not closely connected to the *Timaeus*, but may be influenced rather, as Invernizzi (1976: ad loc.) suggests, by such a passage as *Meno* 81c–d, where Socrates bases his argument for recollection on the soul's having seen 'both things here on earth and those in Hades and all things', and having a knowledge of all things through the kinship of all nature (*kata to syngenes* at 169. 20 may recall *tēs phuseōs hapasēs syngenous ousēs* of *Meno* 81d1), but *Timaeus* 37a–c may be seen as an influence also, since the reference to the *archai* of all things being present in the soul can be taken as a reference to its possession of 'the natures of the Same, and Other, and Being' (37a2–3).

It is also possible that A. is being influenced by a Platonist doctrine going back to Crantor in the Old Academy, as reported by Plutarch, *An. Proc.* 1012f–1013a:

Crantor and his followers, supposing that the soul's peculiar function is above all to form judgements of both intelligible and perceptible objects and the differences and similarities occurring among these objects both within their kind and in relation of either kind to the other, say that the soul, in order that it may know all, has been blended together out of all and that these are four, the intelligible nature, which is ever invariable and identical, and the passive and mutable nature of bodies, and furthermore that of the same and

the different, because each of the former two also partakes of difference and
sameness. (trans. Cherniss, slightly adapted)

This line, which is admittedly readily derivable from Plato's utterances in *Timaeus* 37a–c, may have been followed by Eudorus after
Crantor, since we know from Plutarch that he followed Crantor in
other details (*An. Proc.* 1020c)—it is indeed probable that Eudorus is
Plutarch's immediate source for the Old Academic doctrine in this
work—so it may be that Eudorus (or Arius, following Eudorus) is
A.'s more immediate source.

2. At any rate, with section 2 we move clearly to the *Timaeus*, with
the reference to the 'indivisible essence' and 'that which is divisible
about bodies' (35a)—though the use of the verb 'grasp' (*ephaptesthai*)
shows that 37a is in his mind as well (cf. *ephaptetai*, 37a6). As regards
the identification of the indivisible and divisible essences, we may
note the significant addition of 'intelligible (*noētēn*)' to the indivisible,
a further indication, perhaps, that A. or possibly rather Arius, is following the interpretation of the soul's composition given by Crantor,
quoted above from Plutarch.

Admittedly, Crantor's view is a pretty accurate interpretation of the
meaning of the text (unlike Xenocrates, who saw the soul being
described here as a blend of the Monad and the Indefinite Dyad, *An.
Proc.* 1012e), so that one might not feel the justification for postulating any intermediate influences here, but the identification of the
indivisible essence as that of *nous* is something that Crantor made a
point of, and we may connect with this the fact that in the next section A. makes use of Crantor's preferred meaning of 'generated' as
one of his two preferred meanings. Proclus, at *in Platonis Timaeum
commentarii* 1. 277. 8–10, reports Crantor as declaring that the cosmos
may be said to be 'generated' as being produced by a cause other than
itself, which is essentially A.'s second meaning (cf. below, 169. 34).

[The verb *suneranizō* (169. 29), here translated 'put together', is
worth noting, as being un-Platonic (though occurring in the *Axiochus*,
369a9), but used in Philo in various philosophical contexts (e.g. *Ebr.*
192 (*bis*); *Conf.* 188), though always with slightly derogatory overtones, and then by Plutarch (e.g. *QC* 4. 1. 663b; *Soll. An.* 963b) and
by Atticus, *Fr.* 5. 53 Des Places).]

As for the references to the Pythagoreans and to Heraclitus, that to
the Pythagoreans is supported by Sextus Empiricus (*M.* 7. 92 = 44a29
Diels–Kranz), where Sextus says that the Pythagoreans declare reason

(*logos*) to be the criterion of knowledge because it, 'being conversant with the nature of all things, possesses a certain kinship thereto, since it is the nature of like to be apprehended by like'—very similar to what A. says here about the soul. He then quotes Empedocles (Fr. 109 Diels-Kranz), who is, indeed, credited with this doctrine by Aristotle at *de An.* 1. 2. 404^{b}8 ff. and *Metaph.* 3. 4. 1000^{b}5. In this passage, Sextus seems to be largely dependent on Posidonius' exegesis of the *Timaeus* (*M.* 7. 93), but this need not be the direct source for A. As for Heraclitus, A. seems, as Invernizzi (1976: ad loc.) suggests, to be making a general reference to his doctrine of opposites rather than to any specific known fragment with an epistemological purport.

As for the source of this, the above-mentioned section of Aristotle's *de Anima* may be an influence, since Empedocles is there juxtaposed with the *Timaeus*, but, though Heraclitus is mentioned a little later (405^{a}25 ff.), he is not credited with this doctrine, but rather with the view that what moves is known by what moves—unless the doctrine that unlike is known by unlike can somehow be developed from that. The more probable source, however, is Theophrastus, who at the beginning of his *de Sensu* (499. 1 ff. Diels *DG*) identifies Parmenides, Empedocles, and Plato as basing sense-perception on the action of like on like, Anaxagoras and Heraclitus as basing it on that of opposites on opposites—though also without quoting any particular passages of either of the latter two to support his claim.

For the identification of Empedocles with 'the Pythagoreans', we may compare Sextus Empiricus (*M.* 7. 92), where, to illustrate the Pythagorean position, a reference to Philolaus is curiously combined with a quotation from Empedocles (Fr. 109); and Calcidius (*in Tim.* 51) (probably here dependent on Numenius), where the same passage of Empedocles is again quoted. Indeed, this passage of A. sounds like an abbreviated version of a *Timaeus* commentary. Posidonius may be an important link in the tradition here.

3. We come now to what might be seen as an original insertion by A. into a very largely derivative text, that is, the specification that the account in the *Timaeus* of the generation of the cosmos and of the soul is not to be taken literally. However, in view of the fact that at least one of the proposed senses of 'generated' goes back, as we have just seen, to Crantor, we cannot be sure that even this does not go back to Arius.

One chief focus of the controversy as to whether the *Timaeus* account was to be taken literally was the passage 27c–28c, and in particular the bald assertion at 28b7: *gegonen*, 'it was generated'. If one wanted, as most later Platonists did, to follow Speusippus and Xenocrates in denying that Plato maintained a temporal creation, then one had to explain in what sense Plato meant this statement. By the time of Calvenus Taurus, in the first half of the second century AD, quite a battery of possible senses of this verb, or of the adjective *genētos* as an epithet of the cosmos, had been developed. We have an extended quotation from his discussion of the passage in his *Commentary on the Timaeus*, preserved to us by John Philoponus in his polemical work *On the Eternity of the World* (145. 13 ff. Rabe). Taurus distinguishes four possible meanings of *genētos*, as follows:

Genētos, then, can have the following meanings:

(1) That is said to be *genētos* which is not in fact generated, but is of the same genus as things that are generated. Thus, we describe something as 'visible' which has never in fact been seen, nor will ever be seen, but which is of the same genus as things that are visible, as if for instance there were a body at the centre of the earth.

(2) That is also called *genētos* which is in theory composite, even if it has not in fact been combined. Thus, the *mesē* (in music) is a 'combination' of the *nētē* and the *hypatē*; for even if it has not been combined from these two, its value is seen to be in equal proportion between the one and the other; and the same thing goes for flowers and animals. In the cosmos, then, there is seen to be combination and mixture, so that we can by (mentally) subtracting and separating off from it various qualities analyse it into its primary substratum.

(3) The cosmos is said to be *genētos* as being always in process of generation, even as Proteus is always in the process of changing into different shapes. And in the case of the cosmos, the earth and everything up to the moon is continuously changing from one form into another, whereas those things above the moon, while remaining more or less the same, with very little change as regards their substance, yet change their relative positions, even as a dancer, while remaining the same in substance, changes into many positions by means of gesticulations. Even so the heavenly bodies change, and different configurations of them come about as a result of the movements of the planets in respect of the fixed stars and of the fixed stars in respect of the planets.

(4) One might also call it *genētos* by virtue of the fact that it is dependent for its existence on an outside source, to wit God, by whom it has been brought into order. Thus even according to those for whom the cosmos is eternal, the moon possesses light 'generated' from the sun, although there was never a time when she was not illuminated by him.

Whether A. was acquainted with this triumph of Middle-Platonic scholasticism is not knowable, but not improbable. At any rate, it can be seen that the sense, or senses, which he gives to *genētos* correspond pretty exactly to Taurus' senses (3) and (4). He actually develops somewhat Taurus' fourth sense, by specifying further what God does to the world-soul. The 'rousing-up' of the slumbering world-soul should itself not be a temporal act, but it is possible that A. has in mind a situation such as that presented by Plutarch in his *An. Proc.* (1026e–f), where the soul is envisaged as experiencing periods of latency or 'slumbering', on the model of the myth of the *Statesman* (269c ff.), whence it is roused again in due course by its own intellect reasserting itself. If so, however, A. does not make himself clear.

A case against Albinus' authorship of *Didaskalikos* has been made by Giusta (1961: 173–4) and Whittaker (1974: 451–2) on the basis of the fact that Proclus, in his *Timaeus Commentary* (1. 219. 2 ff. Diehl) attributes a rather different combination of senses to *genētos* to Albinus (Freudenthal and Witt having earlier triumphantly claimed Proclus' evidence in favour of the identification). On the whole, bearing in mind that most second-century Platonists (unless they were advocates of a literal interpretation) would pick one or other of the senses identified by Taurus, Giusta and Whittaker have a point. Proclus attributes to Albinus the view that the world is *genētos* (1) in having a cause of its generation, and (2) in being a combination (*synthesis*) of a multiplicity of dissimilar elements, thus combining Taurus' fourth and second senses. There is a distinction here, which cannot be overlooked even if we assume that Proclus would be drawing on a *Timaeus Commentary* by Albinus (or possibly his collection of the lectures of his master Gaius), rather than the *Didaskalikos*, and it thus constitutes an argument against his authorship of the *Didaskalikos*.

The use of the word *karos*, 'deep sleep'—almost 'catatonic trance' —in relation to the world-soul (169. 39), together with the depiction of it as 'striving' (*ephiemenē*) to receive the thoughts of God, imports an interestingly mythological element into A.'s doctrine here, reminiscent of Plutarch's presentation of Isis in the *de Iside et Osiride* (e.g. 372e–f), though Isis there is assimilated by Plutarch to the Receptacle of the *Timaeus*, rather than to the World-Soul. However, for Plutarch—as also for Atticus (cf. *Fr.* 11 Des Places)—the World-Soul is an essentially irrational entity (cf. the excellent discussion of Werner Deuse (1983: 12–47)), and that is how it is portrayed here, despite the fact that it is presented as having a (potential) *nous* in its 'slumbering' state. It still seeks for the forms to be imprinted on it from outside itself.

[The word *karos*, we may note, is used by Philo, *Legatio ad Gaium* 269 (though in a literal sense), by the second-century Aristotelian Aristocles (*ap.* Eus. *PE* 14. 19. 1), and by Maximus of Tyre (*Diss.* 10. 1) as a description of the *individual* soul's condition in the body. It is much used also in the later Neoplatonic tradition, for example Porphyry, *ad Gaurum* 33. 22–3 Kalbfleisch; Proclus, *in primum Euclidis librum commentarius* 47. 1–4 Friedlein (mathematics rouses the soul, *hōsper ek karou batheos*); *in Platonis Alcibiadem* 226. 6–7 Westerink; anon. *Prolegomena* 8. 5–6 Westerink (again the phrase *ek batheos karou* employed here by A.). What we may have here is a trace of a lost allegorization, perhaps of the myth of the sleep of Kronos, which has found its way into the scholastic tradition. Certainly A.'s rather tentative use of the phrase (*ek karou tinos batheos*) makes it sound as if he is quoting.

As for other linguistic details, his use of the verb *katakosmeō*, 'bring to order' (169. 37), may be intended to recall *Politicus* 273a7, where the verb is used in the middle, of the world bringing itself to order, while the notion of God turning (*epistrephōn*, 169. 38) the soul towards himself doubtless owes something to *Politicus* 273e.]

4–5. We now return to the text of the *Timaeus*, beginning with 30a–b, where we find the concepts that the cosmos is a living thing (*zōon*), ensouled (*empsychon*) and possessed of intellect (*ennoun*), and the 'finest' (*kalliston*)—rather than the 'best' (*ariston*), as A. has it. The concept that anything that is intelligent is superior to what lacks intelligence is to be found at 30b1–2, though not *specifically* the idea that anything ensouled is superior to what is soulless. On the other hand, A. inserts an *isōs* (translated here 'we must presume') to qualify the statement in the *Timaeus* that intellect cannot belong to anything apart from soul (30b2). It is possible, as Invernizzi (1976: ad loc.) suggests, that A. inserts this qualification because of a difficulty that has occurred to many commentators since his time, to wit, does this imply that the Demiurge himself must have a soul, since he is an intellect? The difficulty is that this seems hardly possible, since, in the myth, the Demiurge creates the soul, and even if one demythologizes the account, the divine Intellect should still not require a soul. A possible solution is that Plato is talking here of what *possesses* intellect; his principle need not apply to a being that *is* intellect. This is the solution pointed to by Proclus (*in Ti.* 1. 402. 24 ff. Diehl), when he says that what Plato means is that soul is necessary as a receptacle

for intellect when it enters a body, not that intellect in itself has any
need of soul. Something like this may have been in A.'s mind, but we
cannot be certain. The alternative interpretation, adopted by Louis in
his translation, takes this *isōs* in an 'Aristotelian' sense, and renders it
'*sans doute*', and this may very well be right, after all (though
Whittaker has changed this to '*peut-être*'). I have chosen a rather
waffling translation, reflecting my uncertainty.

[On a detail of terminology, we may note that at 170. 1, A.
employs the word *apotelesma*, here translated 'product', a term not
used by Plato, but identifiably Stoic (cf. e.g. *SVF* 2. 337 (from
Sextus), 351–2 (from Clement)), where Plato uses at 30b3 simply
ergon. We in fact find *apotelesma* and *ergon* in combination at Hipp.
Ref. 7. 24. 2, and Numenius, Fr. 45 Des Places, both times in contexts relating to the soul, indicating, I think, that the former term has
been introduced into the Platonist scholastic tradition as a more
scientifically accurate characterization of a product not created at any
point in time, as an entity *external* to its creator. Some such distinction may be reflected in an interesting passage from Plutarch's *Quaest.
Plat.* 2. 2. 1001c, where he says: 'The soul, however, when it has par-
taken of intelligence and reason and concord (*nou kai logismou kai
harmonias*), is not merely a work (*ergon*) but also a part (*meros*) of
God, and has come to be not by his agency (*hyp' autou*) but both
from him as source (*ap' autou*) and out of his substance (*ex autou*)'—
employing here the technical terms of the 'metaphysic of prepositions'. His point presumably is that the intelligent soul is not just an
ergon—perhaps here implying a criticism of Plato's language at
30b3—but also a *part* of the Demiurge, and the proper term for that
would be *apotelesma*. Plutarch does not, admittedly, use that term
here, but he does, rather pointedly, at *An. Proc.* 1023c, where God's
relation to the soul is explicitly declared to be that of craftsman
(*demiourgos*) to product (*apotelesma*).]

The point about the soul 'binding together and enclosing' (*sundein
kai synechein*) the body of the world (170. 7–9) is interesting, as not
being made by Plato. It is made by Aristotle in the *de Anima* (411b6),
but the use of *synechein* to describe the soul's relation to the body is
characteristically Stoic (e.g. *SVF* 2. 439 and 440), and it is attested
specifically for Posidonius (Fr. 149 Edelstein–Kidd). This may constitute a small indication of a role by Posidonius in the creation of a
body of scholastic exegesis of the *Timaeus*, to which A. would, via
such figures as Eudorus and Arius, be heir.

The latter part of section 4, and all of section 5, reflects *Timaeus* 36b–e, quoted in reverse order, 36e first, describing the extending of the soul through the body of the world from the centre to the periphery, and turning back then to the description of the circles of the Same and the Other, described in 36b–c–d. There is nothing remarkable here doctrinally, though A. is not slavish in his language, and adds some explanatory details, as when he explains why the movement of the inner circle is called 'wandering' (*planētis*, 170. 16), a term not actually used by Plato (it is not attested before the Hellenistic era, and is quite rare), or when he specifies that the rightward movement goes from east to west, and the leftward from west to east. The verb *hypantiazein* (170. 19), also, which I have translated 'move contrariwise' is not attested earlier than Philo (e.g. *Conf.* 31; *Deus.* 71; *Somn.* 2. 121).

The use of *kosmos* to refer, not to the world as a whole (though I have kept the translation 'world'), but specifically the sphere of the fixed stars (as the dominant element in the world) is remarkable. It is justified Platonically by being used at *Epinomis* 987b6–7, but it is interesting that it is picked up by Achilles Tatius, at *Introductio in Aratum* 5. 36. 5–6 Maass, who says, 'The sphere of the fixed stars is the "cosmos"; Plato makes mention of this in the *Timaeus*'—a reference, presumably, to 40a6, where Plato uses the phrase *kosmos alethinos*, in the sense of 'adornment in the true sense' (with, admittedly, a pun on the two senses of *kosmos*, 'adornment' and 'world') to characterize the sphere of the fixed stars. One can see here, I think, a trace of the scholastic fossilizing of Plato's language which would be characteristic of middle-Platonic commentary on the *Timaeus* (and which is picked up later by Proclus, *in Ti.* 3. 118. 22–4 Diehl).

6–7. A. omits the epistemological passage 37a–c, and in the last two sections of the chapter covers the astronomy of 37c–39e, though omitting the speculations on the use of temporal language in 37e–38b. Once again, what we have is a loose, rather than slavish paraphrase, with some explanatory matter.

We may note, first of all, that A. makes a distinction between *astēr* and *astron* (170. 20–1) to describe, respectively, planets and stars, though Plato only uses the term *astra* (I take the *toutōn* of 170. 21, by the way, to refer back to both of these, not just to *astra*, as Whittaker takes it, thus creating a considerable problem as to the meaning of *asteres*, where none, it seems to me, need exist.) There was considerable discussion in later times as to the proper distinction between the two words, of which we have rather confusing testimony. There are, for one thing, two apparently conflicting reports of Posidonius' position on the question, from Arius Didymus (*ap.* Stob. 1. 206. 18 Wachs. = Fr. 127 Edelstein–Kidd) and Achilles, *Introductio in Aratum* 10 = Fr. 128 Edelstein–Kidd). Arius says that Posidonius called the planets (or, more exactly, the sun and moon) *astra* in the strict sense, and then adds that '*astēr* is distinct from *astron*; for if something is an *astēr*, it will necessarily also be termed an *astron*, but not vice versa', while Achilles says that Posidonius' follower Diodorus and Posidonius himself use *astēr* to characterize the planets. It seems, though, from other evidence, (e.g. Macrobius, *in Somn. Scip.* 1. 14. 21, and the scholiast to the *Didaskalikos*, ad loc.) that the distinction settled on by those who made a distinction was that *astēr* referred to a single heavenly body (such as are the planets), while *astron* referred to a combination of units, forming a constellation. I feel that Arius is more likely to be confused on this question than Achilles, whose business is astronomy, and that Posidonius is ultimately behind the distinction which A. is, albeit dimly, adopting here (he leaves it vague whether he means by *astra* individual stars or constellations, but he *could* be understood as meaning the latter).

Another detail of interest is A.'s (or his source's) employment of Chrysippus' definition of time as 'the interval of the motion of the world' (*diastēma tēs tou khronou kinēseōs, SVF* 2. 509–10) at 170. 24–5, plainly treating it as an accurate formulation of what Plato had in mind (it is also attributed to Plato in the doxographic tradition, by Aëtius, *Plac.* 1. 21. 2 = 318. 4–5 Diels *DG*).

More remarkable, though, is the parallel definition which he provides for eternity, 'the measure of the stability of the eternal world'. This might well commend itself to a scholastic mind as a suitable corollary to the traditional Platonist definition of time—'the measure of motion' (*metron phorās*), *Def.* 411b—though in effect it makes little sense to talk of the 'measure' of something unextended and not subject to change of any kind. This might conceivably be a contribution of A. himself, since it occurs nowhere else as such in the surviving tradition. Apuleius, at any rate, at *de Platone* 1. 10. 201, makes no mention of it; nor does Plutarch, in his discussion at *Quaestiones Platonicae* 8. 1007c–d; nor yet does Calcidius, in his discussion of the way in which time is an 'image' of eternity (*in Tim.* 105. 154. 10–20 Wasz.). However, the concept of eternity as a measure of the intelligible world had quite a future in the Neoplatonic tradition. Iamblichus speaks of it as 'the measure of the intelligibles' (*metron tōn noētōn*) in the course of an extended discussion of how time is its *eikōn* (*ap.* Procl. *in Ti.* 3. 33. 1 ff. = *in Ti.* Fr. 64 Dillon), and Proclus speaks of it as 'a measure of things eternal' (*metron tōn aiōniōn*) in *Elements of Theology*, prop. 54, declaring that, in contrast to time, which measures 'part by part' (*kata merē*), it measures 'by the whole' (*kath' holon*), whatever that means.

Another detail is the further specification of the moment when the Great Year comes to completion (170. 37-42). Plato at *Timaeus* 39d declares it to occur 'when all the eight circuits, with their relative speeds, finish together and come to a head, when measured by the revolution of the Same and similarly-moving'. A. adds the specification that 'if one imagines a straight line dropped perpendicularly from the sphere of the fixed stars to the earth, it would pass through the centre of each of them'. This concept is attested also for the Hellenistic interpreter of things Babylonian, Berosus (*ap.* Seneca, *QN* 3. 29. 1), who declared that the world would be consumed by fire when all the planets lined up in the sign of Cancer. A. need not be directly acquainted with Berosus, however; the idea will have filtered into the exegetical tradition long before his time—perhaps, again, through Posidonius. Apuleius, we may note, in the parallel passage of the *de Platone* (1. 10: 203), makes mention of the Great Year, but without the specification added by A.

Since neither Plato nor A. shows any concern with the *length* of the Great Year, we need not dwell long on the problem (see Taylor's commentary on the *Timaeus*, ad loc., for a good survey). Since we learn from A.'s approximate contemporary Theon of Smyrna (*Expos.* 198. 14 Hiller) that the Platonist commentator Dercyllides declared that Oenopides of Chios was the discoverer of the 59-year cycle for the Great Year, we may conclude that that is what Dercyllides assumed was the length of cycle being referred to in the *Timaeus*, and that this may have been in A.'s mind as well, but he gives no indication of this, and many other possibilities had been aired down the years. Proclus, we may note, in his commentary ad loc. (3. 91. 6 ff. Diehl) criticizes all such calculations as misguided.

Section 7 begins with a paraphrase of *Timaeus* 38d, but amplifies this with material from *Epinomis* 987a ff., where the three remaining planets not named in the *Timaeus*, Saturn, Jupiter, and Mars, are specified (though they are also named, we may note, by Timaeus Locrus, 97b).

[We may note, also in this connection that A. appears to read at

38d2, not *heōsphoron*, 'Dawn-bringer', as a name for the planet Venus, but *phōsphoron*, 'Light-bringer', as does Timaeus Locrus 96e–97a, and Calcidius in his translation, 31. 1. Wasz. (*Luciferi*). This variant is attested nowhere in the direct tradition, nor is it recognized by Proclus, but it does seem as if it has crept into some manuscripts available to Middle-Platonic commentators, as an 'ideological emendation', since *phōsphoros* is the more usual title for the planet (cf. e.g. Cic. *ND* 2. 53; Plut. *An. Proc.* 1028d, 1029a–b, *Def. Or.* 430a).]

A problem is caused by the fact that A. refers to the planetary bodies as being composed 'mainly of fire' (171. 2), in which, it must be said, he is simply following *Timaeus* 40a, whereas in the next chapter (4. 171. 34-5), as I have already noted, the spheres of both the fixed stars and the planets are clearly stated to be composed of ether. I do not see how these statements can be reconciled, and the contradiction may simply betoken a change of source on A.'s part.

[Finally, the reference to the sphere of the fixed stars as 'the highest power' (*hē anōthen dynamis*, 171. 13) is striking. The use of *dynamis* can be justified, as Whittaker points out (1990: 118 n. 297), from *Epinomis*, 986a8, but the addition of *anōthen* seems to introduce a note of solemnity, though Whittaker may be going too far afield by adducing Gnostic and Hermetic parallels. A. may, however, be thinking of the 'Intellect of the World-Soul' as having its particular seat in the sphere of the fixed stars.]

CHAPTER 15

1. A. turns now to a brief discussion of daemons, their nature and role in the universe, followed by an equally brief description of the earth, and a note on ether.

His account of daemons takes its start, not from the famous passage of the *Symposium* (202e–203e)—though it ends with an allusion to that—but from *Timaeus* 40d6, where, however, Plato means by *hoi alloi daimones*, not daemons properly speaking, but rather the gods of traditional mythology, whom he then assimilates to the planetary and star-gods. It is to these latter, as 'created gods', that the Demiurge addresses his speech at 41a6 ff. The tradition which A. is following, however, connects this passage with what has gone before at 39e10 ff., where Timaeus is describing the four classes of being to be created in the physical cosmos, the heavenly gods, the winged beings which traverse the air (i.e. birds), the 'watery kind' (i.e. fish), and 'what has feet and goes on dry land' (i.e. man and other land animals). This passage, however, becomes curiously misinterpreted in the later Platonist tradition, by reason of assimilating it to *Epinomis*, 984b–c, which is itself, it would seem, a deliberate misreading of the *Timaeus* (see on this Tarán 1975: 42–7). The author of the *Epinomis*, as mentioned above (Comm., ch. 13), substitutes *five* classes of being for the four set out in the *Timaeus*, but also makes the middle three classes intermediate between the heavenly gods and man, presenting them as daemonic beings fashioned predominantly out of the element, ether, air, or water, in which they reside (birds and fish, like land animals, on this interpretation, are earthy, and not the proper inhabitants of air or water). We find this doctrine also in Apuleius, particularly in the *de Deo Socratis* (6–12), and in Calcidius, *in Tim.* (139–46), and even in Philo, *de Gigantibus* (6–9), we find the argument that the proper inhabitants of the air are not birds, but aery beings. This theory of daemons, then, is established Platonist doctrine by the first century BC, but the evidence of the *Epinomis* indicates that it was already the doctrine of the Old Academy, together with the 'creative misinterpretation' of the *Timaeus* that this involves.

This misinterpretation finds its full flowering later in the commentary of Proclus (*in Ti.* 3. 104. 26–112. 19 Diehl). Proclus does recognize (107. 26 ff.) that there have been differing views in the tradition about the proper reference of 39e10 ff., and that there have been some interpreters, 'sticking closely to the text of Plato', who take the inhabitants of air and water to be mortal beings, while others, 'looking rather to the realities (*ta pragmata*)', and adducing the *Epinomis*, interpret these as referring to classes of being superior to us. Proclus here, interestingly, both attests to the existence of a strictly 'philological' tradition of interpretation of this passage (of which we have no sign in surviving Middle-Platonic sources), and implicitly concedes its correctness on the literal level, though he feels that the passage should be interpreted in the light of *ta pragmata*.

All this, then, lies behind the very succinct account given by A. here (we may note that at the beginning of the next chapter he blandly hitches up 40a1 with 41b7, where the Demiurge speaks of 'three mortal kinds' still remaining uncreated, and recognizes *there* a reference to birds, fish, and land animals).

The argument that 'no part of the world should be without a share in soul or *in a living being superior to mortal nature*' is nowhere to be found in the *Timaeus* (though at least the first part of it is implicit in the doctrine that the world-soul extends throughout the entire body of the cosmos, 36e), but it can be derived from *Epinomis* 984c, where, having described the creation of beings proper to all the elements, the author says, 'having produced all these, it is likely (*eikos*) that soul filled the whole heaven with creatures'. However, there is no talk here of *necessity*, and the author chooses to say 'heaven' (*ouranos*) rather than cosmos, though he seems to mean the latter, nor is it specified that these beings should be superior to man. This latter idea may owe something to *Politicus* 271d and/or *Laws* 4. 713c–d, in both of which places it is described how divine daemons are set over each of the classes of living things, but its formalization may be derived by later Platonists from the demonology of Xenocrates rather than from direct reflection on Plato himself. The argument that every portion of the universe *must* contain rational creatures appropriate to it seems also to have been advanced by Aristotle in the *de Philosophia* (*ap.* Cic. *ND* 2. 42 = Fr. 21 Rose), in support of his claim that the stars are rational beings, and that has been taken on board by the tradition as well.

The first half of the doctrine, at least, is to be discerned in Philo's remark (*de Gig.* 7) that 'the cosmos must necessarily be ensouled through and through (*holon di' holōn epsychōsthai*)', and in Calcidius, *in Tim.* (130), we find the argument: 'Now when the outermost boundaries (of the universe), that is to say the highest and the lowest, and filled with the presence of living beings fitting for their nature, I mean beings making use of reason—the heavenly regions with the stars, the earth with men—consequently also the rest of the places, the regions in the middle, must be held to be filled with rational beings, in order to leave no place in the world deserted' (trans. den Boeft).

2. The second section takes its start from the speech of the Demiurge to his children, the 'young gods', in *Timaeus* 41a–d. In particular, the phrase 'and by his will this universe admits of no dissolution' owes much to 41b2–6, and 'in accordance with his command and in imitation of him' relates to 41c4–6. Finally, the reference to the role of daemons in divination derives from *Symposium* 202e–203a. Cf. the rather rhetorical elaborations of Apuleius in *de Deo Socratis* (6–7).

[The technical terms for omens and presages (*klēdones kai otteiai*) are not found in Plato, nor, indeed, in any Attic prose author. *Klēdōn* is found in Philo, linked with *oiōnos* (*Vit. Mos* 1. 287) and with *manteia* (*Spec. Leg.* 1. 63); *otteia* seems to occur otherwise only in Dionysius of Halicarnassus (the two terms are found interestingly linked in Plut. *de Is. et Os.* 356e, where he is talking about the Egyptian belief in the mantic quality of children's shouts and cries (*tais toutōn otteuesthai klēdosi*)). This later terminology may, as Witt suggests (1937: 79), be an indication that Posidonius' discussions of the role of daemons in divination is an intermediary here (primarily on Arius Didymus).]

There are useful discussions of the Middle Platonist theory of daemons in J. den Boeft (1977), J. Beaujeu (1973: 183–247), and G. Soury (1942).

It may be apposite at this point to remark that the divinity which is the subject in these chapters (Plato's Demiurge) must, if A. is being coherent, correspond, not to his supreme god, but to his secondary god, the intellect of the world.

3. We now turn to the next topic in the *Timaeus* after the description of the four classes of being and the heavenly bodies in particular, and that is the earth (40b9–c3): 'And Earth, our nurse, which is wound around (?) (*heillomenēn* or *illomenēn*) the pole which stretches through all, he framed to be wardress and fashioner of night and day, she being the first and eldest of the gods which have come into existence within the heaven' (trans. Bury, slightly altered). We can see from A.'s paraphrase (*sphingomenē*) of the troublesome verb *heillesthai/ illesthai* of 40b9 that he takes it to mean 'be compressed', rather than 'revolve', as it was understood by Aristotle (*de Caelo* 2. 293^{b}30). For a very full discussion of the history of interpretation of this passage in antiquity see Taylor's commentary on the *Timaeus* (1928: 226–39). I have discussed it also in 'Tampering with the *Timaeus*', (Dillon, 1989: 66–70, repr. in Dillon (1991)). Suffice it here to say that, within the Platonist tradition, Timaeus Locrus (97d—*hidrumenā*), Plutarch (*Quaest. Plat.* 8. 1006c), Theon of Smyrna (200. 7 Hiller), Calcidius (*in Tim.* 122—*constrictam*), and Proclus (*in Ti.* 3. 136. 29 ff.) all agree with A. in taking the earth to be *compressed* about its pole, while only Diogenes Laertius (3. 75) follows Aristotle in assuming motion (*kineisthai peri to meson*).

[It is interesting also to note that A. seems to have a reading *tetagmenon*, 'is arranged', at *Timaeus* 40c1, rather than *diatetamenon*, 'extends'. This undoubted error is not found in the direct tradition, but it is represented also in one group of MSS of Plutarch, *Quaestiones Platonicae* 1006c, and in one of the two chief manuscripts

(D) of Proclus, *in Platonis Timaeum commentarii* (cf. 3. 133. 12 and 136. 30–1 Diehl), so it seems to have got into the late antique vulgate tradition.]

Note also that A., in face of Plato's expression at 40c1–2, 'guardian and creator (*phylaka kai dēmiourgon*) of night and day', omits *kai dēmiourgon*. This might, I think, qualify as an 'ideological emendation' rather than mere inadvertence (although the same omission is to be found in Calc. *in Tim.* 122. 166. 5. Wasz., which might indicate that the omission is at least not original to A.), and is probably to be explained by an unease in Middle-Platonic circles about using the august term *dēmiourgos* to characterize anything other than the cosmic Intellect. Compare A.'s interpretation of *Republic* 7. 530a7, *tōi tou ouranou dēmiourgōi*, back in chapter 7 (161. 30–1), which I have discussed in the commentary, ad loc.

A. feels it necessary to qualify Plato's statement that Earth is first and eldest of all the gods within the heaven by noting that the world-soul, of course, is older (cf. *Ti.* 34b–c). Also, the phrase 'providing us with abundant (*dapsilē*) nourishment' is not in Plato, though it is certainly implied.

[The adjective *dapsilēs* is not Platonic, though it is found in Aristotle, *GA* 4. 6. 774^{b}26, combined with *trophē* (in a context where the pig is being compared to a rich soil). The assertion that the earth is immobile through being 'in a state of equilibrium in the middle' (*isorrhopon . . . en mesōi*) is not to be found in 40b–c, but could be derived from 62d12–63a1, where there is talk of 'a solid body evenly balanced at the centre of the universe' (*kata meson tou pantos isopales*). The word *isorrhopos* is Platonic, but not used in this connection. It may indeed by used here by A. as a deliberate variation on *isopalēs*.]

4. We now come to the troublesome description of the ether mentioned above. There is some Platonic warrant for making ether the stuff or medium of the heavenly bodies in references to it in the myth of the *Phaedo*, 109b8 and 111b5, as well as a rather non-specific reference later in the *Timaeus*, at 58d2, where it is presented as the most translucent type of air, but there is no trace in Plato of its special Aristotelian status. It would seem that A. is on the whole adopting the Aristotelian position for the ether, rather than that of the *Epinomis*, where it comes between fire and air, but he almost seems to want to have things both ways, making a distinction between two levels of ether, that of the fixed stars and that of the planets, perhaps representing the circles of the Same and the Other respectively, and

making no mention of any special motion peculiar to ether. The only way, I think, to reconcile his statement near the end of chapter 14 (171. 2)—admittedly taken direct from *Timaeus* 40a2–3—that the heavenly bodies are 'mainly composed of fire', and the present statement is that A. is assimilating ether to the Stoic pure fire, and feels he has warrant for that from Plato's works (silently setting aside the eccentricity of the *Epinomis*).

The curious impression that is given here of a *three*-tiered universe, composed of ether, air, and earth (with water), as opposed to a four- or even a five-level one, may betoken once again some influence from Xenocrates, who was much attached to such a division, with the air as the daemonic level, median between the two extremes of the divine and the mortal (cf. Fr. 83 IP = Sextus Emp. *M.* 7. 147–9; Fr. 161 IP = Plut. *de Fac.* 493e—although in this latter passage Xenocrates makes the moon part of the median level). Whether or not A. regards the moon as within or bordering on the sphere of air is not clear, but he could well have done; Philo so places it in an interesting passage (*Somn.* 1. 145), where he presents it as general belief (*legetai goun* . . .) 'that the moon is not an unmixed mass of ether, as each of the other heavenly bodies is, but a blend of etherial and aerial substance'.

CHAPTER 16

1. This short chapter follows the *Timaeus* very closely, and contains little that is worthy of special comment. It begins from the middle of the Demiurge's speech, 41b7 ff.:

Three mortal kinds still remain ungenerated; but if these come not into being the heaven will be imperfect; for it will not contain within itself the whole sum of the kinds of living creatures; yet contain them it must if it is to be fully perfect. But if by my doing these creatures came into existence and partook of life, they would be made equal unto gods; in order, therefore, that they may be mortal and that this world-all may be truly all, do you turn yourselves, as nature directs, to the work of fashioning these living creatures, imitating the power showed by me in my generating of you. (trans. Bury)

It is interesting to observe how A., or his source, goes about extracting the 'solid' doctrine from Plato's rather poetical presentation of it. A. excerpts this passage of the speech, and adds to it certain specificatory material from elsewhere, the details of the three classes of mortal being from 40a (where, however, Plato, as we have seen, is now thought to be talking about daemons), and the details about the response of the young gods to their father's command from 42e6–43a1: 'And as he thus abode (in his proper and wonted state), his children gave heed to their father's command and obeyed it. They took the immortal principle of the mortal living creature, and imitating their own maker, they borrowed from the cosmos portions of fire and earth and water and air, as if meaning to pay them back, and the portions so taken they cemented together.' For the mention of the four elements, A. substitutes simply the un-Platonic 'primal matter' (*prōtē hulē*)—derivable from Aristotle (cf. e.g. *Metaph.* 5. 4. 1014^{b}32, 1015^{a}7).

[We may also note the addition of the phrase 'for fixed periods' (*pros hōrismenous khronous*, 172. 2), which is paralleled interestingly in Philo, *Heres*, 282 (*kath' hōrismenas periodous kairōn*), where Philo is drawing on the same passage of the *Timaeus*. It may be that this phrase, which is hardly a significant addition, is borrowed by the scholastic tradition from such a passage as *Phaedo* 107e, where there is a reference to 'many long periods of time' (*pollai kai makrai khronou periodoi*), after which the guardian daemon brings back the soul to begin another life; but one cannot be certain.]

2. This editorial procedure continues in section 2, with the description of the embodiment of human souls, starting from 41d4 ff., where the Demiurge returns to the mixing-bowl to make the 'seconds and thirds' which are to be human souls (though this detail A. omits): 'And when he had compounded the whole, he divided it into souls equal in number to the stars, and each several soul he assigned to one star, and setting them each as it were in a chariot he showed them the nature of the universe, and expounded to them the laws of fate . . .'

A. then summarizes the following passage down to 42e6, concerning the cycle of lives, which connects up with the passage he has utilized at the end of section 1. There is nothing here that goes beyond the text of the *Timaeus*.

[We may note once again, however, certain details of terminology. First of all, the phrase 'creator of the universe' (*ho tōn holōn dēmiourgos*, 172. 7) is not actually Platonic, being only found in second- and third-century AD sources such as Nicomachus of Gerasa (*Ar.* 1. 4. 2. 9. 12–13 Hoche), Origen (*C. Cels.* 3. 56), and the Hermetic Corpus (*Exc.* 24. 1). Then, the verb *katapempō*, 'send down', is not to be found in Plato, but occurs in this sense in Epictetus (*Diss.* 3. 22. 59), and a little later in the Hermetic extract just quoted (24. 3–4). The

Hermetic passage may well reflect contemporary scholastic Platonist terminology, as indeed may Epictetus. Lastly, the description of the Demiurge as a 'lawgiver' (*nomothetēs,* 172. 10), while readily derivable from such passages as *Timaeus* 41e2 and 42d2, is not to be found before Philo (*Vit. Mos.* 2. 48), and then in such authors as Apuleius (*de Plat.* 1. 12. 206), Numenius (Fr. 13 Des Places), and Calcidius (*in Tim.* 188. 212. 24 Wasz.)—another detail of scholastic terminology.]

For a more 'scientific' discussion of the topic of the embodiment of the soul, compare chapter 25 below.

CHAPTER 17

1–2. In this chapter, A. turns to a description of the construction of the human body, beginning from the passage of *Timaeus* (42e–43a) just following that with which he has ended the previous section, but combining with that the later, more detailed description at 72e–75c. We find a broad parallel to the sequence of chapters 17 to 22 in Apuleius, *de Platone* 1. 14–18, and to chapter 17 in particular in *de Platone* 1. 16.

The remarks about 'borrowing certain portions' and 'fitting together with invisible pegs' are taken from 42a9–43a2, while that about the brain being 'a sort of field' is taken from 73c6–d1. The mention of the organs of perception being set in the face is actually taken from 45e6–b2, though the sequel, concerning sight, is only taken up in the next chapter. With the marrow, we are back to 73b–e, and this is followed by a summary of the discussion of the formation of bone and flesh at 73e–74d, and sinews at 74e–75c.

[We may note as further examples of A.'s habit of 'mirror-quotation' the reversal of the order of the adjectives *astrabē kai leia*, 'unwarped and smooth' (*Ti.* 73b6) at 172. 28–9, and *oxeos kai halmurou*, 'acidic and salty' (74c7) at 172. 33.]

3. We now turn back to 72e–73a, for a mention of the bowels, belly, and intestines, and for the windpipe (*artēria*), back to 70d, though A. adds here a mention of the pharynx, running from the mouth to the lungs, a detail not mentioned by, and perhaps not known to, Plato. The word is not used by Plato, though it frequently is by Aristotle (referring, however, to the windpipe). For the description of the process of digestion, we go forward to 78e–79a, though without any close verbal borrowings, and for the description of the two veins

binding the head to the spine, to 77d–e. In all this, apart from the reference to the pharynx, there is nothing that is not derived from the *Timaeus*.

[We may note, however, a small detail, the word *pneumōn* used for 'lung' (172, 44) in place of the form *pleumōn* used by Plato in the *Timaeus* (e.g. 70c5, 70d2, 78c5, 79c2). *Pneumōn* is the more 'modern', rationalized term, arising probably from an etymologizing derivation by Aristotle (*de Resp.* 10. 476ᵃ7–10) from *pneuma*, 'breath'. It is found also in Galen's quotation of *Timaeus* 79a5–c7, at *de Placitis Hippocratis et Platonis* 8. 8. 530. 30 De Lacy, and has worked its way, as a quasi-ideological emendation, into the F, Y tradition of Plato MSS.]

4. This last section concerns the situating of the soul in the body, described first at *Timaeus* 43a–44d, and returned to at 69c–72d, where the apportioning of the different parts of the soul to distinct parts of the body is described. Here it is notable that A. presents a basically bipartite soul (though with the affective (*pathētikon*) part subdivided into spirited and appetitive, as it is back in ch. 5. 156. 35–6), rather than a tripartite soul, such as Plato still seems to be presenting in the *Timaeus*. However, it had been Platonist doctrine since the time of the Old Academy, attested to earliest, perhaps, in the Peripatetic *Magna Moralia*, 1. 1. 1182a24 ff. (although the imagery of charioteer and horses in the *Phaedrus* would appear already to depict such a doctrine, and Xenocrates, at least, would seem—though the sources are pretty wretched (Theodoret = Fr. 70 Heinze/206 IP, and Olympiodorus = Fr. 75 Heinze/211 IP)—to have held it), that the fundamental division of the soul was bipartite, and A. has no hesitation in imposing it here (below, in ch. 24, we may note, he begins by presenting the soul as tripartite, but the basic bipartition reasserts itself before the chapter is over).

We may note also the description of the rational part as *hēgemonikon*, 'ruling element' (173. 7), the characteristic Stoic term (though, of course, for the Stoics the *hēgemonikon* was not in the head but in the heart), which, once again, by this stage in the development of Platonism A. feels quite justified in using, though it occurs nowhere in Plato in a technical sense. Plato does speak, however, at 44d6 of the reason 'reigning over' (*despotoun*) all the other parts within us, and at 45b1–2 of the front part of the head as being 'that which partakes of rule' (*to metechon hēgemonias*), which may even have had some influence on Stoic terminology. The term is used freely by Philo, and in the Platonist tradition proper occurs in the anon.

Theaetetus commentary (11. 28)—where, however, the Commentator is discussing Stoic doctrine. A. uses the term again at 173. 10, 177. 34, and 182. 30, so it is a well-established part of his vocabulary.

At 173. 8 ff., we find a recognition of the brain as the centre of the nervous system, with the term *neura* denoting nerves, and not 'sinews' as it does in the *Timaeus*, where at 75c4 and 77e4 the head is said to be free of *neura*. The discovery that the brain is the centre and origin of the nervous system is to be credited to the physician Erasistratus of Ceos in the third century BC, and so was quite unknown to Plato. A., or more probably his source, has quietly superimposed this on the doctrine of the *Timaeus*. Plato himself, at 73c–d, envisages the marrow (*muelos*) as doing the work of the nerves, but speaks of it in such a way that a loyal Platonist might have felt that here was a poetical description of the nervous system.

The expression *kata tas peiseis paraphrosunai* (173. 7), which I have translated 'losses of reason, occasioned by accidents', is somewhat peculiar. *Peisis* is not to be found in Plato, but is quite common among A.'s contemporaries, such as Marcus Aurelius (13. 6. 2; 7. 55. 3) and Sextus Empiricus (*P.* 1. 22; *M.* 7. 384), apparently to denote something rather broader than *pathos*; meaning 'anything that happens to one'; in this case, 'accident' seems to catch the meaning best. *Paraphrosyne* occurs, not in the *Timaeus*, but in the plural at *Philebus* 36e6, and in the singular at *Sophist* 228d2 and *Epistulae* 7. 331c2. Presumably what A. has in mind here (though his train of thought is somewhat elliptical) is that bangs on the head and suchlike can cause (temporary or permanent) insanity, which would indicate that the reason is situated there (and not in the heart, as the Stoics would have it).

[The image of the sense-organs as 'bodyguards' (173. 10), and the reason as 'king', is not Platonic as such, but may be adapted from Plato's portrayal of the heart being placed in the 'guard-room' (*doryphorikē oikēsis*) at 70b2. It is found, however, (repeatedly) in Philo (e.g. *Opif.* 139; *Leg. All.* 3. 115; *Conf.* 19); in Galen (*Hipp. et Plat.* 2. 4. 120. 1–4 De Lacy, and *UP* 8. 2. 445. 14–17 Helmreich); and in Calcidius (*in Tim.* 231. 245. 3–5 Wasz.). There is also a suggestion of the image in Apuleius, *de Platone* 1. 13. 208.]

There is an interesting small variation in where A. situates the appetitive part (*epithymētikon*) of the soul, as opposed to its place in the *Timaeus*. Plato places it at 70e1–2 'midway between the midriff (*phrenes*) and the boundary at the navel (*omphalos*), and at 71d2 'around the liver' (*peri to hēpar*). A. places it 'around the abdomen (*ētron*)', and the parts around the navel'. In this he agrees with Philo, *Leg. All.* 1. 71, and with Apuleius, *de Platone* 1. 13. 207 (*infernas abdominis sedes*). Whittaker (1990: 123 n. 333) points out, most persuasively, that this seems to be an influence from *Phaedo* 118a, the description of the death of Socrates, where the poison is said to reach first his *ētron* and then his heart, and this must have seemed to later Platonists to make the *ētron* emblematic of the lowest part of the soul, so that it tended to supersede Plato's apparently looser descriptions in the *Timaeus*. This would indeed be a good instance of the workings of the scholastic mind.

The summary remarks at the end of the chapter about the placing of the lower parts of the soul will be developed more fully below in chapter 23, whither A. refers the reader.

CHAPTER 18

1. Still following the order of topics in the *Timaeus*, A. turns to discuss the faculty of vision, dealt with by Plato at 45b2–46a2, and then, arising out of this, mirror-images and the theory of refraction, dealt with by Plato immediately afterwards, at 46a2–c6. There is once again nothing remarkable in A.'s summary of the doctrine of the *Timaeus*. He is not concerned with the intricacies of the theory of vision.

[Certain details, however, may be noted. First of all, if it is correct, as modern commentators such as Taylor and Cornford assume— surely rightly—to take *leion kai puknon*, 'smooth and dense', at 45b7–8 as going, not with *rhein*, 'flow', but rather with the following *holon* and *to meson*, with the result that it is not the fire from the eyes that is smooth and dense, but the eyes themselves, then A. has got the syntax wrong, whereas Calcidius, in his translation, has got it right (*per leves congestosque et tamquam firmiore soliditate probatos orbes luminum*). This involves him in the mild absurdity of describing the visual ray as 'dense', but he presumably took this as meaning 'concentrated' or 'intense'.

The word *phōtoeidēs*, here translated 'luminous' (173. 18), is not Platonic, nor even Classical, but is to be found (perhaps significantly) in Posidonius' commentary (or at least *comments*) on the *Timaeus* (Fr. 85 Edelstein-Kidd), where he is reported by Sextus Empiricus (*M.* 7. 93) as remarking that light (*phōs*) is captured by the sense of sight, which is 'light-like' (*phōtoeidēs*). It is also used by Philo (*Somn.* 1. 217. 220), and is fairly common in later writers, such as Plutarch, Galen, and Alexander of Aphrodisias.

One may note also, once again, an instance of mirror-quotation: 'dissolves and smooths out' (*diakhei kai homalunei*) of *Timaeus* 45e2 becomes 'smooths out and dissolves' at 173. 26.]

2. A. passes on to the description of sleep and dreams, which is the final section of the *Timaeus* passage on vision, and then, as I have said, to a brief discussion of mirror-images and reflection.

At 173. 31–2, A. seems slightly to misinterpret what Plato is saying at 46a1–2. Plato is talking about dreams as images (*phantasmata*) which are first imprinted on the mind in sleep, and then remembered when the sleeper wakes up (thereby, admittedly, causing another *phantasma* to be imprinted on the mind). A. talks here of *phantasiai* appearing to us 'in a waking state' (*hypar*), as well as asleep (*onar*), as if there were some question of waking visions. But perhaps he is simply compressing Plato to obscurity.

From 'direct' (*kat' euthyōrian*, 173. 31) images, he turns to images involving reflection (*kat' anaklasin*, 173. 35). The discussion of mirrors and reflection contains a few points of interest. First of all, A. seems to want to connect mirror-images more closely with dream-images than Plato in fact does, by introducing the connecting phrase 'following on these' (*tautais de hepomenōs*). He may have concluded that this was implied in Plato's juxtaposition of the two topics, or he may merely be reflecting the fact that the topics do in fact follow each other in the *Timaeus*. The two topics are, admittedly, connected in Plato's mind, as both concerning images of a sort, but dream-images cannot be said to *explain* mirror-images. My translation simply preserves the ambiguity of the Greek.

Secondly, he brings in the technical term *anaklasis*, 'reflection', a term not used by Plato, though it is Aristotelian (e.g. *APo.* 2. 15. 98^{a}29; *Meteor.* 3. 4. 373^{a}32 ff.); Aristotle, however, fails to distinguish the phenomena of reflection and *refraction*, both of which are rendered by the term *anaklasis* (see Taylor's discussion (1928:289–90)).

Thirdly, he fills out Plato's account by mentioning convex as well as concave mirrors (173. 31), and producing an explanation to go with it (the rays 'slide off'). For convexity, cf. Euclid, *Optica* 34. 27 Heiberg. Otherwise, he shows no sign of developing Plato's doctrine in this area.

CHAPTER 19

1. A. follows the discussion of sight with disquisitions on the other four senses, hearing, smell, taste, and touch, which Plato does not deal with directly after sight, but reserves to the second half of the treatise (61c–67c). Curiously, A. deals with these in the reverse order to Plato—perhaps just an instance of 'mirror-quotation' on a large scale, but perhaps due to the fact that A. is treating the senses in descending order of importance, following on vision, whereas Plato, in the second part of the *Timaeus*, is treating them in *ascending* order, culminating in a second treatment of vision, or, more specifically, of colours (67c4–68d7), which A. omits. It is also not irrelevant, as Whittaker (1990: 125 n. 345) points out, that this is the order followed by Aristotle in the *de Anima* (2. 7–11), and even by Theophrastus in his exposition of Plato's doctrine in the *de Sensu*, 5–6 (500. 7–18 Diels *DG*). It is another instance of the exegetical tradition taking on Peripatetic material. In Plato, hearing is covered in *Timaeus* 67a7–c3, smell in 66d1–67a6, taste (at greater length) in 65c1–66c7. As for touch, Plato does not treat it as a specialized sense, but rather as the general basis for all the other senses, which are regarded as special kinds of touch, but he deals with it from 61c3 to 64a1 (there is then a section on pleasure and pain, from 64a2 to 65b2, which A. does not reproduce). All this is followed pretty faithfully by A. Note the parallel treatment in Apuleius' *de Platone* 1. 14. 209–10, where, however, touch is dealt with before smell.

There is nothing in the description of hearing that is not in the *Timaeus*, but A. omits any mention of 'smooth' and 'harsh' sounds (67b6–7).

2. The description of smell once again follows the *Timaeus* very closely, though A. somewhat clarifies Plato's account of how smelling takes place. Plato does not actually specify the process, but A. describes it as 'a sensation which comes down from the veins in the nostrils as far as the region of the navel'. This does not necessarily betoken any superior degree of biological knowledge on A.'s part; he (or his source) could be deducing this from the mention of the 'whole bodily cavity which lies between the head and the navel' at 67a4–5. For a more informed contemporary description of the olfactory organs see Galen, *de Usu Partium*, 8. 6. 1. 469–72 Helmreich, where there is no mention of the navel.

[One linguistic detail is interesting: the adjectives *euōdēs* and *dusōdēs*, 'good-smelling' and 'bad-smelling' (174. 12) are not to be found combined in the *Timaeus* (*euādēs* does occur by itself at 50e6), but they do occur in Aristotle, *de Anima*, 2. 9. 421[b]22–3, in his discussion of smelling—a further indication of influence from this source. They also occur, we may note, in the passage of Timaeus Locrus (101a) corresponding to the *Timaeus* passage, and in Philo *Legum Allegoriae* 2. 7, a passage where the senses are listed (in the Aristotelian order).]

3–4. The treatment of taste is much shorter than Plato's, and contains nothing original (though we note A.'s use of the word *chylos* instead of Plato's *chymos* for 'flavour', a usage characterized later by Galen, *de simplicium medicamentorum temperamentis ac facultatibus* (11. 450 Kühn) as Aristotelian—and later Greek—rather than Platonic. Once again, it is interesting that A. presents the flavours in a different (partial-mirror) order to Plato, listing 'sweet' first, which Plato places last (66b7–c7), and then 'acid', which he places second-last, before reverting to the order of the *Timaeus* with 'astringent', 'dry', 'salty' (though here he uses the more usual adjective *halmuros* for Plato's rare *halukos*—as does Aristotle, *de An.* 2. 10. 422[a]19, and Timaeus Locrus, 101a), 'pungent' and 'bitter'; and when he turns to discussing them, he mentions 'bitter' out of order, before 'dry'. There seems no particular reason for this, other than an impulse towards *variatio*.

Throughout the discussion of flavours in section 4 we may note the influence, whether direct or, more probably, indirect, of Theophrastus' *de Sensu*, 84 (525. 4–11 Diels *DG*). Theophrastus, admittedly, keeps the term *chymos*, and his order of topics is different from A.'s, but such a phrase as 'diffusing in a naturally agreeable way the moisture on the tongue' (174. 29–30) is far closer to Theophrastus (525. 10–11) than to *Timaeus* 66c–d, as is the final sentence, 'Of those which contract . . . are the dry' (174. 35–8) to *de Sensu* 525. 6–7, than to *Timaeus* 65d1–4. What seems to be the case is that Theophrastus' work has been taken over by the exegetical tradition, along with Aristotle's *de Anima*, as a means of 'updating' Plato's text.

[In small linguistic details we can observe A.'s liking for *variatio*: at *Timaeus* 65d7, Plato has the compound verb *apotēkein* for 'dissolve'; Theophrastus (525), has *ektēkein*; A., at 174. 33, has *syntēkein*.]

5. As we have noted above, Plato does not treat the sense of touch (*haphē*) in the *Timaeus* as a specialized sense, but regards it as a sort

of generalized sensitive capacity of the whole surface of the body (as, of course it is; all the other senses are based on specific organs, in the head). However, in the *Republic* (7. 523e) he does speak of touch (without naming it) as the *aisthēsis* which is concerned with the hard and the soft, and in the *Theaetetus* (186b) he actually names it (as *epaphē*), so that A. may feel quite justified in treating it as such here.

Nothing in A.'s treatment here cannot be found in the *Timaeus* (apart from the actual mention of a *haptikē dynamis*), though once again he varies the order of topics interestingly. The qualities discernible by touch are first named in the *Timaeus* order (hot–cold, soft–hard, light–heavy, smooth–rough), but they are then dealt with in reverse order, except for 'heavy' and 'light', which are going to be given the next chapter to themselves.

CHAPTER 20

This little chapter is simply an appendix to the previous one, singling out for special treatment the qualities 'heavy' and 'light', since they involve a discussion of the concepts of 'above' and 'below' in the universe, dealt with by Plato at some length at *Timaeus* 62c3–63e7. A. simply reproduces faithfully Plato's definition of weight and lightness, his denial of the meaningfulness of the concepts 'up' and 'down', and his assertion that the heavy is that which is compounded of more homogeneous parts, the light of less, without taking any account of Aristotle's refinements and criticisms in the *de Caelo* (cf 4. 4. 311ᵃ15 ff., on 'heavy' and 'light'; 4. 1. 308ᵃ18 ff. on 'up' and 'down'; 4. 2. 308ᵇ3 ff., on heavy and light as being composed of more or less identical parts)—but there is after all no compelling reason why he should. He is concerned only with expounding the doctrine of Plato.

On the other hand, we may once again see the influence of Theophrastus' *de Sensu*, this time section 83 (524. 26–8 Diels), particularly in the case of the last sentence, 'In fact, heavy . . .' (though the final phrase, 'the light from the minimum amount', is borrowed from *Ti.* 56b1–2). Plato's rather expansive treatment of this topic had to be boiled down for scholastic purposes, and Theophrastus was useful here.

CHAPTER 21

We now turn to a later section of the *Timaeus* (79a5–e9), which
describes the process of respiration, on lines following the theory of
Empedocles, seeking to dispense with the necessity of postulating a
void. A. follows the *Timaeus* quite uncritically, only omitting any reference to the void. The sole notable detail is that A. uses the word
poroi (175. 22) where Plato does not, adding the phrase 'which we are
acquainted with only through reasoning' (*tōi logōi theōrētōn*, 175. 25).
Plato may have avoided the word precisely because it was too closely
connected with Empedocles, but it is implied in his account (he
prefers, however, to use the term *exodoi*, 79a2).

[We may note also A.'s use of the Aristotelian term *eispnoē* for
'breathing in' or 'inhalation' (e.g. *de Resp.* 2. 471ᵃ7–8), in place of the
Platonic *anapnoē* (*Ti.* 79e9, etc.). To judge from Galen's remark in his
commentary on the *Timaeus* (*Plat. Tim.* 21. 30–1 Schroeder): 'Plato
called *eispnoē anapnoē*', it was regarded as the more 'modern' term. A.
does use the term *anapnoē* (below, ch. 25. 178. 7), but in the general
sense of 'respiration'.]

CHAPTER 22

A. turns next to the topic of diseases and their causes, dealt with by
Plato at *Timaeus* 81e6–86a8. This long passage is presented by A. in
brief summary, giving little more than the heads of discussion, and
adding nothing from the intervening centuries of medical discovery.

The first cause of disease, excess or deficiency (*pleonexia kai
endeia*—characteristically reversed and varied by A. to *endeia kai
hyperbolē*), is dealt with by Plato from 81e6 to 82b7; the second, 'the
inverse production of homogeneous parts', from 82b8 to 84c7. Plato
then distinguishes a third class of diseases, resulting from 'air
(*pneuma*), phlegm, or bile' (84c8–86a2), but A. subsumes these under
the second category. Plato then ends his survey with a few lines on
fevers (86a2–8), covered by A. in the last three lines of the chapter.

A. is plainly no authority on medicine. For any creative development on or criticism of the *Timaeus* in this area, one would have to
turn to Galen, who, while maintaining his stance as a philosopher, is
a doctor first and foremost.

CHAPTER 23

1. A. now returns to a discussion of the soul, and in the process makes clear how he (or his source) has been using the *Timaeus*. Basically, we have been following the order of topics introduced at 42e, where the Demiurge handed over the creation of the human body and the binding into it of soul to his 'children'. The details of this have been filled out suitably by splicing in passages from the second part of the work, as we have seen, but now we are essentially back at 44d–e, where the immortal part of the soul is being established in the head, and the two mortal parts are being added to it. However, this must be amplified, once again, by recourse to 69c–72d, where the binding of the lower soul into the various parts of the body is gone into in more detail. By such means is the rather poetical and rambling account given in the *Timaeus* reshaped to serve the needs of a school handbook.

A. begins by apologizing mildly for repeating himself to some extent, referring back to chapter 16, where he started out from the same passage of the *Timaeus*, but with a different end in view, since he was then proceeding to a description of the human body. There is in fact very little overlap. He then makes a reference forward ('as we shall see presently', 176. 9) to chapter 25, where the immortal part of the soul is discussed.

Here he is primarily concerned with the two 'mortal' parts. The move from 44d–e to 69c ff. is made almost at once, since 69c more or less repeats 44e. Note, however, the reference to 'subordinating the rest of the body to its service (*hypēresian*) by attaching it to it as vehicle (*ochēma*, 176. 16–17)', which is taken from 44d–e, while the phrase, 'When they received the human soul in its immortal aspect from the primal god (176. 8–9)' is taken from 69c. The reference here, by the way, to the Demiurge as 'the primal god (*prōtos theos*) is odd, since he is only *relatively* primal in A.'s system, but he may here be simply reproducing without too much thought a source such as Arius, for whom the Demiurge may indeed have been primal.

The reference to the divine part 'being filled with mortal rubbish', is a glancing allusion to *Phaedo* 66c, and the reference to the head as a 'citadel' (*akropolis*), although primarily taken from 70a6, also, perhaps, embodies a reference to *Republic*, 8. 560b, where the desires are described as 'seizing the citadel of the young man's soul'. This image became fairly widespread in later authors, beginning with Aristotle (*PA* 3. 7. 670ᵃ26)—who, however, refers to the *heart* as the *akropolis*; Philo employs it for the head (*Somn.* 1. 32), though recognizing that 'some authorities' (the Stoics, no doubt, rather than Aristotle) claim this role for the heart; and so do Galen (*Hipp. et Plat.* 2. 4. 17) and Apuleius (*de Plat.* 1. 13 207: 'this, he says, occupies the citadel of the head' (*hanc ait capitis arcem tenere*)).

2. The descriptions of the placing of the spirited and appetitive parts of the soul, and of the roles of the lungs, the liver, and the spleen, follow Plato very closely. Lungs are described at *Timaeus* 70c1–d6, liver at 71a3–72c1 (A. suppresses almost entirely the long development on prophecy), and spleen at 72c1–d3. We find a fairly close parallel to this exposition in Apuleius, *de Plat.* 1. 15. 212–13.

[An interesting detail concerns the word *malagma*, 'padding' (176. 25) as a description of the lungs, which occurs also in Ps.-Longinus (*de Sublim.* 32. 5. 39. 9–10 Russell), where Plato is being paraphrased fairly closely. In the corresponding passage of the *Timaeus*, however, 70d3, the MSS. of Plato all have either *halma* (A), *alma* (F), or *hamma* (Vaticanus Palatinus 173, A²) *malakon*. Modern editors have unanimously adopted *malagma* into the text of Plato, but Whittaker (1990: 126 n. 372 and 1989: 86–9) argues acutely for the retention of *halma* or *hamma malakon* (*alma* means nothing). *Halma* could mean 'a place to jump down on to', and *hamma* a 'binding' (though neither meaning is very well attested), and *malakon*, 'soft', would be a suitable qualifier for either noun; but *malagma* is not that common a word either, and there is a case for seeing the various MS readings as corruptions of it, with *malakon* tacked on to make better sense. However, a straw in the wind (adduced originally by Archer-Hind in his commentary, and quoted, but robustly dismissed, by Taylor (1928: n. ad loc.) is a passage of Aristotle (*PA* 3. 6. 669ᵃ18 ff.), where Plato's theory in the *Timaeus* is being referred to, and criticized: 'the theory that the lung is provided as a cushion (*pros tēn halsin*) for the throbbings of the heart is not correct'. It looks very much, *pace* Taylor, as if Aristotle has before him a reading *halma malakon*. In that case, as Whittaker suggests, we have another case of the exegetical tradition introducing a gloss on a slightly troublesome Platonic turn of phrase, and it is this that both A. and Ps.-Longinus are reflecting.]

CHAPTER 24

1. We now leave off the close following of the *Timaeus*, and the treatise becomes somewhat more original and interesting once again. The present chapter, however, dealing with the division of the soul into its parts, is perfectly faithful doctrinally to Plato, making use chiefly of *Republic* 4 (esp. 436a–441e), where the theory of the tripartite soul is worked out, though drawing also on the doctrine of the *Timaeus*, which we surveyed in the last chapter (69b–72d).

The only aspect here of much interest, as I have mentioned above (23. 1), is the way in which A. subsumes the traditional tripartite division of the soul, which he is overtly expounding here, under a bipartite division between the rational (*logistikon*) and the passionate (*pathētikon*), such as became basic to later Platonism, and such as in fact adumbrated, as I have said, both in the 'charioteer and horses' imagery of the *Phaedrus* myth, and in the strong division made in the *Timaeus* between the 'immortal' part of the soul in the head, and the 'mortal' parts in the rest of the body. A. actually employs, at 176. 37–40, a syllogistic argument to prove this, derived from the *Timaeus* (stated most explicitly, perhaps, at 90a–c): 'Things which are naturally separated are different; the *pathētikon* and the *logistikon* are naturally separated; therefore the *pathētikon* and the *logistikon* are different.'

[The adjective *trimerēs*, 'tripartite' (176. 35) is not to be found in the Platonic corpus, but it is used by Aristotle, at *Topics* 5. 4. 133ᵃ31, as a generally agreed characterization of the soul, so it may be assumed to be Old Academic. It is widely used in later Platonist and quasi-Platonist sources (e.g. Cic. *Tusc.* 1. 10. 20: *Plato triplicem finxit animum*; Philo, *Leg. All.* 1. 70: *hēmōn trimerēs hē psykhē*; Aëtius, *Plac.* 4. 4. 1, etc.]

2–3. A. here bases himself upon the argument from 'distinct natural function' of the (two or three) parts of the soul in order to justify the doctrine of the *Timaeus* (69c–72d) about their difference in location within the body, and this in turn serves to introduce the argument of *Republic* 4. 436a ff., that a single thing cannot be in conflict or contradiction (*machesthai*) with itself, and so at least three distinct elements must be distinguished within the soul (though only two seem to be in prospect here).

It is possible that these arguments, which can be seen as directed against the Stoic concept of the unitary soul, owe something to the polemic of Posidonius in his treatise *On the Passions* (*peri Pathōn*) against Chrysippus and orthodox Stoicism, as is suggested, for example, by Witt (1937: 81); cf. Posidonius, Frs. 142–6 Edelstein–Kidd (all from Galen's *Hipp. et Plat.* books 5–6). In particular, Galen, in Fragments 145 and 146, testifies that Aristotle and Posidonius called the different elements of the soul not 'kinds' (*eidē*) or 'parts' (*merē*), as did Plato, but rather 'powers' or 'faculties' (*dynameis*), which is the term preferred by A. here (176. 36). Since, however, this use of *dynamis* is also a feature of Aristotle's doctrine in the *de Anima* (cf. esp. 2. 3. 414^{a}29 ff.), it cannot be claimed as distinctive of Posidonius, who in fact (as is pointed out by Kidd (1988) in his notes ad loc.) objected to Plato's doctrine of the local separation of the parts of the soul, and based all the *dynameis* in the heart, in accordance with Stoic theory, whereas A. recognizes the supremacy of the head. Also, Posidonius used the term *hēgemonikon* for the reason, while here *logistikon* is used.

On the other hand, we have the two quotations from Euripides in section 3, produced to buttress the argument, the one from the *Medea*, the other from the lost *Chrysippus*, at least the former of which we know to have been used by Chrysippus (Galen, *Hipp. et Plat.* 4. 6. 382 = *SVF* 3. 473)—though, as Galen remarks, it is strange that he does not perceive that he is testifying against himself when quoting it! The *Medea* passage is used later by Calcidius in his commentary (ch. 183), when discussing the same topic, and the *Chrysippus* passage by Plutarch, twice, at *Quomodo Adulescens Poetis Audire Debeat* 33e and *de Virtute Morali* 446a (though it is only from A., here, that we learn to which play it belongs). It is also quoted by Stobaeus, *Anthologia* 3. 3. 205. 4–5 Wachsmuth–Hense, under the rubric *On Practical Wisdom* (*peri Phronēseōs*), and it is pretty certainly alluded to already by Cicero in *Tusculanae Disputationes* 4. 71, a place where Posidonian influence may reasonably be suspected. Both were plainly by A.'s time commonplaces in discussions of the passions and of the parts of the soul; it is possible that they were employed for this purpose by Posidonius when arguing against Chrysippus in the *peri Pathōn*, but we cannot be sure.

On the whole, then, the question of Posidonian influence in this chapter remains no more than an intriguing possibility. If present, however, it will, as far as A. is concerned, be second-hand, filtered through Arius Didymus. The doctrine remains Platonic, though modified by Peripatetic influence.

4. This section consists of an argument which seems to have been extracted from *Republic* 7. 518d–e, where Socrates first speaks of that art of true education which involves turning the vision of the soul in the right direction, and then goes on to say that 'the other so-called virtues of the soul' (that is, those of the affective part) are brought into being 'by habituation and training' (*ethesi te kai askēsesin*), a phrase that seems to be echoed here by 'the training of one's habitual behaviour' (*tēs tou ethous askēseōs*)—although the influence of the beginning of book 2 of Aristotle's *Nicomachean Ethics* (1103ᵃ14–18) is also perceptible, in the contrast between teaching (*didaskalia*) and habituation (*ethos*).

CHAPTER 25

1. We now embark on a series of arguments in favour of the immortality of the soul, taken mainly (naturally enough) from the *Phaedo*, though drawing also on the *Republic* and the *Phaedrus*, but including, in the latter part of the chapter (sects. 5–7), some interesting material from the later Platonist tradition. We may note here that the emphasis is quite different from that given to the discussion of the nature of the soul in chapter 14 above, but there what was under discussion was the role of the soul in the world, and the *Timaeus* was the source being used.

The first argument here is taken from the last argument of the *Phaedo*, 105c–107a, embellished with a series of epithets of the soul taken from the argument from affinity (78b–84b), 'intelligible' (80b1), 'invisible' (79b14), 'uniform' (80b2), 'incomposite' (78c7), 'indissoluble' (80b2). Only the first two epithets, interestingly, are not to be found in the *Phaedo*: 'incorporeal' (*asōmatos*), an obvious characteristic of the soul, but applied to it only in the *Epinomis* (981b); and 'unchanging' (*ametablētos*), an adjective used by Aristotle (twice in the *Metaphysics*, to refer to the cosmos), and by Timaeus Locrus (to refer to the cube as one of the primary cosmic figures), but not by Plato. Both epithets are firmly attached to the soul in the later Platonist tradition (e.g. Philo, *Somn.* 2. 72–3 (*asōmatos*); Plot. *Enn.* 4. 4. 2. 25), but it is possible that incorporeality, at least, was introduced by A. at the head of the list with the Stoics in mind. The corresponding epithets of body are all taken from the same passage of the *Phaedo*.

The latter part of the section (177. 26–35) is also taken bodily from this passage of the *Phaedo* (79c–80b), without any notable variation or addition (note, however, the characteristic inversion 'becomes dizzy and is thrown into confusion' for 'is thrown into confusion and becomes dizzy' of 79c7), but this time to present a separate argument, derived from the affinity argument.

2. We proceed now further backwards through the *Phaedo*, to the first argument, that from the interchange of contraries, or the 'cyclical argument' (69e–72e), though presented in a somewhat more formalized way than we find it in Plato. Although the principle that 'things which are direct contraries (*amesa enantia*) of one another, not in themselves (*kath' hauta*) but in virtue of their accidents (*kata symbebēkos*), naturally come to be from one another' is derivable in essence from 71c ff., the further specification seems to owe something to Aristotle's doctrine on contraries in the *Categories*, 10 (11^b35 ff.), particularly the notion of a *direct* contrary, and the *kath' hauto/kata symbebēkos* antithesis.

It is not quite clear to me, I must confess, why this latter distinction is introduced here. What we are talking about, surely, are states like sleep and waking, death and life, which *are* contraries 'in themselves', but A. may have in mind that the true subject of discussion is rather the waking or sleeping *person*, or the live or dead *body*, which can only contain one or other of these attributes at any time.

The term 'direct contraries' (*amesa enantia*) is not found in Plato, but the distinction between *amesa* and *emmesa* (i.e. opposites with an intermediate state between them)—with a reference to sleep and waking as *amesa*—is attributed to him by Hippolytus (*Ref.* 1. 19. 14), so it was part of the Platonist tradition.

3. A. next takes up the argument from recollection, presented in *Phaedo* 72e3–78b3 (though A. borrows chiefly from 72e3–73e3). However, he amplifies this with an argument against Aristotelian induction (*epagōgē*), which is of some interest, since we find it also used by Sextus Empiricus (*P.* 2. 204) from a sceptical viewpoint, to prove the method invalid, as a survey of a limited number of instances will never attain absolute reliability, while a complete review of particulars is impossible, since they are infinite, or at least incomprehensibly numerous. For A., however, this is an argument in favour of the limitation of the role of *epagōgē* to 'activating the natural concepts (*physikai ennoiai*)', as he defines it at the end of chapter 5 above (158. 3).

A. presumably adduces, as an example of inductive reasoning, 'only that which breathes is an animal', because Aristotle produces this as the Atomist definition at *de Anima* 1. 404ª10, whereas the implication is that further investigation has shown that certain animals do not breathe.

[The reference to the evidence provided by the senses, on the basis of which our memory of general concepts is awakened, as 'sparks' (*aithygmata*) may, as Witt (1937: 83) suggests, be a deliberate reference to the Stoic use of this term, or something like it, to describe the first intimations of the virtues (and of common notions in general) that dawn in us as children—if at least we may deduce from this Cicero's use of the terms '*scintillulae*' at *de Finibus* 5. 43, and '*igniculi*' at *Tusculanae Disputationes* 3. 2, in contexts which are either Stoic or Antiochian. If so, A. is using a word which for the Stoics had a literal sense (common notions *are*, after all, a form of pure fire) deliberately in a metaphorical sense (as we find it used later by Iamblichus, at *Comm. Math.* 22. 68. 11–12 Festa—if indeed this is Iamblichus himself, and not some earlier authority he is quoting).

A further linguistic detail: the rare verb *ensōmatousthai*, 'to be embodied' (178. 11) employed here (and below, 178. 43) by A., turns up as well in the anonymous *Theaetetus* commentary at 53. 7, also in the context of a discussion of the doctrine of recollection.]

4. A. now turns to book 10 of the *Republic* (608c–611a) and to the *Phaedrus* (245c–d) for his last two proofs. In the case of the *Republic* proof, he merely summarizes the Platonic argument, but with the *Phaedrus* proof he systematizes and clarifies somewhat, bringing 'self-motion' to the head of the argument instead of 'eternal motion', as in Plato, since self-motion is the more basic concept (as, indeed, is noted by Hermias in his *Commentary on the Phaedrus*, 108. 6 ff. Couvreur). He also specifies that the argument applies to both universal soul and individual souls, a point rather fudged by Plato in the opening phrase 'all soul'. The discussion of the reference of this in Hermias' *Commentary*, 102. 10 ff. bears witness to the disputes of earlier commentators on this question. Hermias singles out Posidonius and the Middle Platonist Harpocration of Argos as representing two extreme interpretations of which he disapproves, the former restricting the application of the argument to the world-soul, the latter extending it to soul of every sort, 'even those of ants and flies'. Hermias holds, as, it would seem, does A. here, that the reference must be restricted to the rational soul, both divine (including cosmic) and human,

especially in view of the fact that Plato has said just above (245c2–3) that he is going to investigate 'the soul divine and human'. In his anxiety to maintain that all rational soul is of a uniform nature ('both partake of the same mixture', 178. 20–1), A. glosses over the obscure pronouncements in the *Timaeus* (41d–e) about 'seconds and thirds'; as far as he is concerned the significant division is not between divine and human soul, but between rational and irrational.

The final sentence of the section, which speaks of life being innate (*symphytos*) in the soul, besides summarizing 245e, seems to embody a reference back to *Phaedo* 105c–d, utilized in the first argument, though the actual adjective is not used there either. It is perfectly Platonic, however.

5. This section is of considerable interest, since it raises the question of the immortality of the irrational soul, a matter of some controversy in later Platonism, since Plato's own position is somewhat obscure. In the *Phaedo*, on the one hand, it is plain that the soul whose immortality is being argued for is a rational one, since all irrational impulses are identified as arising from the body. In book 10 of the *Republic*, however, the whole business of the choice of lives seems to presuppose the survival of a passionate element in the soul, and the image of the charioteer and horses in the *Phaedrus* myth, if pressed, also implies some correlates to the irrational parts of the soul in a discarnate state. As for the Old Academy, we have the rather dim evidence of Damascius, *in Phaedonem* 1. 177 Westerink, that Speusippus (Fr. 55 Tarán) and Xenocrates (Fr. 211 IP) 'attribute immortality to all soul down to the irrational (*mechri tēs alogias*)'. Among A.'s contemporaries, this same passage declares that Numenius (= Fr. 46a Des Places) postulated immortality for everything from the rational soul to the *empsychos hexis*, however we are to understand that (Westerink, 1977: 106, translates it 'the animate condition of the body', a reasonable rendering). I would take this to be another term for the 'pneumatic vehicle', that accreted soul which the discarnate soul acquires on its journey downwards through the spheres to join the body, and which enables it to commune which and rule the body. If so, then Numenius, like Iamblichus after him, believed in the immortality of the 'vehicle'.

Iamblichus' views are revealed in another important passage on this subject, in Proclus' *in Platonis Timaeum commentarii* 3. 234. 8 ff., where we also learn that such Platonists as Atticus and Albinus grant immortality only to the rational soul. This passage has been adduced by those who seek to prove discrepancies between our testimonia to Albinus and the text of the *Didaskalikos*, but I cannot see that any serious discrepancy emerges. A.'s position here, as befits a handbook of Platonism, is that whether the irrational soul is immortal is 'a matter of dispute', but I should say that he makes his own view pretty clear in what follows. While this measure of agreement *proves* nothing as regards A.'s identity with Albinus, it certainly cannot be said to disprove it.

On later Platonist views in general on the immortality of the soul see Dörrie (1957 = 1976, 420–40). Galen has some interesting comments on the controversy, and on the difficulty of deciding Plato's true views on the matter, in *de Placitis Hippocratis et Platonis* 9. 9. 8–14, in the course of which he remarks that 'many of the Platonists' believe that the irrational parts of the soul are also immortal.

The present passage also throws an interesting light on A.'s view of *phantasia*, here translated as 'representation'. It can be distinguished from any rational activity, such as *logismos* or *krisis*, and the results of this, such as the formation of general concepts (the phrase 'general concepts' (*katholikai dialēpseis*, 178. 29) is notable—the adjective is attested in both Stoic and Epicurean sources, the noun only in Epicurean), and is something that the irrational soul shares with any other animal.

A.'s final claim is a strong one, that the irrational soul cannot even possess the same *ousia*, 'essence', as the rational—which in turn, as we have seen above, is of the same 'mixture' (which should imply the same *ousia*) as the divine. This seems almost to imply a doctrine of two souls, which is a distortion of Platonic doctrine, but accords with the views of A.'s contemporary Numenius (Frs. 43–4 Des Places). See my discussion (1977: 375–6).

6. The immortality or otherwise of the irrational soul should have some bearing on the next question raised by A., that of metempsychosis, but it is not clear what bearing it in fact has. Apparently ignoring the doubt he has just cast on the immortality of the irrational soul, A. now points out that immortality involves the consequence that souls 'should pass through many bodies both human and non-human'. The problem is, then, how there can be metempsychosis of souls into irrational animals, unless somehow the souls that undergo the metempsychosis are in fact rational souls, but in some cases their rationality is rendered inoperative or latent by their material conditions, and they pick up a new irrational soul on each incarnation. That

is a possible solution, I think, but if that is what A. means he is less than clear about it.

The second topic raised in this section is the possible reasons for the descent of souls into bodies, and here again A. is interesting. First we may note the doctrine that souls enter bodies 'following upon the natural processes which form the embryo', that is, as a by-product of the formation of the embryo, which is in contrast to Stoic doctrine that the soul enters the body at the moment of birth (*SVF* 2. 804–8), and in agreement with Porphyry's position later in the *Ad Gaurum*. This is the standard later Platonist position.

The reasons for the soul's descent may be viewed against the background of those attributed to Calvenus Taurus 'and his followers' by Iamblichus in his *de Anima* (*ap.* Stob. 1. 378. 25 ff. Wachs.):

The Platonists of the school of Taurus say that souls are sent by the gods to earth, *some*, following the *Timaeus*, for the completion of the universe, in order that there may be as many living beings in the cosmos as there are in the intelligible realm; *others* declaring that the purpose of the descent is to present a manifestation of the divine life; for this is the will of the gods, for the gods to reveal themselves (*ekphainesthai*) through souls; for the gods come out into the open and manifest themselves through the pure and unsullied life of souls.

It is not clear what Platonic warrant these followers of Taurus have for talking of the purpose of descent being the self-manifestation (*ekphansis*) of the gods, unless it be based on speculations as to why, at *Phaedo* 113a, the gods are said to send back souls to be born again; the first explanation, at least, is clearly derived from the speech of the Demiurge to the young gods at *Timaeus* 41b. But both have some bearing on the reasons offered by A., which are presumably intended as a full conspectus of Platonist views on the question. Let us examine them in turn.

1. *following their turn in a numbered sequence*: this is my rendering of the troublesome phrase *arithmous menousas*, 'waiting for numbers'—perhaps 'waiting for their number to come up'. There seems to be a notion here of a fixed quota of embodied souls to be kept up, and this would in turn seem to relate to the first reason given by the followers of Taurus, derived from *Timaeus* 41b; but the expression is extremely elliptical. There might also here be a reference to *Phaedo* 113a, where it is said that the souls of the dead, after remaining at the Acherusian Lake 'for such times as are appointed (*tinas heimarmenous chronous*),

are sent back to be born again into living beings'. This would seem to imply both divine decision-making and a sort of rota system, such as A. appears to be alluding to here.

One should mention, though, Freudenthal's suggestion (1879: 320), rejected as unnecessary by Whittaker, but which seems to me to have some merit, *isarithmous menousas*, which would mean something like 'waiting to make up the number', which comes to very much the same thing, but is somewhat better syntactically, perhaps.

2. *The will of the gods* (*boulēsis theōn*): once again, this could be taken as a very condensed version of the second reason advanced by the followers of Taurus, and thus derivable from *Phaedo* 113a. We are not here told what the gods have in mind, but presumably their own honour and glory.

3. *Intemperance* (*akolasia*): that is, sinful wilfulness on the part of the soul—a rather Gnostic conception, though it finds various echoes in Plotinus, e.g. *Enneads* 5. 1. 1, where he speaks of 'audacity (*tolma*) and the process of generation (*genesis*) and the primal otherness (*prōtē heterotēs*) and the wishing to belong to themselves', which I take to be all aspects of one basic reason, which is also adumbrated here, a certain restlessness on the part of the soul (originally the world-soul, but ultimately all souls), which leads it to break away, or 'fall', from the intelligible world, and set up an imperfect imitation of it, which is the physical world.

It is interesting in this connection, though without proving very much one way or the other, that Iamblichus in the *de Anima* (*ap.* Stob. 1. 375. 2 ff.), in the course of a doxography of reasons for the descent of soul, gives as that of Albinus 'the erring judgement of a free will' (*hē tou autexousiou diēmartēmenē krisis*), which has some relation to the reason given here. However, A. only airs this impartially as one of his list of touted reasons, whereas Albinus seems to have adopted it unequivocally.

4. *Love of the body* (*philosōmatia*): this notable noun, attested before A. only in Andronicus of Rhodes, no doubt owes something to *Phaed.* 68c1, where Socrates remarks that 'when you see a man troubled because he is going to die, that is a sufficient indication that he was not a lover of wisdom (*philosophos*), but rather some sort of body-lover (*tis philosōmatos*)'. This category of reason seems to some extent to overlap the previous one, but in this case there is no willfulness postulated, but rather a sort of natural affinity (*oikeiotēs*), or weakness, for embodiment. The explanatory sentence which follows would seem

to confirm this. If we press this interesting simile about fire and asphalt (which is of uncertain provenance; certainly not Platonic; a similar image involving fire and *naphtha* is to be found in Porphyry, *ad Gaurum* 48. 26–8 Kalbfleisch), it would imply that when a soul in the course of its peregrinations through the universe comes into a certain degree of proximity to body, it must spring towards it and ensoul it, and this would happen without any forethought on the part of the soul in question, but simply as a natural reaction. Embodiment is thus a necessary consequence of the arrangement of the universe, and not a fault to be imputed to soul.

If one could attach any weight to the fact that this reason is presented last, one might conclude that this was A.'s preferred one. It is, after all, the only one furnished with a sentence of explanation. But A. is keeping his cards pretty close to his chest here.

7. The final section of the chapter contains a most interesting piece of doctrine on the structure of the divine soul (and of the disembodied soul in general). Partly, at least, as a result of the imagery of the *Phaedrus* myth (246a–b) in which the souls of the gods are also portrayed as charioteers and pairs (each horse of the pair, however, being of noble birth and good behaviour), later Platonists seem to have developed the theory that even in divine souls, but also in souls destined to be human, before embodiment, there must be archetypal equivalents of the spirited and libidinous parts of the human soul. A. here gives the details. The disembodied soul has three aspects, the critical (*kritikon*) or cognitive (*gnōstikon*), corresponding to our rational part, the appetitive (*hormētikon*) or 'dispositional' (*parastatikon*), corresponding to our spirited, and the 'appropriative' (*oikeiōtikon*), corresponding to our libidinous.

This is a most interesting theory, which finds a remarkable development later in the first part of Plotinus' *Enneads* 6. 7 (1–15), where he is arguing for the existence of an archetype of sense-perception already in the disembodied soul. There seems here to be a recognition that a soul would not be a soul without something corresponding to *thymos* and *epithymia*, although those aspects of the soul as we know them are intimately involved with bodily organs. So if the gods have souls, as it is agreed that they do, they must have these parts of the soul in some sublimated form, since a soul without them would be simply intellect, and not soul at all. All this might seem to be in contradiction to the account in the *Timaeus* of the 'mortal' parts of the soul being added by the young gods at the moment of embodiment, outlined by A. at the beginning of chapter 23 above, but it need only be seen as an amplification of it—the archetypal faculties would be there to be activated by the young gods in their corporeal mode.

Such a theory should arise out of an exegesis of the *Phaedrus*, but it is notable that Hermias later, in his commentary on *Phaedrus* 246a (*in Phaedr.* 122. 10 ff. Couvreur), shows no sign of knowing the exact system of equivalences propounded here by A., although he does discuss the nature of the 'horses' of the divine souls, identifying them respectively with the 'circle of the same' and the 'circle of the other' of *Timaeus* 35a–36d. He also (following his master Syrianus) gives a series of equivalences for all levels of soul superior to the embodied. Proclus also makes mention of the horses of the divine and daemonic souls at *in Platonis Parmenidem commentarii* 674. 26 ff., apropos *Parmenides* 126c.

As regards the terminology produced here by A., if we take the first terms given for the three analogical parts of the divine soul, *kritikon*, *hormētikon*, and *oikeiōtikon*, we can find at least the first two used together by Numenius (Fr. 18 Des Places) as epithets for parts of the soul of the Demiurge, his second god. The Demiurge derives his *kritikon* from his contemplation (*theōria*) of the primary god, and his *hormētikon* from his concern (*ephesis*) with the physical world. As for *oikeiōtikon*, it has an obviously Stoic ring to it (though it occurs, in a different context—the definition of the sophist—in Plato, *Sph.* 223b2), but nowhere else is it to be found referring to a part or function of the soul. If it is originally Stoic, it is being used in an interestingly un-Stoic sense here, as an archetype of *thymos*. As such, it seems quite well chosen; if we are to postulate a sublimated, purely spiritual form of *thymos*, it could well be seen as the sort of basic consciousness of self as a subject to which attributes could belong which one could imagine even a god possessing, and which could well be described as *oikeiōsis*.

As for the two subsidiary terms which A. produces, 'cognitive' (*gnōstikon*) and 'dispositional' (*parastatikon*), the former may be found in Plato's *Statesman* (258e–261b), but only to describe a division of *technē* (as opposed to *praktikē*), not a faculty of the soul; as such, it has, if anything, Gnostic overtones. The latter is rather more peculiar, but it occurs in Sextus Empiricus (*M.* 7. 162), in a definition of *phantasia* explicitly attributed to Antiochus of Ascalon, though referring to the doctrine of Carneades. This proves nothing much about provenance, however, and from the way in which A. introduces it here, one might be tempted to see it as an original contribution of his own in this sense.

CHAPTER 26

1–2. A. now turns to a topic which counted in ancient times as part of physics, but which is also closely linked to ethical speculation, that of fate and free will. It thus forms a suitable conclusion to the physical section of his work. We may note in the outset that A. shows no trace of the very distinctive doctrine on fate, providence, and free will which we find set out in two sister treatises, Pseudo-Plutarch, *On Fate* (ed. E. Valgiglio, Rome, 1964, hereinafter PP) and the essay on fate preserved by Calcidius in his *Commentary on the Timaeus* (ed. J. den Boeft (1970), as *Calcidius on Fate: His Doctrine and Sources*), chapters 142–90 (*in Tim.* 41e)—and summarized by Nemesius of Emesa (*Nat. Hom.* 38) (we can also observe distinct traces of it in Apuleius, *de Plat.* 1. 12). We do, however, find in A. the bare bones of a theory which may probably be regarded as the basic Middle-Platonic one. It seeks to base itself on the inadequate suggestions of a theory provided in the Platonic dialogues, but its form is primarily conditioned by the necessity of countering Stoic doctrine on the subject. It may be summarized as follows:

1. All things are within the sphere of (lit. 'in') fate, but not all things are in accordance with fate.
2. Fate has the status of a law, and utters its decrees in the form of hypotheses,

that is, it does not say 'individual *x* will perform this particular act; *y* will suffer this particular consequence' but rather 'if a soul chooses such-and-such a life (a reference to the choice of lives at *R.* 10. 617e ff.), and performs such-and-such actions consequent on that, then such-and-such results will follow from it'.

3. If all things are fated, freedom of choice (*to eph' hēmin*) is nullified, and no place is left for praise or blame.

There is nothing in this brief chapter of the distinctive doctrines of PP's *de Fato*, the distinguishing of fate 'in activity' from fate 'in substance', and the identification of the latter with 'the soul of the world in all three of its divisions' (568e), together with the triadic division of the universe that follows on this, and the bringing in of the three Moirai (Fates) to preside over these divisions. On the other hand, all the general principles enunciated above are found also in the *de Fato*: (1) and (2) are discussed at 570c ff. (with a preliminary definition of fate at 569d), while (3), the point about the undermining of the rationale for punishment, is referred to at the end of the treatise (574d), though not discussed. It is found in Cicero's *On Fate* (ch. 17), however, and is developed by the Peripatetic Alexander of Aphrodisias in his treatise *On Fate* (34. 206. 1 ff. Bruns). Compare Sharples (1983: 13–14).

Of the heads of doctrine given here, the second, to the effect that fate has the status of a law, and that it operates hypothetically—that is, a theory of 'conditional fate'—seems most worthy of discussion. It would seem to be a basic principle of the standard Middle-Platonic doctrine on fate and free will. Aëtius (*Plac.* 1. 28. 2) declares that 'Plato defines the essence of fate as an eternal reason-principle (*logos*) and an eternal *law* of the nature of the universe.' PP (569d) describes fate as 'having the quality of the law of a state, which in the first place promulgates most, if not all, of its commands as consequents of hypotheses (*ex hypotheseōs*), and secondly, so far as it can, embraces all the concerns of the state in the form of universal statements (*katholou*)'.

This comparison is found also in Calcidius (*in Tim.* 150 and 179), and in Nemesius (*Nat. Hom.* 38). The point being made is one that is vital for the preservation of the doctrine of free will against Chrysippan determinism. Our own powers of decision are to be taken as answering to the basic precepts of the law, or, as in Calcidius' comparison (150), the primary hypotheses of a science such as geometry. What follows from these is fixed, or 'fated', but the principles are in our power to establish and observe or not. In Nemesius' example, 'it is in our power whether to undertake a sea voyage; this has the status of a hypothesis (*kath' hypothesin*). Once it is established that we make the voyage, however, there then follows from this hypothesis that we are either shipwrecked or not.'

The Platonists do not permit us to consider, however, the causes that might have led us to decide to take the voyage in the first place—or, to take A.'s literary examples, what led Paris to seduce Helen, or Laius to beget a son. On their argument, these decisions must have no external motivation, as if we were to take, for no conscious reason, one of two equally good roads home. But even in such a case as this Chrysippus would probe further. *Something* must have induced us to take the left fork rather than the right. Unless one denies absolutely any causation here, one is surely caught up again in the ineluctable chain of cause and effect. The Platonist argument, then, is only another way of declaring dogmatically that the mind is 'self-causative'.

In his summary of the doctrine, A. contrives to combine the myth of *Republic* 10 (617d ff.), with a verbal reminiscence of the ordinance of Adrasteia in the *Phaedrus* myth (248c). The phrase 'if a soul (*hētis an psychē*)' (179. 9) is the beginning of Adrasteia's statement. This is quoted in full in the *de Fato* (570a). Calcidius (chs. 153–4) adduces the oracle to Laius, and adds the prophecy of Thetis to Achilles. He also quotes *Republic* 617e. These proof texts and exempla, then, are part of the common Platonist inheritance (the quotation from Euripides' *Phoenissae* is also to be found in Alexander's *de Fato* (ch. 31), showing that the Peripatetic and Platonist doctrine on fate and free will is largely a shared one—though the use of the quotation seems to go back to Chrysippus (cf. *SVF* 2. 956–7).

The first principle, that all things are 'within the sphere of fate' (*en heimarmenēi*), but not all things are 'in accordance with fate' (*kath' heimarmenēn*)—of which A.'s *katheimartai*, 'are fated', is an equivalent—is properly explained in the *de Fato*, and constitutes an introduction to the concepts of the possible, the voluntary, and chance. Again the comparison with law is used (570c–d):

For neither is everything included in law 'lawful' or 'in accordance with law'; for law includes treason, desertion, adultery, and a good many other things of the sort, none of which one would term 'lawful'; indeed I should not even call an act of valour, the slaying of a tyrant, or the performance of any other right action (*katorthōma*) 'lawful'.

There is a certain amount of linguistic juggling going on here, but yet a valid point is, I think, being made. Treason, for instance, is dealt with by law, it comes within its sphere of activity, but it plainly cannot be described as being 'in accordance with law'. Even thus, it is argued, chance, for instance, comes within the sphere of fate, but is not in accordance with it.

This is a pretty vacuous comparison, perhaps, but the second part of the argument is rather better. Conspicuous bravery, for example, is not 'in accordance with law', for otherwise lack of it—ordinary performance of duty—would be unlawful, and thus punishable. Yet such bravery concerns matters within the sphere of law, such as perform-

ing one's military duty. What is in our power (*to eph' hēmin*), similarly, operates within the sphere of fate, but it is not 'in accordance
with' it.

It can be seen that the comparison with the operation of law is of
basic importance to the Platonist response to the Stoics. Platonists
wanted to see the physical world as a series of law-like chains of causation, ineluctable once they were set in train, but needing to be trig-
gered by acts of human free will, and thus 'conditional'. Whether or
not this is a coherent notion it is fortunately not incumbent on us to
determine at present (see the useful discussion in Sharples (1983:
intro., 3–14), and also Theiler (1945: 35–90)).

3. A. now goes on, following what seems to be a traditional Middle-
Platonist format, to give brief definitions of 'the possible (*to dunaton*)',
the voluntary, or 'what is in our power (*to eph' hēmin*)', and then a
discussion of potentiality and actuality. These topics are all discussed,
in a more scholastic manner, as being 'things contained by fate', in
PP, *de Fato* (570e ff.), but all this goes back a very long way, ultimately to Aristotle's treatment of these questions in the *Nicomachean
Ethics*, 3. 1–3, and *Physics*, 2. 4–6, along with the definitions of 'the
possible' and of 'realized state (*hexis*)' in *Metaphysics* 5. 12 and 20
respectively; though Chrysippus' discussions of 'the possible', as evid-
enced in *SVF* 2. 201–2 and 959–64 (mainly from Alexander's *de
Fato*), are also an important influence.

The definition of the possible, first of all, seems to owe something
to Aristotle's definition in *Metaphysics* 5. 12. 1019^{b}27 ff.: 'The possible, then means (1) what is not of necessity false; (2) what is true;
(3) what *may be* true', but goes beyond it in characterizing the possible as 'indefinite' (*aoriston*) as between true and false, and thus providing a field for the exercise of our free will (the imagery in the verb
epocheisthai, 'ride upon', here (179. 19) is notable). Truth and falsehood only arise once we have exercised our free will to make a choice.

A. now passes on from the possible to the potential (*to dynamei*),
which he distinguishes both from being something 'in a realized state
(*kath' hexin*) and being something 'in actuality' (*kat' energeian*). Again,
the definition of *hexis* may owe something to Aristotle's definition of
the word in *Metaphysics* 5. 20, but the distinction which A. is making
here between *kath' hexin* and *kat' energeian* (a boy is *dynamei*, e.g. a
carpenter; he becomes a carpenter *kath' hexin* when he (grows up
and) learns the trade of a carpenter; he is a carpenter *kat' energeian*
only when he actually carpenting, not when he is asleep, or eating, or

listening to music) is not to be found in that passage. On the other hand, it seems analogous to the distinction made by Aristotle in *de Anima* 2. 1. 412ª22 ff., between primary and secondary actualization (*entelecheia*), but the use of *hexis* and *energeia* to characterize these two states seems to have come into the Peripatetic (and Platonist) tradition only later. Certainly we find it in Alexander of Aphrodisias (e.g. *de An.* 9. 20 ff.; 33. 3 ff.; 107. 21 ff.).

The point of introducing this distinction between the possible and the potential is made plain in the last sentence of the chapter. The potential is already 'programmed' in some direction—it is 'fated' to be actualized. The possible, on the other hand, remains purely undetermined, and is thus the proper domain of 'what is in our power'.

PP, as I have said, gives a more scholastic account of the possible, the contingent (*to endechomenon*), and the voluntary, or 'what is in our power' (570f–571e). The possible is first declared to be prior to the contingent, which in its turn underlies the voluntary as substratum (*hylē*). A. simply says that the voluntary 'presides over' (*epocheitai*) the possible. The *de Fato* notes that chance (*tychē*) intervenes accidentally in the sphere of the voluntary (571e ff.), A. does not mention chance at all—although he does, we may note, use a phrase, 'inclination in either direction' (*tēn eph' hopoteron rhopēn*), to characterize the possible (very close to that (*tēn eph' hekatera rhopēn*) used by PP to describe chance in the above passage), which would seem to indicate that such a phrase is part of the traditional Platonist discussion of fate and free will.

The *de Fato* makes a threefold distinction between potentiality (*dynamis*), 'the potent' (*to dynamenon*)—that is, that which is capable of acting, and the possible. The potent agent, as a substance, is logically prior to the possible, while potency is prior in reality (*prohyphistatai*) to the possible (571a). All this may not solve any substantial philosophical problems, but it bespeaks a level of scholastic sophistication of which A. is not aware—or just perhaps that he was not impressed by.

A. seems, then, to be representing here the more traditional Platonist position on fate and free will, though no doubt in a somewhat abbreviated form, while the *de Fato* tradition (of which Apuleius also is cognizant) appears as a later elaboration.

CHAPTER 27

We now turn to the final section of the work, the exposition of Plato's ethical theory. Here A. begins, quite properly, with a definition of the ultimate good for man, which consists in the contemplation of the supreme good, which is God. This in turn is the essence of happiness (*eudaimonia*).

We may note here the order of topics which A. follows, and compare it with that of Apuleius, in book 2 of his *de Platone*. Following on the present chapter he deals in order with: the *telos*, or end (28); Virtue and the virtues (29); *euphyiai*, or 'good natural dispositions', and progress towards virtue (30); the thesis that vice is involuntary (31); the emotions (32); friendship and love (33); and lastly, a chapter on political theory, dealing with the various types of states and constitutions (34).

Apuleius provides a more extended treatment, but broadly observes the same order. He begins with the classification of goods, from the supreme good, through the virtues, to external goods (chs. 1–2); he then discusses the state intermediate between virtue and vice, which involves the topics of good natural dispositions and progress towards virtue (3); then the vices, including the emotions (4). So far so good, but Apuleius then turns to further discussion and classification of the virtues, culminating with justice (5–7), which leads in turn into a discussion of rhetoric and politics, the teaching of virtue, and the choice between good and evil (8–12). Only in chapters 13–14 does he turn to the topic of friendship and love, but this is in turn followed by an extended disquisition on the topics of guilt and punishment, and the worst and best types of man (15–23), and not till chapters 24–8 do we get an exposition of political theory, which ends the book. What we have here, though, as I think can be readily seen, is the basic pattern observed by A., amplified by Apuleius in certain directions of special interest to him as a rhetorician and lawyer, so A.'s choice and order of topics may be taken with probability as constituting the basic Platonist school order of topics. It may be noted that it has little in common with the elaborate division of topics attributed by Arius Didymus to Eudorus of Alexandria (*ap.* Stob. *Ecl.* 2. 42. 7 ff. Wachs.), but is no doubt essentially the order followed by Arius himself.

1. A. begins with a subtly altered quotation from *Timaeus* 28c. Where Plato talks of 'the maker and father of this universe' as being neither

easy to discover nor safe to reveal to all, A. substitutes 'the most valuable and greatest good', thus identifying the Demiurge of the *Timaeus* with the Good of the *Republic*. This is certainly far from revolutionary—Aëtius before him makes this identification (*Plac.* 1. 7. 31), as does his approximate contemporary Atticus (Fr. 12. 1–2 Des Places)—but it is interesting none the less, as it betokens a non-literal interpretation of the *Timaeus*, which takes the Demiurge to be simply the creative aspect of a supreme Intellect, such as we have discerned earlier as being A.'s true position (cf. above, 10. 3), and which he confirms just below, at the end of this section, when he identifies the Good with 'God and the primal intellect (*prōtos nous*)'.

[On a small but significant detail of terminology, we may note that A. substitutes for Plato's *adunaton legein* ('impossible to declare'), *oute . . . asphales . . . ekpherein* ('not safe to reveal'). Apuleius also quotes the passage with *ekpherein* (*de Plat.* 1. 5. 191); and the Jewish writer Josephus, in his *contra Apionem* (2. 224), at the end of the first century AD, paraphrases it using both *ouk asphales* and *exenengkein*. I would suggest that this points to a handbook previous to Josephus, probably that of Arius, having introduced the rephrasing, perhaps with the idea of introducing a mild 'tightening-up' of Plato's language.]

The observation that he 'only imparted his views on the good to a very small, select group of his associates' might be seen as embodying a reference to the famous discourse on the Good mockingly reminisced about by Aristotle (*ap.* Aristoxenus, *Harm.* 2. 30), but in fact cannot refer directly to that fiasco, precisely because there Plato was making an effort to take his teaching to a wider audience. In the version of the story given by Proclus in his *Parmenides* commentary (688. 10 ff. Cousin), however, we find a clue which connects with A.'s remark here:

At this point in the narrative some persons ask whether philosophers should read their compositions to others, as Zeno does here, and if they do so on occasion, they want them to restrict their reading to what their hearers can understand, to avoid what Plato experienced, it is said, when he announced a lecture on the Good. A large and miscellaneous crowd gathered to hear him; but as he read, they did not understand what he was saying and left him, a few at a time, until eventually almost all had left the hall. *But Plato knew this would happen, and forbade his associates to prevent anyone from leaving, for thus only those who understood would hear the reading.*

Here the story has been turned to Plato's advantage by some faithful Platonist prior to Proclus (and probably prior to A.), and connected with a tradition of which A. himself constitutes an important testimony, that of the *secret* doctrine of Plato. This is to be distinguished, I think, from the tradition of simply *unwritten* doctrines (*agrapha dogmata*), such as Aristotle himself mentions on occasion, since there is nothing necessarily *secret* about the unwritten doctrines; they are just doctrines or ideas (such as, for instance the One and Indefinite Dyad as ultimate principles, or the theory of 'mathematicals') which Plato and his pupils kicked around in the daily interchange of the School, but which were never embodied as such in a dialogue. Obviously their currency was thus restricted, but there is no necessary implication of 'initiation' or 'mystery'. The rather Pythagorean overtones of secrecy may only have been introduced in the first century BC, by the same people who advanced the notion that the New Academy had 'dogmatized in secret' (cf. Aug. *contra Acad.* 3. 20. 43, quoting a lost portion of Cicero's *Academica*). There is a useful discussion of this subject now in Dörrie (1987– , 1. 277–94).

The identification of the Good with God and the primal Intellect has been mentioned above. The works of Plato which A. will have particularly in mind for 'examination with care' in this connection will be primarily, no doubt, books 6 and 7 of the *Republic*.

2. The idea of all particular goods being so called from their 'participation' in the primal Good, even as sweet things and hot things are by participation in the Sweet Itself and the Hot Itself, is inspired ultimately by *Phaedo*, 100c: 'It seems to me that if anything else is beautiful besides the Beautiful itself, it is beautiful for no reason at all other than that it participates in (*metechei*) that Beautiful; and the same goes for all of them.' A. seems somewhat to undercut this point, however, immediately below, when he suggests that most things regarded by the majority of men as 'good', such as health, wealth, and physical beauty, are not really good at all, but at best 'matter' for goodness, if combined with virtue. This is not the way in which beautiful things are beautiful, or hot things hot. What has happened, I think, is that A. is combining two thoroughly Platonic thoughts, the doctrine of the participation of particulars in forms, and the doctrine that most 'goods' are unreal, but is being careless in juxtaposing them. Such relative incoherence arises, as often, from the fact that he is shifting between proof-texts, from the *Phaedo* to the *Timaeus* to the *Laws*. We may note that Apuleius, in *de Platone* 2. 1, makes very similar distinctions between 'primary' and 'secondary', divine and human, goods, the latter being good only by participation (either

taking *per praeceptionem* of the MSS in this sense, or emending it to *per participationem*), also making the point that external goods may be good for the wise, but bad for the stupid. All this, then, is thoroughly traditional.

In fact, the dominant influence in the next part of this section (180. 5–7) is the end of the *Timaeus*, where the theme is the correct method of attaining likeness to God, and specifically 87c–d, 88b, and 90a. At 87c4–5 it is stated that 'all that is good is fine, and the fine is not devoid of proportion' (*ouk ametron*), and, just below, that every living thing that is fine must be well-proportioned, while at 87d8 it is described as 'most fine and lovely (*erasmiōtaton*)'. At 88b2, the soul is described as 'our most divine part'; and the passage at 90a2–8, in turn, contributes the idea that the ruling element of our soul may be regarded as our *daimon*, or guardian spirit. This may hold the clue to the solution of a textual problem at 180. 9, where the MSS read *daimoniōs proskaloumenon*, 'summoned or invoked in a marvellous way', which makes no sense in the context. R. E. Witt has proposed here *daimonion pōs kaloumenon*, which may be rendered 'called, in a manner of speaking, daemonic', and I am inclined to accept this.

The final part of the section takes its inspiration from *Laws* 2. 661a–b: 'For the things which most men call good are wrongly so described. Men say that the chief good is health, beauty the second, wealth the third; and they call countless other things 'goods', such as sharpness of sight and hearing, and quickness in perceiving all the objects of sense . . . But what you and I say is this: that all these things are very good as possessions for men who are just and holy, but for the unjust they are very bad.' The description of the 'lower' goods as 'mortal' (*thnēta*), with which the section ends, owes something to an earlier passage in the same work (1. 631b–c), where Plato makes a distinction between 'divine' and 'human' goods (strength being also mentioned among the latter), but the characterization of the lower goods as 'mortal' is interesting, since it is not an epithet that Plato himself attaches to them. It turns up in Philo, however (*Deus* 152), so it is not an original contribution by A., and may best be seen as a conflation of the *Laws* passage with the descriptions of the lower part of the soul as 'mortal' in the *Timaeus* (cf. 65a, 69c).

3. The influence of *Laws* 631b–c continues here, with the specification that *eudaimonia* is to be found among the divine goods, which are identified in that passage as the four virtues (the lower goods being now characterized as 'human'), but the inspiration behind the rest of

the section is plainly that of the central myth of the *Phaedrus*, particularly the heavenly ride of the gods and pure souls (247a–248b). The *Phaedrus*, however, gives a picture of the joys of the disembodied soul; for a source for A.'s statement that Plato attributes 'great and marvellous things' to the virtuous soul in this life we may turn, perhaps, to the latter part of the *Republic*, and particularly to book 9, where it is shown that the pleasures of the intellect are superior to those of the other parts of the soul, and that the life of the sage is 729 times as happy as that of the tyrant (586e–588a), a passage picked up in book 10. 608c, just as Plato is about to embark upon the myth.

The reference to purifying the 'eye of the soul' is (as noted in the text) an allusion to *Republic* 7. 533d2, but mainly to a slightly earlier passage, 527d–e, where Plato talks of 'purifying and rekindling an organ of the soul which had been destroyed and blinded by our ordinary pursuits'—with, finally, a glancing reference back to 6. 486a5–6 (*eporexasthai*, 'grasping').

4. We begin this section with an interpretation of the Allegory of the Cave in *Republic* 7, with few exact verbal reminiscences, but not adding anything interesting to the source-text, except, perhaps, the use of the evocative word *zophos*, 'gloom', the Homeric term for the darkness of the underworld—and, more distinctively still, the phrase *biōtikos zophos*, 'the gloom of (earthly) life'. The introduction of this term into the context of the cave allegory may not be original with A., since we find it used by Philo (e.g. *Leg. All.* 3. 171; *Praem.* 36), to describe the life of the senses as opposed to the 'bright light' of reason (Philo also uses the adjective *biōtikos*, but not in this connection). It would seem to be a product of the allegorizing of Homer, and the equation of Hades with the sublunar realm, such as emanated from the Stoic theorists of the School of Pergamum.

The doctrine embodied in the cave allegory is now declared to be 'concordant' (*symphōnon*) with the principles that 'only the noble is good', and that 'virtue is sufficient for happiness', both thoroughly Stoic doctrines (*SVF* 3. 29–37 and 49–67), but derivable also from utterances of Plato's. Indeed, we learn from Clement of Alexandria (*Strom.* 5. 14. 97. 6) that the Stoic Antipater of Tarsus composed three books to demonstrate, against Carneades, that Plato held precisely these doctrines (Fr. 56). Indeed, the former doctrine is reasonably derivable from such passages as *Gorgias* 474c–d, *Symposium* 201c, or *Timaeus* 87c, while the latter is derivable, though less explicitly, from *Gorgias* 527c or *Laws* 2. 660e. Unfortunately, we have no idea how Antipater proved his case, but from the evidence of doxographers such as Arius Didymus (*ap.* Stob. *Anth.* 2. 55. 22 Wachs.) and Diogenes Laertius (3. 78) we can see that these propositions were readily accepted from the first century BC on as Platonic (cf. also Apuleius, *de Plat.* 2. 13. 238).

A. now asserts that the proposition that the good (or, *our* good) consists in knowledge of the first principle (or perhaps, the primal Good) 'is demonstrated throughout whole treatises (*syntaxeis*)'. What he has in mind is not quite clear, but probably such works as the *Republic* (or more particularly, books 6 and 7) and the *Symposium*. For an account of those things that are good 'by participation' (*kata metochēn*)—the actual noun phrase is not Platonic, but Aristotelian (e.g. *Metaph.* 7. 3. 1030ᵃ13)—he can turn to the passage of *Laws*, 1 (631b) of which he has already made use earlier in the chapter.

[It is interesting here that, in quoting 631b6–7, he accords with Arius Didymus (*ap.* Stob. *Anth.* 2. 54. 12 Wachs.) in using *ditta* for Plato's *dipla*, 'of two kinds', another small indication of his source. Arius in fact quotes the whole passage; A. here contents himself with an 'and so on' (*kai ta hexēs*), indicating that he expects the passage to be familiar to his readers (who will therefore not be complete novices in Plato); or perhaps just that the *Didaskalikos* is primarily a *lecturer's* handbook, the lecturer being expected to complete the quotations either from memory or from the texts available to him.]

The reference to *Euthydemus*, 281d–e, is interesting. It was of some notoriety, being quoted again later by Iamblichus in chapter 26 of his *Protrepticus*. The argument there is that none of the popular goods— the 'human' goods of the *Laws*—are of any advantage to their possessor without prudence and wisdom (*phronēsis kai sophia*); indeed they may just as well be accounted evils. It sounds as if this passage has been excerpted by doxographers before A.'s time.

5. The statement that virtues (*aretai*) are choiceworthy (*hairetai*) in themselves seems to be a reference to one of Plato's etymologies in the *Cratylus* (415d4–5): 'he perhaps calls *aretē* (h)*airetē* because this state is most choiceworthy', a notion taken up by Aristotle in the *Nicomachean Ethics* (6. 13. 1144ᵃ1–2), and, once again, by Arius Didymus (*ap.* Stob. *Anth.* 2. 100. 24). Presumably what A. is thinking of in identifying this as the pervasive theme of the *Republic* is the fact that Socrates at the beginning of book 2 is explicitly challenged to prove that justice (as the combination of all the virtues) is preferable *in itself* to injustice (cf. esp. 366e–367e), and that that is what he

spends the rest of the dialogue doing. The rest of the section, indeed, is a development of this passage and what precedes it—though (as Whittaker (1990: 137 n. 448) notes) utilizing turns of phrase from elsewhere in the dialogues: for example, 181. 10, *eutychestaton kai eudaimonestaton* certainly seems to be a borrowing from *Euthydemus* 282c9, *eudaimona kai eutychē*, with A.'s characteristic inversion; while in the mention of wealth, health, and beauty (181. 16–17) we may see again the influence of *Laws* 2. 661a–b. This is the procedure of a mind saturated with Plato.

CHAPTER 28

We now turn to a discussion of the *telos*, or final good for man (defined by the Stoics as 'that for the sake of which everything is done, but which is not itself done for the sake of anything', *SVF* 3. 16), a fundamental aspect of any Hellenistic or later exposition of ethical theory. Most of the chapter consists of the quotation (to an extent unusual for A.—note, however, the summarizing 'and so on' (*kai ta toutois hexēs*) in the *Laws* and *Phaedrus* references at 181. 39 and 41, on which see my comments above, in ch. 27) of a series of proof texts (though not, we may note, of *Ti.* 90a–d, which is the only place (90d5) in which the word *telos* actually occurs in this connection), but this is followed by some scholastic exegesis, which raises a few interesting points.

The specification of the Platonic *telos* as 'likeness to God' (*homoiōsis theōi*) seems to have been made in the context of the Pythagorean-influenced tradition of dogmatic Platonism arising in Alexandria in the latter part of the first century BC, with which the figure of Eudorus is associated (cf. Dillon (1977: ch. 3)). For Antiochus of Ascalon, the *telos* had been the Stoic one of 'living in accordance with nature' (cf. Cic. *Fin.* 2. 34); only the access of renewed interest in the Pythagorean tradition, and the concern to attach Plato more closely to the wisdom of Pythagoras (one of whose basic precepts, as handed down in the tradition, was 'Follow God' (*hepou theōi*), cf. Arius Didymus, *ap.* Stob. *Anth.* 2. 49. 16 Wachsmuth–Hense), led Platonists to identify those passages in the dialogues which could be said to advance this doctrine. Philo of Alexandria is the first author after Eudorus to adopt this formula (e.g. *Fug.* 63)—though he also sticks to the concept of concordance with nature (e.g. *Dec.* 81)—and *homoiōsis theōi* remained the Platonist *telos* thereafter to the end of antiquity and beyond. See on this Merki (1952).

It is interesting in this connection to compare Arius' exposition (*ap.* Stob. 2. 49. 16 Wachs.) with that of A. Arius (perhaps following Eudorus) divides Plato's treatment of the topic into three, answering to the tripartite division of philosophy. He sees the subject being dealt with from the 'physical' perspective in the *Timaeus* (90a–d), from the ethical in the *Republic* (possibly the same passage as A. quotes, but Wachsmuth thinks of 585b–c and 608c ff.), and from the logical in the *Theaetetus* (176a–e), while he sees the *Laws* (4. 715e ff.) passage as a comprehensive treatment. He ends, however, by emphasizing that the variety of approaches adopted by Plato does not betoken any variation of doctrine. A., as we see, does not make any such distinctions as this, but simply declares that Plato presents the doctrine 'in various forms' (*poikilōs*), and notes slight variations in the particular virtues mentioned. He could, however, be dimly reflecting the distinction made by Arius. The proof-texts employed are common to both authors (*Ti.* 90a–d is not, admittedly, quoted as such by A., as I have noted above, but verbal reminiscences of it abound in the latter part of the chapter, as will become apparent).

1–2. The *catena* of texts begins with the most basic one, *Theaetetus* 176a–b, followed by *Republic* 10. 613a, and *Phaedo* 82a–b, with some attempt being made to draw distinctions of emphasis between them. Basically, however, the doctrine of Plato being propounded here is that 'likeness to God' is to be attained through the exercise of the virtues— wisdom (*phronēsis*), justice, moderation, and holiness; only courage is passed over (by Plato) in the texts, as not so obviously relevant.

[Certain details show, I think, the scholastic origin of these proof-texts. In the *Phaedo* text, we first have 'blessed' (*makarioi*), which is not in the text of Plato, subjoined to 'happiest' at the beginning of the quotation. As Whittaker suggests (1990: 56 n. 452) it is doubtless introduced from other Platonic contexts where the two adjectives are conjoined, such as *Republic* 354a1, or *Laws* 660e3 and 730c2–3. Then there is the detail that 'the *social and civic* virtues' are joined by *te kai*, thus agreeing with two Plato MSS, but also—more significantly, perhaps—with Stobaeus' quotation of the passage at *Anthologia* 1. 433. 18 (cf. Whittaker, 1990: 56 n. 453).]

3. A. now adduces two texts where the more Pythagorean formula 'follow God' is used, *Laws* 4. 715e ff. and *Phaedrus* 248a ff., both of

which are too long to be quoted in full, but with which he expects his readers to be familiar.

[Again a significant detail: at the beginning of the *Laws* text, A. agrees with Ps.-Aristotle, *de Mundo* 7. 401^{b}25 in omitting the *kai* after *hōsper* (in 'as old tradition has it') present in the MSS of Plato—another indication of the handbook tradition.]

A. goes on to propound the doctrine that the good is the first principle (*archē*) of the advantageous (*ōphelimon*), a thought derivable from a passage of the *Hippias Major* (296e), where Socrates argues, first, that the fine (*to kalon*), and then that the good, is 'advantageous', but the principle had been taken up in the scholastic tradition before A.'s time, as we find it in Arius Didymus (*ap.* Stob. *Anth.* 2. 53. 22 Wachsmuth–Hense): 'The good is that from which advantage accrues.' The principle seems also to have been adopted by the Stoics, if we may attribute to a Stoic source a very Stoic-sounding argument in Clement's *Paidagogos* (1. 8. 63. 1 ff. = *SVF* 2. 1116), the conclusion of which runs: 'God is agreed to be good; therefore God is advantageous (*ōphelei*).' A. will have derived from some such argument as this, presumably, his claim that 'this is dependent on God' (though the actual phrase 'is dependent' (*ērtētai*) is borrowed from *Laws* 631b7). The point of the remark, presumably, is that since God, *qua* 'the advantageous', is the *archē*, the *telos*, which should be to one's ultimate advantage, should consist in likening oneself to him, this being an exegesis of the *Laws* 715e passage (though the compound *exomoiōthēnai* is plainly borrowed from *Ti.* 90d4).

The next point is somewhat more substantial, that the God to which one is likening oneself will not be the primal God, the God 'above the heavens' (*hyperouranios*), but the God 'in the heavens' (*epouranios*)—presumably the heavenly Intellect of chapter 10 above. The terminology here derives ultimately from *Phaedrus* 247c, but the point being made relates to a controversy in Middle-Platonic circles as to whether the supreme principle could be meaningfully said to possess virtue, or at least the four virtues as attainable by humans, and so whether it made any sense to say that likeness to God was to be achieved by the practice of virtue. Originally, perhaps, this argument was directed against the Stoics, who maintained, in a simplistic way (from the Platonist point of view), that God was the acme of all the virtues (cf. the argument of Cleanthes reported in Sextus, *M.* 9. 88 = *SVF* 1. 529, and also the testimonia gathered at *SVF* 3. 245–52 to the doctrine that the virtue of men and gods is the same); but there were Platonists too who had to be reminded of the problems of such a doctrine. Plotinus, in the first chapter of his tractate *On Virtues* (1. 2. [19]), sets out the problem with much more subtlety than A. accords it here, showing that there are difficulties involved in attributing virtues in their ordinary, 'civic', senses even to the Demiurge, the *epouranios theos* in A.'s terminology. It is actually Aristotle, in *Nicomachean Ethics* 7. 1. 1145^{a}25-7, and 10. 8. 1178^{b}7-22, who seems first to have pointed out the absurdity of attributing the ordinary virtues to God, but his arguments (picked up by Plotinus) apply just as forcefully to the *epouranios* as to the *hyperouranios theos*, so it is not quite clear in what sense A. feels that the Intellect of the World Soul (if that is what he is referring to) possesses virtue.

It is not clear to me how the last sentence of section 3 connects with what precedes it. It does not follow, certainly, from what immediately precedes it, but perhaps A. saw it as following from the paragraph as a whole. The etymologizing of *eudaimōn* ('fortunate') and *kakodaimōn* ('unfortunate') as referring to the state of, or of one's relations with, one's guardian spirit (*daimōn*) is a conceit attributed originally to Xenocrates (Arist. *Top.* 2. 6. 112^{a}32 ff. = Xen. Fr. 81 Heinze/236 IP)—though Democritus (Frs. 170-1) may have said something of the sort as well. According to Aristotle, however, Xenocrates identified the (rational) soul as the *daimōn*, whereas here A. is taking it to mean the divinity in general. However, both Xenocrates and the late Platonist tradition doubtless had Plato's remarks at *Timaeus* 90c very much in mind, where the *daimōn* is presented as both immanent (as the highest element in the individual soul) and part of the divinity, so that in assimilating ourselves to it we are at the same time assimilating ourselves to God as a whole.

[A terminological detail: the word *euexia*, 'good state' (182. 2), is doubtless taken from *R.* 4. 444e1, where virtue is described as an *euexia* of the soul.]

4. The last section of this chapter provides a scholastic specification of the methods whereby likeness to God may be attained, utilizing first of all a triadic listing of requirements for success in philosophy, derived ultimately, perhaps, from the beginning of Aristotle's *Eudemian Ethics* (1214^{a}16 ff.): natural ability (*physis*), learning (*mathēsis*), and practice (*askēsis*)—though Aristotle there produces these as possible *alternative* ways of attaining happiness. At

Nicomachean Ethics 10. 9. 1179ᵇ20 ff., however, Aristotle presents a triad of *physis*, *ethos* (habituation), and *didachē* (instruction) as *complementary* components of successful education, and this became fixed in the scholastic tradition. We see this happening, for instance, in the Neopythagorean writings, in 'Archytas', *On Moral Education* 3. 41. 20 ff. Thesleff, where *physis*, *askēsis*, and *eidēsis* (comprehension?) are three stages in education, and in Philo, *Vita Abrahami* 52–4 (*physis*, *mathēsis*, *askēsis*—identified each with one of the patriarchs). Arius Didymus (*ap.* Stob. *Anth.* 2. 118. 5 ff.) produces a slightly different formulation, when he identifies *physis*, *ethos*, and *logos* (reasoning) as the requirements for attaining perfection in virtue.

A.'s purpose here is to connect this formulation as far as possible with Plato. For 'habit and practice' he can appeal to *Republic* 7. 518e, where it is said of the virtues that 'where they do not pre-exist, they are afterwards created by habit and practice' (*ethesi te kai askēsesin*, 518e1). The insertion here by A. of 'way of life' (*agōgē*) may be provoked by Plato's use of it in *Laws* 1. 645a1 and 5—the well-known 'puppet on a string' passage—though there *agōgē* is used in a rather literal sense, as a 'leading-string'. The combination of *agōgē* with *ethos*, however, is never employed by Plato, as Whittaker points out (1990: 140 n. 461), but is by Aristotle, at *Politics* 4. 5. 1292ᵇ16 and at *Eudemian Ethics* 2. 2. 1220ᵃ39–b3, which latter passage seems to be the inspiration of Arius Didymus in his summary of Peripatetic ethics (*ap.* Stob. *Anth.* 2. 116. 2 ff.), so that A. may be picking this conjunction up from the tradition rather than creating it himself.

[For the conjunction of *didaskalia* and *paradosis* ('education' and 'tradition') we must turn to *Laws* 7. 803a1–2, a passage concerning musical education, which leads into another characterization of man as puppet (803c), while the immediately following phrase ('distance ourselves . . . from human concerns') is taken from a significant passage of the *Phaedrus*, 249c–d, which is plainly an influence on the thought of this section.]

The terms *proteleia* and *prokatharsia* ('introductory ceremonies' and 'preliminary purifications') are interesting, as exemplifications of the widespread tendency in Middle Platonism to depict progress in philosophy in terms of stages of initiation into a mystery religion, the most elaborate version of which is to be found in Theon of Smyrna (*Expos.* 14. 17–16. 2 Hiller). However, the idea of preliminary studies as 'lesser mysteries' preparatory to the 'greater mysteries' of philosophy itself, or dialectic in particular, can be traced back to such a passage as *Symposium* 209e5 ff., where Diotima distinguishes between the lesser and the perfect, or 'epoptic', mysteries of love. We have also, from the Old Academy, a significant remark of Crantor's, preserved by Stobaeus (*Anth.* 2. 206. 26–8), to the effect that 'even as no one can be initiated into the greater mysteries before the lesser, so no one can come to philosophy before working his way through the "encyclical" sciences'. Mystery-imagery is popular with Philo of Alexandria (e.g. *Vit. Abr.* 122, where he makes a contrast between the great and lesser Mysteries; but also *Sacr.* 62, and *Vit. Mos.* 1. 62), and Plutarch makes use of it in a passage of his *Table Talk* (718c–d), where the talk is of the status of geometry as a science.

[The two nouns used by A. here are both notable. *Prokatharsion* is attested otherwise only in a scholion of Maximus Planudes on Sophocles, and the verb is not much commoner (though it occurs, with *proteleo*, in an interesting passage from the first oration of Aelius Aristides (12. 9–11 Lenz-Behr), which is evidence for the use of these terms in connection with preliminary rites of purification). *Proteleion*, on the other hand, is not uncommon from Aeschylus (*A.* 227) on as a term for a preliminary sacrifice. There is a particularly relevant use of it, however, in Philo (*Deus*, 148), *ta proteleia tēs sophias*, 'the preliminaries of wisdom'; and another in Pseudo-Galen's *History of Philosophy* 16 (608. 11 Diels *DG*), *ta proteleia tōn kata philosophian*, 'the preliminaries to philosophy'. It is plain that A. is here utilizing fairly well-worn imagery, but the conjunction of these two nouns may be original to him.]

The mention of 'our innate spirit' (*tou en hēmin daimonos*, 182. 9) is a further reference to *Timaeus* 90a–c.

The basic idea behind this passage is derived from *Republic* 7. 531d, where, however, Plato uses musical imagery—the study of the preliminary sciences is, as it were, the *prooimion*, 'prelude', to the main *nomos* (in this context, 'musical composition'). There now follows a listing of the preliminary sciences in the order 'music–arithmetic–astronomy–geometry', disregarding the order in which they are presented in *Republic* 524d–531c, and omitting stereometry, while throwing in 'gymnastics' from earlier in the dialogue (3. 403c–405a), whence also derives the rather grimly practical remark about preparing the body for the demands of both war and peace.

CHAPTER 29

1. A. now proceeds to a definition of virtue (*aretē*), and a distinction of its various kinds, according as it is concerned with the rational or irrational parts of the soul. He begins with the characterization of *aretē* as a 'divine thing' (*theion khrēma*), which may, as Whittaker (1990: 58 n. 467) suggests, be derived by a scholastic mind from Socrates' rather ironical remark at the end of the *Meno* (99e–100a, cf. 100b), to the effect that virtue has been shown by the argument to be neither natural nor teachable, but acquirable only 'by divine dispensation' (*theiāi moirāi*), but if so, it has been thoroughly purged of its ironic context. The fact that the same statement about virtue is made by A.'s approximate contemporary, the Peripatetic commentator Aspasius (*in EN* 99. 4–5 Heylbut), and linked to the statement that it is 'a sort of likening to God (*homoiōsis tis tōi theōi*)' would seem to indicate that this has become a fairly well-worn formula by A.'s time.

The basic definition of virtue is very close to that provided by Apuleius, in *de Plat.* 2. 5. 227 'a supremely good and noble state of mind, which secures for him in whom it is established that he be in harmony with himself, calm, firm, and consistent, not only in words but also in deeds, both with himself and with others' (*habitus mentis optime et nobiliter figuratus, quae concordem sibi, quietem, constantem etiam eum facit, cui fuerit fideliter intimata, non verbis modo sed factis etiam secum et cum ceteris congruentem*), which is evidence of its thoroughly traditional nature. The phrase 'most excellent state' (*diathesis hē beltistē*) occurs as a definition of virtue in the Platonic *Definitions* (411d), but also in Aristotle (*EE* 2. 1. 1218ᵃ38), in a context where he seems to be referring to an established definition. Again. at *Physics* 7. 3. 246ᵃ13, Aristotle produces the remark that virtue is 'a sort of perfection' (*teleiōsis tis*), which contributes the other half to A.'s formula here. The definition also turns up (if one accepts the probable supplement of De Lacy), in Galen *Hipp. et Plat.* 7. 1. 24. 434. 1–2 De Lacy. Variations on what will originally have been the Academic definition found their way into the Stoic tradition (cf. *SVF* 3. 197–200, *diathesis homologoumenē, teleiōsis*), and into Arius Didymus' account of Peripatetic ethics (*ap.* Stob. *Anth.* 2. 51. 1–2 (*hexis hē beltistē psychēs, teleia*), so we are dealing with commonplaces here. The second part of the definition, however—closely paralleled, as we have seen, in

Apuleius—is not attested elsewhere than in these two sources, but would seem to be ultimately derived from such a passage as *Republic* 3. 413d–e, where the training of the prospective guardian is being described, designed to render him 'graceful' (*euschēmōn*, e2) and 'harmonious (*eurhythmos kai euarmostos*, e4, cf. A.'a *symphōnos*), and by implication 'firm' (*bebaios*)—though the adjective may be borrowed from *Republic* 7. 537c4.

Following on the basic definition of virtue, we proceed to a consideration of its species. Here, unfortunately, the text is corrupt, a phrase or so having fallen out. My version accepts in substance an emendation proposed by Harold Cherniss, in his review of Louis's Budé edition (1949: 76 n. 5), though its grammatical plausibility does not impress me. Something like this, however, is what A. intends to say, namely that there are two types (*eidē*) of virtue, the one 'rational', concerned with the rational part of the soul (*to logistikon*), which consists in wisdom (*phronēsis*), the other 'irrational', which is concerned with the irrational parts of the soul, that is to say, courage (*andria*) and self-control (*sōphrosynē*), concerned respectively with the 'spirited part' (*thymikon*) and the 'passionate part' (*epithymētikon*). All this is taken, without notable alteration or development, from *Republic* 4. 441c–443b, though filtered through the scholastic tradition (of which we can see an earlier stage in, for example, Philo, *LA* 1. 70–1).

2–3. We now pass to the definitions of the individual virtues, in which again there is much that is patently traditional.

For the definition of (practical) wisdom (*phronēsis*), cf. Apuleius, *de Plat.* 2. 6. 228: 'the science of knowing what is good and evil, and those things that are median between the two'. The basic definition 'knowledge of goods and evils' figures already in the Platonic *Definitions* (411d); the addition 'and of what is neither' seems to be a contribution of the Stoic tradition. It occurs in Arius Didymus' summary of Stoic ethics (*ap.* Stob. *Anth.* 2. 59. 5–6 Wachsmuth–Hense = *SVF* 3. 262). It is also to be found in Cicero (*de Inv.* 2. 160; *ND* 3. 38)—borrowed by him either from Posidonius or Antiochus or both—and in Sextus Empiricus (*P.* 3. 271).

There is slight incoherence in A.'s exposition here, since the definition he provides is only of the *ethical* virtue of practical wisdom, not of the corresponding *intellectual* or theoretical virtue, which would be the virtue most proper to the rational part of the soul in Platonist theory (though practical wisdom is certainly proper to it as well). The explanation for this doubtless is that by A.'s time (and indeed ever since the Platonic *Definitions*), definitions of the four virtues in an ethical context are concerned only with *phronēsis* as practical wisdom. A. has in fact dealt with theoretical wisdom back in chapter 2. 153. 4–9. We may note, however, that Apuleius, in the parallel passage of his work (*de Plat.* 2. 6. 228) gives a definition of both levels of wisdom, *sophia* (*sapientia*) as concerning things divine and human, *phronēsis* (*prudentia*) as concerning the knowledge of good and evil.

The definition of self-control can be related to such Platonic passages as *Republic* 4. 430e: 'self-control is a kind of order (*kosmos*) and control of certain pleasures and desires', together with the slightly later passage 432a, where it is described as a unanimity (*homonoia*) and concord (*symphōnia*) between the various parts of the soul as to which should rule and which should be ruled. Plato, however, speaks of 'pleasures and desires'; the term 'impulse' (*orexis*) which A. uses here is taken from the Aristotelian tradition. The noun *eupeitheia*, likewise, to describe *sophrosyne*'s relationship to the reason does not occur in the Platonic tradition before Plutarch (cf. esp. *Virt. Mor.* 446d), though Plato uses the adjective *eupeithēs* at *Phaedrus* 254a1, of the good horse's obedience to the charioteer, which may well provide the origin for the term. Although A. borrows a Stoic term, *hēgemonikon* ('ruling element'), to describe the reason, the concept of the rule of reason is taken from *Republic* 441e.

Courage (which should properly, if one is following the scheme of *Republic* 4, be dealt with before self-control, but A. seems here to be influenced by the normal Stoic order of the virtues, cf. *SVF* 3. 264) is defined in terms taken from *Republic* 433c: 'the maintenance of a law-abiding opinion (*ennomos doxa*) as to what is and what is not to be feared' (cf. also 429b–c). The force of *ennomos* is not entirely easy to render: 'lawful' or 'legitimate' is not quite sufficient; it really denotes a state of mind that assents to rules of conduct laid down by a higher authority. This definition was taken into the Stoic tradition, at least by Zeno's pupil Sphaerus (Cic. *TD* 4. 53 = *SVF* 1. 628), and is implied also by the second-century Platonist Hierax in his definition of cowardice (*ap.* Stob. *Anth.* 3. 345. 4–6).

Finally, the definition of justice is dependent ultimately on *Republic* 4. 443c–d, where its role in harmonizing the three parts of the soul and disposing each of them towards its proper duties is set out. Substantially the same definition can be found in Philo (*Leg. All.* 1. 72—part of his extended treatment of the virtues in 1. 63–73), though

Philo also employs the Stoic definitions for this and the other virtues
(e.g. 1. 65).

[The noun *panteleia* (here translated 'supreme perfection') is
notable. It is not used by Plato, but would seem to be a
Neopythagorean coinage. At any rate, it appears in 'Hippodamos', *On
the State* (*ap.* Stob. 4. 1. 94. 99. 18 Thesleff), where the political community is compared to the *panteleia* of a lyre (presumably something
like 'overall composition'—we may note the musical context), which
requires constant tuning and harmonizing; and Philo tells us (*Spec.
Leg.* 2. 200) that 'wise men' (presumably the Pythagoreans) called the
number ten *panteleia* because it embraces all the numerical and musical ratios. Philo himself also uses the expression *panteleia aretēs*,
'supreme perfection of virtue' at *Opif.* 156, to describe the Tree of
Life in the Garden of Eden. Plutarch also uses it (*Comm. Not.* 1061e)
in an ethical context ('*panteleia* of goods'), but it remains a rare and
interesting word.

The term *peithēnios* (lit. 'obedient to the reins') embodies a reference to the 'good horse' of the *Phaedrus* Myth. The actual adjective is
not used by Plato, but it is to be found in both Philo (*Sacr.* 105;
Conf. 54) and Plutarch (*Virt. Mor.* 442c; *de Gen. Socr.* 592c; *An. Proc.*
1029e), all contexts where the obedience of the irrational part of the
soul to the rational is being discussed, amid equestrian imagery.]

For a good discussion of the treatment of the virtues in the
Middle-Platonic tradition see Lilla (1971: 60–84). It is notable that A.
and Apuleius do not employ the standard Stoic definitions of the
virtues, whereas they are taken over without hesitation two centuries
earlier by Antiochus of Ascalon, and are obviously dominant in Philo
of Alexandria also. Despite the fact that the Stoic definitions are doctrinally unobjectionable, A. is concerned to derive his formulations
more explicitly from Plato's *Republic* (though, as I have observed, he
is betrayed into using the Stoic order of the virtues in giving his
definitions).

4. Section 3 ends with a reference to the doctrine of the mutual implication (*antakolouthia*) of the virtues, but since this is developed in section 4, it seems best to discuss it here. This doctrine is originally Stoic
as regards its formalization (cf. *SVF* 3. 295–304), being first set out,
perhaps, in Chrysippus' treatise *On Virtues*, but it could be discerned
as operative in Plato's *Protagoras* (cf. esp. 329e ff., where Socrates
raises the question, 'Do some men possess one of these parts of *aretē*

and some another, or if someone has one must he have them all?', and
then proceeds to prove to Protagoras the latter alternative), and is also
recognized by Aristotle in *Nicomachean Ethics* 6. 13. 1144^{b}30 ff. (referring perhaps to arguments of the real Socrates, perhaps to the argument in the *Protagoras*). Both in the *Protagoras* and in Stoicism, the
doctrine of mutual implication is bound up with the doctrine that
virtue is knowledge, or that all the virtues are exercised according to
rational judgement; it is a consequence of intellectualist ethics.

The mutual implication of the virtues is accepted by all Middle
Platonists from Antiochus on (Cic. *Fin.* 5. 67). We find it in Philo
(e.g. *Vit. Mos.* 2. 7; *Sacr.* 82); Hippolytus, *Refutatio Omnium
Haeresium* 1. 19. 18; the Anonymous *Theaetetus* Commentator, 9. 39 ff.,
and 11. 16 f.; and Apuleius, *de Plat.* 2. 6. 228 (with the specification,
as here, that it applies only to the 'perfect' virtues). Later, Plotinus
also accepts it (*Enn.* 1. 2. 7. 1–2), and it is unchallenged in
Neoplatonism. Cf. Lilla (1971: 83–4).

It is possible, however, that A. is here in conflict with contemporary Peripatetic doctrine. If we may judge from Diogenes Laertius'
summary of Aristotelian ethics (5. 30), it was later Peripatetic doctrine
that the virtues 'are not reciprocal' (*mē antakolouthein*), 'for a man
might be prudent (*phronimos*), or again just, and at the same time
intemperate and incontinent (*akratēs*)'—perhaps, therefore, a reference
to Aristotle's theory of *akrasia*. Aspasius, on the other hand (*in EN*
80. 14. Heylbut), declares that '*some* of the virtues are reciprocal', not
specifying which. This may or may not contradict Diogenes, but it is
in any case less than a full commitment to a doctrine of *antakolouthia*.

A. singles out courage to make his point about *antakolouthia* precisely because this was the most plausible exception to the rule, as
had been noted already in the *Protagoras* (349d ff.), and by Aristotle
(*EN* 1144^{b}30 ff.). To establish his proof, he equates the 'law-abiding
doctrine' (*ennomon dogma*) of his previous definition with 'right reason' (*orthos logos*), once again utilizing a term which might seem to be
associated with Stoicism, but which is in fact derivable from both
Plato and Aristotle. Plato uses it on numerous occasions (e.g. *Phd.*
73a10; *Ti.* 56b4; *Lg.* 2. 659d2), but always with the meaning 'correct
account' (rather than anything more cosmic), as does Aristotle in the
same passage of the *Nicomachean Ethics* as referred to above (1144^{b}23)
and, for example, in book 2, 1103^{b}31 ff., and that is all that A. means
by it here, though he may also be affected by the Stoic belief that the
laws of human morals are the same as the laws of nature.

The definition of *phronēsis* as 'knowledge of what is good' shows affinity with one of the basic Stoic definitions (e.g. *SVF* 3. 262), 'knowledge of what is good, what is evil, and what is neither' (it occurs also in the Platonic *Definitions*, 411d, but that may just as easily constitute proof of Stoic influence on the *Definitions*, as evidence of Old Academic influence on Stoicism).

For the idea that courage is required along with wisdom to achieve the good, we may compare the observation of Philo, again in the course of his major discussion of the virtues (*Leg. All.* 1. 86), that wisdom and courage 'are able to construct an enclosing wall against the opposite vices, folly, and cowardice, and capture them'. He goes on to say that self-control by itself 'is powerless to encircle desire and pleasure' (it needs wisdom and courage). Philo is presumably borrowing here from some Stoic (or Antiochian Platonist?) treatise on the virtues.

The image of the soul's view of the good being obscured (*episkotoumenos*) by cowardice, etc., is interestingly paralleled, as Whittaker (1990: 59 n. 482) points out, in Aspasius (*in EN* 134. 26 Heylbut), where he is discussing *akrasia*. He remarks that when a *pathos* falls upon people of hasty disposition, their vision is as it were obscured (*episkotēthentes*) by a kind of mist, so that they do not see the *logos* within them. In both cases, the image may go back to an exegesis of Homer (either *Iliad* 5. 127 or elsewhere—Aspasius' use of *akhlys*, 'mist' is significant, I think), discussing the mist of ignorance in which mortals normally walk.

The reference to Plato in 183. 14 is to *Protagoras* 357d–e, though the actual term 'folly' (*aphrosynē*) is taken from earlier in the dialogue, 332a. The conjunction of terms *akolastos kai deilos* ('intemperate and cowardly') is to be found in Plato at *Gorgias* 477d5, while the nouns *akolasia* and *deilia* occur at *Republic* 4. 444b7–8. A. may have either or both of these passages in mind.

Finally, for the concept of 'perfect' (*teleiai*) virtues, we may turn again to the above-mentioned passage of Aristotle's *Nicomachean Ethics* (1144^{b}30 ff), where the contrast is made between *physikai aretai*, 'virtues on the natural level', which may be possessed separately (e.g. one may possess *natural* courage without self-control or practical wisdom), and *kyriai aretai* ('virtues properly so-called'), which cannot be separated from *phronēsis* (or from each other); but also to *Eudemian Ethics* 2. 1. 1219^{a}35 ff., where virtue is distinguished into perfect and imperfect (*teleia* and *atelēs*). This latter terminology is picked up by

Arius Didymus in his summary of Peripatetic ethics (*ap.* Stob. 2. 131. 14 ff.), and by Aspasius in his *Commentary* (e.g. 40. 11; 99. 35), and, as was mentioned above, is also recognized by Apuleius (*de Plat.* 2. 6. 228). Philo, on the other hand, employs more Stoic contrast between *teleiai aretai* and *euphyiai*, 'good natural dispositions' (e.g. *Leg. All.* 3. 249–50, where he introduces a three-way contrast between *aretē teleia*, *prokopē*, 'moral progress', and *euphyia*). It is this latter contrast that A. adopts, as we shall see in the next chapter.

CHAPTER 30

1. A. proceeds in this chapter to a discussion of the thoroughly Stoic concepts of 'moral progress' (*prokopē*) and 'good natural dispositions' (*euphyiai*), which may also be termed 'not perfect virtues; (*ou teleiai aretai*—he avoids, we may note, the Peripatetic term *ateleis*, 'imperfect' (interestingly enough, a scholion of Bishop Arethas of Caesarea, in MS V, writes in *ateleis* over the *allōs* ('in a different sense') in the first line, showing that that learned clergyman felt the lack of this term). He then goes on to propound the doctrine of the virtues as means between extremes.

A. begins with a distinction between perfect virtues, or virtues in the true sense, and their homonyms, the 'natural' or 'imperfect' virtues of Peripatetic theory, for which he uses the Stoic terms *euphyiai* and *prokopai*—using the latter term, rather unusually, in the plural, to denote virtues in a state of development. There are ambiguities here that merit discussion. Both the *physikai aretai* of *Nicomachean Ethics* 6. 13, and the Stoic *euphyiai* comprise both such natural advantages as good memory and quickness to learn (such as are mentioned, indeed, at the beginning of the *Handbook*, 1. 152. 24), and the instinctive (or at least non-intellectual) qualities of justice, self-control, or bravery, which we share even with certain of the animals (such as are alluded to by Aristotle at *EN* 1144^{b}30 ff), which (*a*) admit of degrees of intensity, and (*b*) are compatible with lack of any of the other virtues. Only these latter are in question here, since we are really talking about the 'imperfect' homonyms of the four canonical virtues. A similar use of terminology may be found in Arius Didymus' summary of Peripatetic ethics (*ap.* Stob. 2. 131. 14 ff.), where Arius first distinguishes between *teleiai* and *ateleis* virtues, and then identifies the *ateleis* as *euphyia* and *prokopē* (using the singular).

The examples of the soldier and of the foolish (*aphrōn*) person are taken from this discussion of the nature of true bravery in the *Laches* (cf. esp. 193a–d), but may also be influenced by Aristotle's discussion at *Nicomachean Ethics* 3. 11 (indeed Aristotle himself seems to refer to Plato's discussion here at 1116^{b}4–5, and Aspasius explicitly does so in his commentary on the passage at *in EN* 84. 23 ff.).

A. seems now to be about to go on to make a contrast between perfect and imperfect virtue (as do Apuleius, *de Plat.* 2. 6. 228, and Hippolytus, *Ref.* 1. 19. 18), but instead turns to a contrast between virtue and vice (*kakia*). This could be the result of carelessness in summarizing a source, but it could also be the case that A. feels that the contrast between perfect and imperfect virtues is sufficiently clear from what has already been said, and that it may reasonably be subsumed under the opposition between virtue and vice. The result, however, is to leave it less than clear whether he holds (as he presumably does) that imperfect virtues admit of variations in intensity.

The vices, at any rate, are not reciprocal, some being even incompatible with others, e.g. opposites, such as cowardice and recklessness, or miserliness and dissoluteness. This is presumably an intentional contradiction of Stoic theory that all vices are equal (cf. *SVF* 1. 224–5 (Zeno) and 3. 524–43 (Chrysippus))—a position already argued against by Antiochus (Cic. *Acad.* 2. 133; *Fin.* 4. 67), and later by Plutarch (*Virt. Mor.* 449d). The Platonists have common sense on their side, certainly, but they do not appear to appreciate the force of the Stoic argument that, if a given quality, like virtue, admits of no variation of degree (as the Platonists are prepared to accept), then its opposite must admit of no degrees either—or at any rate there can be no degrees of approximation to virtue in anything that is not a virtue.

The view that no one could possess all the vices, because a single body simply could not tolerate them, may owe something to Aristotle's remark (*EN* 4. 11. 1126^{a}11–13): 'Still, it must not be supposed that the same man is guilty of all these modes of excess. That could not happen, because evil destroys even itself, and, when it is total, cannot be borne.'

2. Still countering Stoic doctrine, A. now advances the thesis that there is a neutral mean between the states of virtue and vice. For such a thesis he can appeal to the authority of Plato in *Phaedo* 90a (though there Socrates is only saying that extremes of badness and goodness are comparatively rare) and *Lysis* 216d (where he states

more definitely that there are three types of person, the good, the
bad, and the neither good nor bad). For A., the process of *prokopē* is
not, as it was for the Stoics, a process which takes place in a soul
which is still evil, and which precisely *does* result in a sudden qualitative change from vice to virtue (Plut. *On Moral Progress* 75c; *Comm.
Not.* 1063a–b = *SVF* 3. 539/61s–t LS), but rather something which
is proper to this intermediate state, the existence of which the Stoics
denied. Plutarch, in criticizing the Stoic doctrine in the texts referred
to above, supports the same position as A.

3. The distinction between 'predominant' (*proēgoumenai*) and 'subsidiary' (*hepomenai*) virtues is not to be confused with that between
perfect and imperfect virtues. This is a distinction between types of
perfect virtue, and is to be related rather to that made back at the
beginning of chapter 29 between 'reason-related' and 'irrational-
related' virtues. The terminology here is Stoic (cf. *SVF* 2. 1157; 3.
116), but the doctrine of the dominant role of rational or theoretical
virtue is readily derivable from such Platonic passages as *Republic* 7.
518d–e and *Phaedo* 82a–b, where the derivative nature of what in the
Phaedo passage is called 'social and civil (*demotikē kai politikē*) virtue
is emphasized, as is the 'habituation and practice' (*ethos kai meletē*) by
which they are acquired.

The specification that only rational virtue is a science or an art
(*epistēmē kai tekhnē*) seems to take its origin from a Stoic distinction
between the virtues proper and natural qualities such as great-spirit-
ness (*megalopsychia*) or strength, if we may judge from Arius
Didymus' account of Stoic ethics (*ap.* Stob. 2. 58. 9–14), though an
acute scholastic mind *could* derive at least the seeds of such a doctrine
from the remarks of Adeimantus in *Republic* 2. 366c that a man would
only abstain from injustice if he either was endowed with a divine
nature or 'attained to knowledge (*epistēmē*)'. The same Arius makes a
similar distinction in his summary of Peripatetic ethics (*ap.* Stob. 2.
117. 18–118. 4), where he describes 'ethical' virtue as not being a science, but rather a habit of mind (*hexis*) which tends to choose what is
noble. The basic doctrine that the virtues proper are *epistēmai*, however, does accord well with Stoic theory, while it may be Arius himself who adapts it to the Aristotelian distinction between theoretical
and practical virtue (cf. *EN* 2. 1)—the one acquired by teaching
(*didaskalia*), the other by practice (*ethos*)—as is done in the latter passage. It is this equation that A. adopts here, as does Apuleius in the
parallel passage of the *de Platone* (2. 9. 234). Since, however, Apuleius

makes some slightly different points, it is worth while, I think, to quote him in full:

He [sc. Plato] considers proper matter for teaching and study those virtues which pertain to the rational soul, i.e. theoretical and practical wisdom (*sapientia et prudentia*); as for those which, in their role as preservatives, resist the vicious parts (of the soul), that is to say, courage and self-control, they are certainly rational, but, whereas the two higher virtues are regarded by him as sciences (*disciplinae*), he only describes the others as virtues if they are perfect. If they are only semi-perfect, he does not consider that they should be called 'sciences', though he does not consider them totally alien from sciences. As for justice, since it is extended over the three parts of the soul, he considers it to be the art of living and a science, and at one time to be teachable, at another to arise from practice and experience (*usu et experiendo*).

This last piece of vacillating over the status of justice is presumably the result of conflating Plato's treatment of it in *Republic* 4 with his presentation of *sophrosynē* and *dikaiosynē* at *Phaedo* 82b as acquired by 'nature and habit' (*ex ethous te kai meletēs*), which is what Apuleius is rendering here by *usu et experiendo*. Otherwise, Apuleius makes a distinction between perfect and semi-perfect virtues which A. does not make as such at this point (though he has just been talking about an 'intermediate disposition', and earlier about *prokopai*); and A. develops the point about the 'subsidiary' virtues deriving their rational aspect from outside themselves (i.e. from the 'predominant' ones), which Apuleius takes no cognizance of.

The image of the helmsman and the sailors is both respectably Platonic (e.g. *R.* 1. 341c–d, *Plt.* 296e–297a, *Lg.* 12. 961e and of course *Phdr.* 247c, where the intellect is called the 'helmsman of the soul'—the 'Ship of Fools' passage in *R.* 6. 488–9, though famous, is hardly apposite), and can be paralleled in various of A.'s contemporaries (e.g. Plut. *Quaest. Plat.* 1008a; Aspasius, *in EN* 40. 31–41. 2), but A. gives it a distinctive twist by laying stress on the fact that the 'helmsman' is able to see things (sc. with the 'eye of reason') that the sailors cannot. He has also thrown in the general and the soldiers for good measure.

4–6. In the last three sections of the chapter, A. first takes a moment to reject the Stoic dogma that all vices are equal (*SVF* 3. 526–35), and then passes on to an exposition of the doctrine of virtue as a mean, borrowed, of course, from the *Nicomachean Ethics*, book 2 (although we must not neglect to note that at least an adumbration of this doctrine might be discerned, and no doubt *was* discerned, in

Plato's *Statesman*, 284d). His first remark, that the virtues are extremes (*akrotētes*)—in the sense of 'high points'—as well as means (*mesotētes*) is taken from *Nicomachean Ethics* 2. 6. 1107^{a}6–8, where Aristotle specifies that 'looked at from the point of view of its essence (*ti ēn einai*) as embodied in its definition (*logos*) virtue is a mean, but from the perspective of what is best and right it is an extreme'. This formulation appears in the pseudo-Pythagoric corpus ('Metopos', *On Virtue* 120. 6–8; 'Theages', *On Virtue* 191. 27 ff. Thesleff), and is attributed to Plato also by Apuleius (2. 5. 228) and by Hippolytus (*Ref.* 1. 19. 16), though without the interesting comparison of virtue to a straight line, the provenance of which is rather problematical. It is possible, as is suggested by Donini (1974: 86 n. 63), that it owes something to Aristotle's advice at *Nicomachean Ethics* 2. 9. 1109^{b}3 ff., where he suggests that we will best attain virtue by pulling hardest away from our favourite of the two extremes on either side of it— even as people do when they want to straighten a warped plank. But this, as Whittaker (1990: 145 n. 502) points out, relates to virtue as a mean, not an extreme. Whittaker in turn proposes a solution based on a passage of Simplicius' *Commentary on the Categories* (237. 29 ff. Kalbfleisch), where he is explaining the difference between the Stoic concepts of *hexis* and *diathesis*, and why they say that the virtues are *diatheseis* (this being, no doubt, a dig at Aristotle, who in *EN* 2. 5 declares that virtue is a *hexis*). A *hexis*, they say, admits of variations of intensity (*epitasis* and *anesis*), while a *diathesis* does not. It is like the straightness of a rod, which may bend, but always returns to its straight position; and so it is with the virtues. This seems to me an excellent suggestion. A. would surely be acquainted with this Stoic image, which is presented also by Diogenes Laertius (7. 227 = *SVF* 3. 536) in the form of saying that a stick may be straight or crooked, but there are no variations in straightness; even so, there are no variations of degree in virtue. A., like other Platonists, has little sympathy with, or understanding of, the dialectical (and paradoxical) aspects of Stoic ethics, but he is perfectly willing to use Stoic terminology or imagery when it suits him. The straight line can, of course, be seen just as readily as an extreme (of perfection) as it can a mean, and this makes it a doubly suitable image for his purposes.

We now pass on to a survey of a number of virtues and vices, very largely taken from *Nicomachean Ethics* 2. First of all, the concept of vices as excesses or deficiencies is taken from 2. 8. Then, generosity (*eleutheriotēs*), and the pair of vices surrounding it, are taken from 2.

7. 1107ᵇ8-10—except that A. has substituted for the Aristotelian *aneleutheria* the term *mikrologia*. The same is the case with the term *ametria*, for 'lack of measure', which does not occur in Aristotle. Both these words occur in Plato, in the same passage of *Republic* 6 (486a5, d5), so that A. may be 'Platonizing' here, but it is also the case that both terms occur contiguously in the Peripatetic treatise *On Virtues and Vices* (1251b15-16), so that A. may simply be inheriting them from the scholastic tradition (*ametria* is also used by Philo, *Virt.* 195, and by Aspasius, *in EN*, 92. 35 Heylbut).

At 184. 24, we find the term *metriopathēs*, 'moderate of passion', to describe the mean of righteous indignation between insensibility and irascibility. This, and its noun *metriopatheia*, is the key term in later times to describe the Peripatetic position in ethics as against the Stoic ideal of *apatheia*, but the actual noun and adjective do not occur before the first century BC, notably in Philo of Alexandria. Diogenes Laertius also employs the term in his account of Aristotelian ethics (5. 31), contrasting it with the Stoic *apathēs*. For a discussion of the Platonist position in this Stoic–Aristotelian dispute, see my article '*Metriopatheia* and *Apatheia*' (Dillon, 1983: 508-17 = 1991: essay 8). There is a good deal of semantic juggling involved in the controversy (is a properly moderated passion a passion at all, after all?), and Plato could be quoted on either side of it. In the *Phaedo*, for instance, he would seem to be on the side of the extirpation of the passions, while in the *Republic* the passionate part of the soul cannot be done away with, but only moderated by the reason and spirit, acting in unison. Platonists on the whole tended to side with Aristotle (though Antiochus of Ascalon seems to have adopted the Stoic ideal of *apatheia*, if we may judge from Cic. *Acad. Pr.* 135, and the Platonist fellow-traveller Philo manages to combine the two ideals by relating them to different degrees of moral progress, cf. the contrast between Aaron and Moses, *Leg. All.* 3. 129-32).

The two extremes in the sphere of anger are mentioned at *Eudemian Ethics* 2. 3. 1221ᵃ15 ff., but also by Arius Didymus (*ap.* Stob. 2. 139. 11 ff.), which is verbally rather closer than A., though the example of an outrage done to one's parents is not attested elsewhere. Similarly, the example of the death of parents, apropos the passion of grief, may be original, though Plato in the *Republic*, both at 3. 387e and 10. 603e-604b, mentions the death of children or siblings as prime sources of grief. This discussion of grief has no parallel in Aristotle.

[In this context, A. uses two terms, *hyperpathēs* and *ametriopathēs*, for which no other source is attested (some late writers use *hyperpathēs*, but only in the sense of 'very grievous', not in this technical sense of 'over-sensitive'). It is even possible that he has coined them himself, though I would doubt this.]

The final example, of excess, deficiency, and the mean in the sphere of courage, is solidly Aristotelian, being discussed in *Nicomachean Ethics* 2. 2. 1104ᵃ20–2 and 2. 7. 1107ᵃ33 ff. (although in this latter passage Aristotle declares that excess in the direction of fearlessness is something we have no name for, and makes 'rash' (*thrasys*) the name for an excess of confidence; but that is a small point).

His final summation (184. 32–6) may owe something to Aristotle's praise of the mean (*EN* 2. 6, esp. 1106ᵇ10 ff.), but it is not particularly close, either verbally or conceptually.

CHAPTER 31

1. This short chapter expounds the Socratic–Platonic doctrine of the involuntariness of vice, by contrast with the voluntariness, or 'autonomy' of virtue. A. begins by once again (cf. ch. 26. 179. 10, above), referring to *Republic* 10. 617e3. Virtue is itself exercisable only in conditions of free will, and one attains to it by the exercise of free will, or 'impulse' (*hormē*)—a term with undeniable Stoic overtones. That is why one is praised for acquiring virtue, which one would not be if it were attainable merely by natural aptitude (*physis*) or a gift from God (*theia moira*)—here a reference to the end of the *Meno*, 99e and 100b (where, however, Socrates comes to the ironic conclusion that virtue, since it is neither natural nor teachable, must be acquired, if at all, by *theia moira*).

[The characterization of the impulse that drives us to virtue as 'ardent (*diapyros*) and noble (*gennaios*), and abiding (*emmonos*)' is notable. All the adjectives are thoroughly Platonic, though they are not recorded as being ever combined with *hormē*. *Diapyros* is used in the *Laws* (2. 664e4) as an epithet of youthful vigour, and *gennaios* in the *Republic* (2. 375a2) as an epithet of a well-bred puppy, with whom the young prospective guardian is being compared, while *emmonos* is used at *Republic* 7. 536e4 to characterize the right sort of learning (*mathēma*)—sc. not that which is dinned in forcibly. One cannot be sure that A. derived this selection of epithets from these sources (he may well have inherited them from the tradition), but at least one can say that the passages referred to have a certain relevance as background to what he wants to say here.]

The corollary of virtue being 'voluntary' (*hekousios*) is that vice is 'involuntary' (*akousios*). Here we run up against a problem of translation. The words *hekōn*, *hekousios*, and their opposites, have a rather wider range of meaning than their usual translations, 'voluntary' and 'involuntary', and this can lead to misunderstanding. The Platonic position, as expounded by A., is obviously not that vice is involuntary in the sense of something one cannot help, but rather that it is something which one cannot *will*, as such. To do something *akōn* may be *either* to do it against one's will, *or* to do it unwittingly, while one thinks one is doing something else. It is this latter meaning that is relevant here. *Kakia*, 'vice', is by definition *kakos*, 'evil', and no one wills himself evil; so that anyone who adopts a vicious course of action does so thinking it to be in some way *good*, if only in so far as it avoids a greater evil. So stated, the Socratic 'paradox' makes reasonably good sense. Even people in the grip of an addiction, let us say, can be seen as reaching for tobacco, whiskey, or cocaine either as a good, or to avoid a greater evil (sc. being deprived of those substances). Vice is therefore a kind of ignorance, even as virtue is a kind of knowledge.

Apuleius presents a very similar account of the doctrine in *de Platone* 2. 11. 236, though expressing himself somewhat more clearly on the subject of the deceptive nature of vice; and so, in a very compressed form, does Hippolytus (*Ref.* 1. 19. 19–21). At 184. 42 ff., A. produces a composite quotation from *Laws* 5. 731c ('And most precious in very truth to every man is, as we have said, the soul. No one, therefore, will voluntarily admit into this most precious thing the greatest evil and live possessing it all his life long'), and *Clitopho* 407d ('Then how, pray, could any man voluntarily choose an evil of such a kind? Any man, you reply, who is mastered by his pleasures. But is not this condition also involuntary, if the act of mastering be voluntary? Thus in every way the argument proves that unjust action is involuntary'). The fact that this same composite reference is to be found also in Hippolytus (*Ref.* 1. 19. 19–21) and in Apuleius (though not in the above parallel passage, but somewhat later, at 2. 17. 244) indicates that we are dealing here with a fairly well-worn piece of school exposition.

[The verb *apoikonomoumai*, 185. 5, here translated 'divest oneself', is worth noting, as not otherwise being attested before Plotinus (*Enn.* I. 4. 6. 16; 5. 9. 1. 6), but from the fact that the noun *apoikonomia* is found in Alexander of Aphrodisias (*de An.* 160. 25 and 163. 35 Bruns), both times in a Stoic context (as the opposite of *eklogē*, 'selection', and synonym of *ekklisis*, both Stoic technical terms), it may be taken to be Stoic in origin.]

The phrase 'by the fear of some greater evil', 185. 7, may embody a verbal reminiscence of *Phaedo* 68d8, but the more immediate source is certainly Aristotle's discussion of the various senses of *akousion* (*EN* 3. 1, cf. esp. 1110^{a}4).

There is also some influence here, in the argument that one is always striving for some good (185. 1–8), from the argument of Socrates against Polus in the *Gorgias* (468b–c) that people do everything they do, whether good or evil or neutral things, 'for the sake of the good (*heneka tou agathou*)' (cf. also *Prt.* 358c–d). The influence of the *Gorgias* becomes increasingly important in the latter part of the chapter, as we shall see.

2. The argument of this section simply develops A.'s previously stated doctrine, by specifying that acting in accordance with *kakia* is that much worse than the simple possession of it, even as action (*energein*) according to a characteristic is more significant than mere possession (*echein*) of it. There is some suggestion of this point in Apuleius (2. 17. 244), but it is closely linked to what follows in A. at the beginning of section 3, rather than to what follows immediately here: 'When witless persons come to possess evil (*possessio*, *hexis*), then the practice (*usus*) of it and actions (*actiones*, cf. *energein*) in accordance with it are committed in ignorance, and so it is worse to do harm than to suffer harm.' It sounds as if both A. and Apuleius are reflecting, in variously garbled forms, a line of argument which first contrasted the basic possession of vice with action in accordance with it, and then went on to make the argument (derived from the *Gorgias*, 469b–c and elsewhere) that doing evil is worse than suffering it. Into this A. has, it seems to me, inserted the independent point that the acceptance that evil acts are *akousia* should not inhibit one from punishing them, since, whether they are committed from ignorance or under the influence of some passion, they are susceptible to reason (*logos*, 're-education') and training (*ethos*, *meletē*—probably another reminiscence of *Phd.* 82b). This latter thesis is a reflection of the position

advanced by Aristotle in *Nicomachean Ethics* 5. 10. 1136ᵃ5 ff., where he says, 'Of involuntary actions (*akousia*) some are to be pardoned, some not to be pardoned. When offences are committed not merely *in* but *as a result of* ignorance, they are pardonable; when made in ignorance but as a result of some passion contrary to both nature and common humanity, they are not to be pardoned.' Aristotle here makes a contrast between ignorance in the normal sense of the word and ignorance in the special, 'Socratic' sense, which is the result of the influence of *pathos*, and it is this latter that A. here is speaking of as ignorance. Actions committed in real ignorance are not crimes at all, and he is not concerned with them.

3. The final section, as I have mentioned above, is very much dependent on various theses advanced in the *Gorgias*. The first has just been alluded to—'it is worse to do evil than to suffer it'—which Socrates presents not only at 469b–c, but at 474b ('For I think that you and I and other men believe that doing injustice is worse than suffering it, and that not paying the penalty is worse than paying it'), and again at the end of the dialogue (527b).

The remark that doing injustice is the mark of a wicked man, but suffering it the mark of a *weak* one is a reference to the statement of Callicles at *Gorgias* 483a–b that doing injustice is only disgraceful *nomōi*, 'by convention', whereas suffering it is disgraceful *physei*, 'by nature'—but laws (*nomoi*) have been made by the weak to shield them against nature.

For the idea that committing injustice is worse (*kakion*) in so far as it is more shameful (*aischion*) we return to *Gorgias* 474c ff.; while for the principle that it is advantageous for the wrongdoer to undergo punishment, and for the comparison with medicine, we may turn to 478b–480b (though the argument occurs also at *R.* 9. 591a–b, whence the expression 'it is advantageous' (*lusitelei*) seems to have been borrowed, 591a6).

The section ends with a definition of punishment derived from the Platonic *Definitions*, 416a33: 'Punishment is a cure (*therapeia*) for the soul after a crime has been committed'—a definition reflected in (if, indeed, it is not stimulated by) Aristotle's dictum in *Nicomachean Ethics* 2. 2. 1104ᵇ16–18 (and at *EE* 2. 1. 1220ᵃ35–6) that 'punishments are sorts of medical treatments (*iatreiai tines*)'. A. is thus solidly behind the remedial theory of punishment.

CHAPTER 32

1. A. now turns, logically enough, to an exposition of the Platonist theory of the emotions (*pathē*), since the *ethical* values, at least, are concerned with the control of these. There are four basic emotions, pleasure (*hēdonē*), distress (*lypē*), desire (*epithymia*), and fear (*phobos*). I choose the term 'distress' to render *lypē*, since we are dealing here, not with the physical sensation, but rather with its psychological counterpart, for both of which the Greek is *lypē*; 'grief', on the other hand, is too narrow in meaning.

The (rather obvious) observation that the virtues are concerned with the emotions goes back ultimately to Aristotle in the *Nicomachean Ethics* (3. 1. 1109^{b}30 ff., and 10. 8. 1178^{a}9 ff.), but we also find it reflected in the Pseudo-Pythagorean corpus, itself dependent here on later Peripateticism (e.g. 'Theages', *On Virtue* 192. 5–6 Thesleff: 'Since ethical virtue is concerned with emotions, and the chief emotions are pleasure and distress (*lypa*), it is obvious that the task of virtue is not the removal of the emotions from the soul, that is, pleasure and distress, but rather in the harmonizing of these.' Compare also 'Metopos', *On Virtue* 119. 8 ff. Thesleff, where the emotions are categorized as the 'matter' (*hyla*) of the virtues).

The definition of emotion which now follows (185. 26) is attested as being Stoic, cf. *SVF* 1. 205: 'emotion according to Zeno is the irrational and unnatural motion of the soul'; and 3. 378 (though the more popular Stoic definition is simply 'excessive impulse', *hormē pleonazousa*), but more probably A. derives it, immediately or otherwise, from the Peripatetic Andronicus (as reported by Aspasius, *in EN* 44. 21–2), who defines it as 'an irrational motion of the soul, prompted by an apprehension (*di' hypolēpsin*) of good or evil'. The additional mention of an apprehension of good or evil would also seem to be Stoic, on the evidence of Aspasius (*in EN* 45. 16 = *SVF* 3. 386), so that Andronicus may simply be borrowing a formulation from the Stoics (Aspasius notes, 44. 20–1, that 'among the older Peripatetics we find no definition of emotion'), but if so, he is introducing an important modification, in that he omits (as does A.) the characterization of emotion as *para physin*, 'contrary to nature' (Pseudo-Andronicus, *On the Emotions*, 1, on the other hand, we may note, gives the basic Stoic definition, including *para physin*!). This denial is an important feature of the Peripatetic opposition to Stoic theory, as Aspasius makes clear, 43. 33–45. 20.

The idea that pleasure and distress are 'motions' in the soul is advanced at *Republic* 9. 583e, but the addition of 'irrational and unnatural' is not to be found in that passage (though at least the former is no doubt implied), while the idea of a *pathos* being *para physin* is to be found at *Timaeus* 64d1 (though this only refers, in fact, to physical pain). This does not all add up, however, to a Platonic definition of *pathos*.

The statement that the emotions are *not* judgements or opinions (*kriseis, doxai*), but rather motions of the irrational parts of the soul is a direct contradiction of the doctrine of Chrysippus (cf. *SVF* 3. 380, 394, 456–63) that they are judgements. In opposing Chrysippus and orthodox Stoicism on this, Platonists and Peripatetics had on their side the figure of Posidonius, as Galen has much satisfaction in relating in *de placitis Hippocratis et Platonis* (e.g. 5. 1. 405 Mü. = Fr. 152 Edelstein–Kidd), but it is not clear that we need to postulate any direct influence of Posidonius on A. here (though he could have been an influence on Arius, and even on Andronicus). Posidonius does, however, refer his definition of emotion (as 'a motion of irrational powers of the soul') directly back to Plato, which would suit A. well.

A. adds an explanatory clause (185. 29–31) which is unfortunately marred by a lacuna. I accept for the purposes of the translation an emendation suggested by Cherniss in his review of Louis (1949: 77), and read *oude* ('not'), after *kai*. Whittaker, more cautiously, leaves a lacuna after *synistatai*. According to the emendation, what A. would be saying is that emotions, as motions of the irrational part of the soul, do not count as actions by *us*, or as being properly in our power. This certainly does not imply that we are not responsible for acts committed under the influence of an emotion. All that A. means here is that a sudden pang of distress or fear, for example, is not in our power to control, and so not properly to be counted as an act of ours. What happens after that, however (i.e. whether we resist the emotion or not), *is* our responsibility. This, at any rate, is what is explained further in the next sentence. All this is by way of refutation of Chrysippus' position that emotions are judgements. If the sensation of fear, for instance, were nothing other than the judgement that *x* is to be feared, we could simply dismiss it from our minds once we had satisfied ourselves intellectually that there was no basis for it; as it is, however, the sensation lingers (although we may well have it under control) even after we have convinced ourselves intellectually that x is not to be feared.

The exegesis of the latter part of the definition permits A. to provide a framework for the distinguishing of the chief emotions: in respect of goods and evils, the presentation or appearance (*emphasis*, a term used by Aristotle and by the Stoics, but not by Plato) of the *presence* of either of them generates either pleasure or distress respectively, while the presentation of the *probable future appearance* of either generates either desire or fear.

2. Once again, on the question of the structuring of the emotions, A., representing the Platonic-Peripatetic tradition, is at pains to contradict the Stoics. The Stoics notoriously declared that all four emotions, pleasure, distress, desire, and fear, were equally basic (e.g. *SVF* 3. 378). Indeed, this passage, from Stobaeus' account of Stoic ethics (*Anth.* 2. 88. 6 ff.), presents desire and fear as the most basic (*proēgeisthai*), with pleasure and distress supervening (*epigignesthai*) on these. This makes quite good sense, in fact, since desire and fear correspond, in Stoic theory, to the basic appetition towards or 'declination' (*ekklisis*) from phenomena which the human organism experiences, and pleasure and distress may logically be seen as supervening on these. A., however, disregards this point, and presents a different argument for the opposite view that desire and fear are secondary. This argument in its turn has something to be said for it. Logically, fear can be 'broken down' into a certain quotient of pleasure (on the slightly odd premiss that one could not even survive without a minimum of pleasure—in just being alive?), and a predominance of distress; while desire is more easily seen as a compound of pleasurable anticipation, and distress at the postponement of actual pleasure (some influence here, no doubt, from the discussion at *Phlb.* 35e–36b about the mixture of pleasure and distress involved in anticipation).

The doctrine that pleasure and distress are the basic emotions could well be derived from such a passage as *Timaeus* 64c–d—where this is not·said, admittedly, but could be seen to be implied by the basic role that they play there. In the later tradition, the basic role of pleasure and distress is recognized by Arius Didymus, in his review of Peripatetic ethics (*ap.* Stob. 2. 138. 21–6, and 142. 20–2), and by Aspasius (*in EN* 42. 13 ff.). Apuleius, we may note, does not include a discussion of the emotions as such, though he mentions pleasure (as being not unqualifiedly evil) in *de Plat.* 2. 12. 238.

3. This short section concerns the ruling out of all other emotions as candidates for being primary (*arkhikoi*), since they too exhibit the mixture of pleasure and distress that characterize desire and fear. The list of secondary emotions is borrowed from *Philebus*, 47e–48a, where '*anger*, fear, *longing*, sorrow, love, *envy*, malice *and suchlike*' are listed as combining distress with 'an unexpected degree of enjoyment'.

4. We next find a division of emotions into 'wild' (*agria*) and 'tame' (*hēmera*), a division which takes its start from a famous passage in the *Republic*, 9. 589a–b, where Plato is depicting justice as the control by the 'inner man' of the lion and the many-headed beast within us, 'like a farmer who cherishes and trains the cultivated (*hēmera*) plants but checks the growth of the wild (*agria*)' (cf. also the earlier passage 588c, where the many-headed beast itself is described as a compound of all beasts, tame and wild). The distinction being made here is of interest, as it focuses on one of the chief points of contention between Peripatetic and Stoic ethics, the ethics of *metriopatheia* as against that of *apatheia*.

This can be seen clearly if we compare this use of the imagery with that of Philo in a notable passage of the *Quaestiones in Genesim* (2. 57), preserved only in the Armenian, but useful none the less. There Philo makes a distinction (since the passage is a comment on Genesis 9: 3 (LXX): 'Every reptile that lives shall be to you for food') between poisonous and tame reptiles, but since he is more under the influence of Stoicism than A., the distinction he makes, in his allegorical exegesis, is between emotions (the poisonous) and the *eupatheiai*, or 'equable states' of Stoic theory (the tame). For A., the distinction is between duly moderated, 'natural' emotions (e.g. being angry to the correct degree at the right things), and immoderate, unnatural ones—though strangely enough, he does not here contrast e.g. moderated anger with immoderate anger, but rather pleasure, distress, anger, etc.—the 'normal' emotions—with such perverse (*ek diastrophēs*, 186. 25) states of mind as *gelōs*, 'mockery', *epichairekakia*, 'Schadenfreude', and *misanthrōpia*, 'misanthropy'. The contrast actually seems to be, not between moderated and immoderate versions of the same emotion, but rather between those emotions which admit of a moderated ('tame') form, and those which do not. Aristotle does recognize a class of *pathē* which do not admit of a mean (*EN* 2. 6. 1107ᵃ8 ff.), on the ground that an idea of badness (*phaulotēs*) is built in to them, and *epichairekakia* is one of these, but the others are shamelessness (*anaischyntia*) and envy (*phthonos*), so A. seems to be innovating somewhat here.

He is innovating, though, in a Platonic direction, since both of his other 'wild' *pathē* have possible Platonic pedigrees. The use of *gelōs* in a pejorative sense is notable, though it is not uncommon in ordinary Greek usage, e.g. the expression *gelōta ophlein*, 'to be laughed at' (lit. 'to incur a liability to laughter')—though *katagelōs* would be a more explicit term. Its inclusion among the 'wild' passions, though, may owe something to such a passage as *Philebus* 49e–50a, where 'laughter at the misfortunes of one's friends' is being discussed (*phthonos*, we may note, is also brought in here, 50a2, etc.). As for *misanthrōpia*, it could be derived from *Phaedo* 89d, though it is not there explicitly condemned as a *pathos*. For Philo later, however, it is a serious vice (e.g. *Spec. Leg.* 3. 102, ranked with murder of one's children).

5–7. A. turns for the remainder of the chapter to a discussion of pleasure, based heavily on *Philebus* 31–55, as is suitable, since that is Plato's major discussion of pleasure.

The initial point about pleasure and distress being kinds of motion in the soul, distress being motion *away from* the natural state (*para physin*), pleasure motion *towards* the natural state (*kata physin*), and the natural state as a sort of quiescence median between the two of them, is taken from *Philebus* 31d–33a, and also from 42c–d, where the doctrine is resumed (though the topic also occurs at *R.* 9. 583c–584a and *Ti.* 64c–d).

[The only notable innovation in terminology here is A.'s use of *katastēma*, 'state' (186. 34), for Plato's *katastasis* (*Phlb.* 42d6). It is a Hellenistic word, though not the exclusive property of any one philosophical school (if anything, it has Epicurean associations, cf. their category of 'catastematic' pleasures, Usener, *Epicurea* 416). Aspasius uses it (*in EN* 143. 22), we may note, in very much the same context, where he is discussing the state intermediate between pleasure and distress.]

The distinction of various kinds of pleasures is taken from *Philebus* 31d–32c; the contrast between those which mix with their opposites and those which remain 'pure and uncontaminated' (*katharai kai eilikrineis*) is made at 32c–d, cf. *eilikrinesin te . . . kai ameiktois*, 32c7–8), but developed at greater length later, at 50d–52d; pleasures involving memory are mentioned at 33c ff.; hope is mentioned at 32b–c, but again at 36a ff. The contrast between immoderate and moderate pleasures is set out at 45d ff., while the remark that there is nothing 'proper to true being' (*ousiōdes*, 187. 4) in pleasure is taken from 53c, where it is stated that 'pleasure is always a process of becoming (*genesis*)—that with pleasure there is no such thing at all as being (*ousia*)'. Likewise, the statement that 'pleasure and pain are intermingled' is taken from 46c.

Apuleius provides a parallel, but more summary account of pleasure at *de Platone* 2. 12. 238. Plainly a coherent doctrine of pleasure has been abstracted from the *Philebus*, with some appeal to the other passages mentioned above from the *Republic* and the *Timaeus*, at some earlier point in the tradition. Arius' account of the relation of pleasure to happiness in Platonic doctrine at Stobaeus, *Anthologia*, 2. 53. 11 ff. does not concord with A. particularly closely, but he is not really discussing the same subject. He does, however, at 53. 17–18, describe pleasure as 'supervenient' (*epigennēmatikon*)—a term originally Stoic, compare *SVF* 3. 504—while rationality (*eulogistia*) is 'primary' (*proēgoumenon*), in the constitution of happiness, language which finds an echo in this chapter, at 187. 3–4. I feel that we cannot dismiss the possibility that in a different context Arius might have presented an exposition of the Platonic doctrine of the emotions very close to this.

CHAPTER 33

A. next turns to a discussion of friendship (*philia*) in its various forms, beginning with the most perfect kind. His treatment of this topic is heavily dependent on Aristotle's exposition in book 8 of the *Nicomachean Ethics*, while drawing whenever possible on Platonic passages. There is a parallel treatment by Apuleius in *de Platone* 2. 13–14. 238–9, indicating a fairly immediate common source (Arius' surviving summary of Aristotelian doctrine on friendship, however, we may note (*ap.* Stob. 2. 143. 1–16), is not particularly close). Aristotle had made a discussion of friendship an accepted part of ethical (and political) theory, and the two main Hellenistic Schools dealt with the topic. Chrysippus wrote a work *On Friendship*, in at least two books (*SVF* 3. 724), and one *On Love* (*SVF* 3. 716), and Epicurus dealt with it at various places in his works (22e–i, o Long–Sedley). Some aspects of the Stoic doctrine are reflected here, as we shall see.

Aristotle had in *Nicomachean Ethics* 8. 2. (1155[b]18–19) distinguished three types, or grades, of *philia*, according as it was entered into for the sake of the good, or of pleasure, or of usefulness, and they are all dealt with here, though not distinguished in quite this way. A. deals first with the highest form of friendship, then briefly mentions family ties and business relations (sect. 2), and lastly (sects. 3–4) deals with erotic relationships, of which he distinguishes three types.

One might perhaps expect a Platonist to try to make some use of the *Lysis* in a discussion of *philia*, but there is very little sign that A. has that dialogue in view at all. Its eristic and aporetic nature may be sufficient explanation of that, though a faithful Platonist might have felt that in fact Aristotle's doctrine in *Nicomachean Ethics* 8–9 was little more than a formalization of various doctrines present in solution in the *Lysis*. For instance, the idea that to be 'dear' one must be useful (*khrēsimos*) is expressed at 210c–d, though Aristotle takes this as only one cause of friendship; then, the concept that 'like is friend to like', provided that both be good, is aired at 214a ff. (only to be shot down, however), and accepted by Aristotle at 8. 3. 1156^{b}7 ff. (though A. here produces a quotation, not from the *Lysis*, but from the *Laws*, where the doctrine is stated more positively). However, it remains true that no substantial reference is made to the *Lysis*.

1. A. begins with a definition of friendship derived from Aristotle, *Nicomachean Ethics* 8. 2. 1155^{b}33–4: 'Friendship, then, consists in mutual goodwill (*eunoia en antipeponthosi*).' Apuleius produces very much the same definition (*de Plat.* 2. 13–14. 238): 'Friendship is sociable, consists in unanimity (*consensus*), and is reciprocal (*reciproca* = A.'s *antistrophos*), giving a fair exchange of enjoyment, when one returns love equally.' This latter sentiment, which A. renders as 'wishing one's neighbour to flourish equally with oneself', while derivable from such passages as *Nicomachean Ethics* 8. 4. 1156^{b}9–10, or 8. 7. 1157^{b}31– 1158^{a}1, also reflects Stoic doctrine that 'we treat our friends as we treat ourselves' (*SVF* 3. 631)—which is in its turn derived from the Pythagorean dictum that a friend should be 'another I'.

He then caps this with a (lightly modified) quotation from Plato, *Laws* 4. 716c, which is actually part of a discussion, not of friendship, but of means of attaining likeness to God (the same position is, however, presented already, albeit in aporetic form, in Plato's *Lysis*, 214a–216b). In fact, this quotation of Plato can also be seen as validating Stoic doctrine (*SVF* 3. 631), to the effect that 'friendship exists only among the good (*spoudaioi*), on account of their similarity (*homoiotēs*) . . . But no friendship exists among the bad (*phauloi*), and no bad man has a friend.'

At this point, Apuleius inserts a short disquisition on enmity (*de Plat.* 2. 13–14, 239), which may be a development of his own, but which follows on logically enough from the definition of friendship. Arius Didymus, however, in his discussion of the Peripatetic doctrine of friendship, *ap.* Stob. 2. 143. 1–16, gives no place to enmity; but his treatment, as I have said, differs significantly from those of A. and Apuleius.

2. A. now briefly surveys the other two types of *philia* distinguished by Aristotle, which he terms the natural (*physikē*) and the political or 'club' variety (*politikē–hetairikē*).

Aristotle discusses *philia* between family members at some length in *Nicomachean Ethics* 8. 12. 1161^{b}16 ff., though he only describes this type of friendship as *physikē* much later, at 1163^{b}24, and then only incidentally. Aspasius, however, gives it this term in his discussion of the subject (*in EN* 178. 16), where he uses the formulation to resolve the problem as to whether love between family members is based on pleasure or utility—a natural tie of this sort transcends that dichotomy. Arius (*ap.* Stob. 143. 5–6) uses Aristotle's own term for this type of friendship, *syngenikē* ('kin' or 'congenital'), but gives its base as *physis*. Apuleius does not use the adjectival form, but is otherwise very close to A.: *necessitudinum et liberorum amor naturae congruus est.*

Friendship of the 'political' type (under which he would subsume both the comradeship of political-social clubs, or *hetaireiai*, and a wide range of business relationships), Aristotle deals with in 8. 9. 1159^{a}25 ff., but mentions again at the beginning of chapter 12. The point about 'reciprocity of goodwill (*to antistrophon tēs eunoias*)' is not made in so many words by Aristotle, but is implied in his treatment of business relationships in 8. 3–4, and in his discussion of *eunoia* later in 9. 5—certainly if *antistrophon* can be understood to comprehend not just the return of any affection or goodwill at all, but the return of an *equal degree* of affection. It is certainly inequalities in this regard that characterize the lower sorts of *philia* in Aristotle's theory.

[The word *epikechrōsmenai* (187. 17), here rendered 'having a superficial colouring', is very probably borrowed from a well-known passage of the *Seventh Letter* (340d7: *doxais epikechrōsmenoi*).]

3. To this discussion of friendship is appended a discussion of erotic love (*erōs*), which is admittedly closely involved with it, both in the *Lysis* (where it constitutes the lead-in to the discussion of *philia*), but also in Aristotle, *Nicomachean Ethics* 8, where it comes under the heading of 'friendship for the sake of pleasure'. Arius Didymus men-

tions *erōs* just before *philia* in his review of Peripatetic ethics, defining it as follows (*ap.* Stob. 2. 124. 24–6): 'Of love, one sort is concerned with friendship, another with sexual intercourse (*synousia*), and another with both; for which reason one is noble (*spoudaios*), the other base (*phaulos*), the third median between the two.'

A.'s discussion of *erōs* here seems to be influenced by that of Plato in *Laws* 8. 837a–d, though without direct verbal echoes. However, I think it is worth quoting the passage at some length. The Athenian Stranger is here concerned to formulate proper laws for regulating relations between the sexes, and in that connection he feels it necessary 'to discern the true nature of friendship and desire and what are called "loves"', because there are two distinct kinds of love (confusingly called by the same name), and a third type that is a mixture of the two.

Friendship is the name we give to the affection of like for like, in point of virtue (*kat' aretēn*), and of equal for equal; and also that of the needy for the rich, which is of the opposite kind; and when either of these feelings is intense we call it 'love' . . . The friendship which occurs between opposites is terrible and fierce and seldom reciprocal (*koinon*) amongst men, while that based on similarity is gentle and reciprocal throughout life. The kind which arises from a blend of these presents difficulties—first, to discover what the man affected by this third kind of love wishes to obtain, and in the next place, because the man himself is at a loss, being dragged in opposite directions by the two tendencies, of which the one bids him enjoy the bloom of his beloved, while the other forbids him. For he that is in love with the body and hungering after its bloom, as it were that of a ripening fruit, urges himself on to take his fill of it, paying no respect to the disposition of the beloved; whereas he that counts bodily desire as but secondary, and puts looking (*horōn*) in place of loving (*erōn*), with soul lusting really for soul, regards the bodily satisfaction of the body as an outrage, and, reverently worshipping temperance, courage, nobility, and wisdom, will desire to live always chastely in company with the chaste object of his love. But the love which is blended of these two kinds is that which we have described just now as third. (trans. Bury, slightly altered)

This passage is itself dependent to some extent on the myth of the *Phaedrus* (esp. 253c–256d), but sets out more clearly than is the case there the three types of love with A. is concerned to distinguish here. Apuleius too distinguishes three sorts of love at *de Platone* 2. 14. 239–40, in very much the same terms, though he characterizes the best sort of love explicitly as 'divine', and the basest sort as 'earthy' (*terrenus*).

[The description of the lowest form of love at 187. 29 as 'bestial' (*boskēmatōdēs*) is probably derived from the description at *Republic* 9. 586a of those devoted to sensual pleasures: 'like beasts (*boskēmatōn dikēn*), looking downwards always, and bowed down over their tables, they feed themselves (*boskontai*), grazing and copulating', though the adjectival form only occurs later (e.g. Ocellus Lucanus, p. 57. 25. 3 Harder).]

4. We now turn to the proper object of love—*ho axierastos*, 'the truly lovable', or 'worthy object of love', a term first attested in Xenophon (*Cyr.* 5. 2. 9), but after that primarily in the Stoics, and then in such authors as Philo (e.g. *Migr.* 36; *Vit. Mos.* 1. 59) and Plutarch (*Comm. Not.* 1073a–b = *SVF* 3. 719), who are themselves influenced by Stoic terminology. Indeed, the rather curious way in which the *object* of love is characterized here as 'neither bad nor good', rather than Love (*Erōs*) himself, as in the *Symposium* (202b), may have something to do with the fact that one of the Stoic 'paradoxes' concerning the Sage was that he alone was *axierastos* (*SVF* 3. 598. 719). This would then be a Platonist contradiction of that position. If so, however, it surely results in an incoherence. It would make sense to say that the object of love in general may be either good, or bad, or middling between the two, since there are three varieties of love, but such a point should not have been tied in with the characterization of Eros himself, which follows on from it immediately, taken from the same section of the *Symposium* (202d–e)—'a daemon . . . transmitting to men what comes from the gods'—with a little phrase thrown in, significantly, from *Phaedrus*, 246c3, where the soul that loses its wings is described as ending up in an 'earthy body'. The object even of noble love may indeed be initially 'neither bad nor good', in the sense that he/she would have potentialities in either direction, but ultimately becomes good, if the love is successful; Love itself, however, remains a 'daemon', and thus intermediate.

The remark that only the noble sort of love can be reckoned as *tekhnikē*, an 'art' or 'craft', is notable. Whittaker (1990: 68) may be right to make reference back to *Symposium* 186c5, where Eryximachus declares that the essence of following his art (as a doctor)—being *tekhnikos*—consists in satisfying the good and healthy elements in the body, and refusing to satisfy bad and unhealthy elements—this being a sort of scientific 'love'—but the true influence may lie in another direction. We find a mention of an 'art of love' (*erōtikē tekhnē*) in the *Phaedrus* (257a7), where Socrates is rounding off his palinode. The

Neoplatonist Hermias, in commenting on this (*in Phaedr.* 207. 17 ff.
Couvreur), makes reference to the *Alcibiades*, as follows:

> What is the nature of this 'art of love'? It is what he himself has demon-
> strated in the *Alcibiades*, where he teaches that one must first seek out the
> worthy object of love (*ho axierastos*) and discern whom one should love (for
> one should not love everyone, but only the large-minded (*megalophrōn*), who
> despises secondary things); then, after deciding to love, not even speak to him
> until the critical moment comes when he is ready to listen to philosophical
> discourses; and then, when he is ready to listen, take him in hand and teach
> him the principles of love, and so generate in him a reciprocal love (*anterōs*).

Here there seems to me to be a reference not to any particular passage of the *Alcibiades*, but rather to the theme of the whole dialogue,
which constituted for later Platonists a paradigm case of how the wise
man should love (Hermias was presumably not the first to think of
seeing this reference in the *Phaedrus* passage). I would suggest that it
is in fact the *Alcibiades*, or at least a scholastic interpretation of it,
that is the dominant influence in the present passage also.

There may also be some influence from the Stoic doctrine (which
itself may be influenced by the *Alcibiades*) that any love that the sage
would indulge in would be a 'science' (*epistēmē*, *SVF* 3. 717), and
therefore an 'art' (Cleanthes, we may note, wrote a work entitled
Erōtikē Tekhnē (*SVF* 1. 481), but we do not know whether he made
this point in it).

At any rate, such an art of love would have its seat in the rational
part (*logistikon*) of the soul. The *theōrēmata* (what I have translated
'aims', but which could also be rendered, perhaps, 'principal heads')
of this art or science are listed as three: (1) 'getting to know' (*gnōnai*)
or discerning (*epikrinein*) the *axierastos*; (2) 'gaining possession'
(*ktasthai*) of him, by making his acquaintance; and (3) 'making use'
(*chrēsthai*) of him, by exhorting him to, and training him in, virtue, so
that he may become a 'perfect practitioner' (*askētēs teleios*) of it, and
that thus true friendship may result (as between equals who are also
good), instead of the relationship of lover and beloved—in other
words, that *anterōs* should be generated in the beloved, as Hermias
discerns as being prescribed in the *Alcibiades*—and as is certainly
attested to by 'Alcibiades' himself in his famous tribute to Socrates in
the *Symposium* (222b).

The postulation of a triad of *gnōsis*, *ktēsis*, and *chrēsis* is obviously
relevant to the acquisition of the tools of any art or craft, but it may
be that A. is being original in applying it to the art of love. At any

rate, Apuleius shows no sign of such a development, though he otherwise closely parallels A. What we may be seeing here is the bare bones of a Platonist *Ars Amatoria*, a sort of philosophic answer to the much less edifying handbooks which must have abounded by this time, and of which Ovid's treatise is a good example, on how to succeed in love. Cleanthes' treatise, mentioned above, may be an earlier example of this philosophic genre, and we find a later, very much Neoplatonized exposition in Proclus' *Commentary on the Alcibiades*, 30. 5–37. 18 Westerink (on the various classes of love), and 133. 17–140. 2 West. (on the proper object of love).

We may also, I think, see a reference to such treatises in the Anonymous *Theaetetus* Commentary (8. 23–7), where the author, apropos *Theaetetus* 143d, remarks that 'in treatises on Love (*en tois erōtikois*) it is declared that it is the task of the good man (*ho spoudaios*) to identify (*gnōnai*) the proper object of love (*axierastos*)'. This has been thought, both by Diels and Schubart, and by Whittaker (1990: 151 n. 548), to be a reference to dialogues such as the *Phaedrus* or the *Symposium* (though indeed the *Alcibiades* would be more apposite, one would think), but it does not seem to me necessary that the author is referring to Plato at all, though doubtless to works which draw on Platonic doctrine.

Although I suggest that an exegesis of the *Alcibiades* is the chief inspiration for this passage, some study of the *Lysis* may also play its part. Certainly the point about not spoiling the beloved (under the heading of *ktēsis*) seems to owe much to *Lysis* 205b–206b, where Socrates is instructing Hippothales in how *not* to approach his beloved.

Lastly, the reference at 188. 4 to 'demonstrating to him that life in his present state is not worth living' is a direct quotation from *Symposium* 216a1–2, where Alcibiades is paying tribute to Socrates' effect on him, showing clearly that the relationship between Alcibiades and Socrates is paradigmatic for the whole later Platonist discussion of friendship.

CHAPTER 34

The topic of friendship leads for A., as it does for Aristotle (cf. particularly *EN* 8. 12–13), from the study of ethics to that of politics, since friendship concerns relations of various sorts within civil society.

Apuleius, we may note, does not follow on directly from friendship and love to politics, but interposes a number of chapters (on punishments, the man of moderate virtue, the Sage, and likeness to God) before turning, in chapters 24–8 (sects. 255–63) to the topic of politics, starting with a discussion of the ideal city of the *Republic* (255–8), and then turning to an examination of the institutions proposed in the *Laws* for an actual state (259–63), along with some discussion of corrupt types of citizen and regime, taken from *Republic* 8. As we can see, this corresponds in broad terms to the procedure followed by A.

1. A. begins by making a distinction between 'non-hypothetical' (*anhypothetoi*) constitutions (188. 8), such as that of the *Republic*, and those 'based on an hypothesis' (*ex hypotheseōs*, 188. 36), such as those of the *Laws* and *Letters* 7 and 8. The terminology here is interesting. *Anhypothetos* must in this context mean 'without any limiting conditions', in the sense of natural or social features which one would have to take into account, or 'hypothesize'—that is to say, an ideal state built up from nothing, as is the case with that of the *Republic*; while the states of the *Laws* and the *Letters* postulate certain limiting conditions of situation and population. This terminology is reflected also in Apuleius (26. 259), as a distinction between a *civitas sine evidentia*— perhaps, 'without clear limiting conditions'—and one *cum aliqua substantia*, 'with certain postulates', but the actual Greek terms used in this connection (though the terms *anhypothetos* and *ex hypotheseōs* are Platonic (*R.* 6. 510b7, 511b6)) do not seem to occur in conjunction in any other extant authority before the late Neoplatonic anonymous *Prolegomena to Platonic Philosophy* (26. 35–45). There, however, the distinction is presented as basic Platonic doctrine (a third type, the constitution *ex epanorthōseōs*, 'resulting from reform', is presented as distinct here, whereas A. recognizes it only as a subdivision—*ek diorthōseōs*, 188. 37—of those *ex hypotheseōs*). It is worth presenting the whole passage, as it agrees closely with A.'s exposition, and helps to clarify it:

There are three kinds of constitution: the reformed (*ex epanorthōseōs*) state, the hypothetical (*ex hypotheseōs*) state, and the non-hypothetical (*aneu tēs hypotheseōs*—later, *anhypothetos*) state. The reformed state is attained when we mend our own evil ways and return to our natural uncorrupted condition; the hypothetical state, when certain laws and inherent characteristics of the state are taken as given; and the non-hypothetical state when nothing is regarded as given by tradition, but everything is common property, so that mine is

yours and yours is mine, and the possessions of the individual are his own
and at the same time not his own. The reformed state is treated in the
Letters, the hypothetical state in the *Laws*, and the non-hypothetical in the
Republic. (trans. Westerink, slightly adapted)

The 'hypothetical' and 'non-hypothetical' types of constitution
could be seen as being contrasted by Plato in *Laws* 5. 739a–e, where
he first recalls in general terms the ideal state of the *Republic*, and
then makes clear that on this occasion he is going to accept certain
limitations (though he does not use the term *hypothesis*), such as the
preservation of private property and the family; and also by Aristotle
at the beginning of book 4 of the *Politics* (1288^b21 ff.), where, in contrasting the ideal constitution with that which is best in given circumstances, he actually uses the term *ex hypotheseōs*—from which the later
scholastic terminology doubtless takes its start.

There now follows, for the rest of section 1 and all of section 2, a
summary sketch of the ideal state of the *Republic*, without notable
additions or deviations. The term *apolemos*, 'free from war' (188. 10),
to describe the first state of *Republic* 2 (369b–372e), is not Platonic,
and actually rather poetical, but apt enough; war is brought on by the
onset of luxury, and that in turn leads to the creation of a guardian
class, such as is characteristic of the second, 'fevered' state. What follows is primarily taken from books 3 and 4, though with some
phrases borrowed from elsewhere. The actual expression 'divided into
three elements' (*diēirēmenē trichēi*, 18. 14) is only used later, in book 9.
580d3–5; and the word *phrouroi* used to characterize the Guardians in
the same line is not used by Plato in this context (though he uses it
in another one later, at 8. 560b9), but by Aristotle, at *Politics* 2. 5.
1264^a26, to gloss Plato's term *phylakes*. Such details simply serve to
show once again that a scholastic tradition has been at work.

2. This section is chiefly taken up with an exposition of the famous
paradox about the necessity of kings becoming philosophers, or vice
versa, uttered first at *Republic* 5. 473c–d, but repeated later in *Letter*
7. 326a–b, and the language here is a complex mixture of the two
passages—with, however, the latter predominating, perhaps because
more succinct. The principle of each of the three classes in the state
doing the work proper to it is expounded in the *Republic* at various
points, but cf. especially book 4. 433a–434c and 443b–c.

3. The sequence of five types of constitution is first adumbrated at
the end of *Republic* 4 (445d), but only taken up again in book 8

(543d–544a), when the thread of Socrates' discourse is resumed after his long digression. Notable here is A.'s ranking of democracy ahead of oligarchy, contrary to Plato's own preference in the *Republic* (cf. 545c, 555b ff.). As Whittaker (1990: 152 n. 562) suggests in his note, the strong probability is that A. is here accommodating the scheme of the *Republic* to the discussion of types of constitution presented at *Statesman* 291d–292a, in which monarchy, aristocracy, and democracy are first listed as three types of law-based constitution, from which two more, lawless or 'violent', ones may then be derived, oligarchy and tyranny (democracy, the Eleatic Stranger says rather dismissively, is given the same name whether the masses rule by force or by consent). This is no doubt the explanation of the order of constitutions, rather than that A. is concerned to promote democracy. There is no need to propose a transposition of *dēmokratikēn* and *oligarchikēn*, the expedient resorted to by Hermann. Apuleius, we may note, at *de Platone* 2. 262, preserves the order presented in the *Republic*.

4. A. now turns to the constitutions *ex hypotheseōs*, 'based on the presence of certain conditions'. I have discussed the basis for this distinction above, in the Commentary on section 1. The subdivision 'emended' (*ek diorthōseōs*), in reference to Plato's legislative suggestions in *Letters* 7 and 8, alludes to the circumstance that Plato is there trying to rectify a given situation, brought about by Dion's expulsion of Dionysius II, and then his own murder by Callippus (cf. esp. *Ep.* 7. 334c–337e, and 8. 355a–357d—where the proposals for reform are put into the mouth of the dead Dion).

The reference to 'diseased' states is presumably a reference to *Laws* 1. 628d, where Plato compares the usual sort of legislation, which makes its provisions with a view to warfare, to medical regulations for the care of a sick body. A. generalizes this, then, to a reference to all antecedent conditions which might limit one's discretion in creating an ideal state, such as the possession of a certain population or physical situation (cf. *Lg.* 1. 625c–e, where Clinias specifies conditions in Crete).

[The phrase *hoi en mesogaiāi oikountes* ('those situated inland') at 188.44, A. may indeed, as Whittaker (1990: 71) suggests, have borrowed from the *Phaedo* (111a4–5), but if so, it is a purely verbal reminiscence, since the phrase has a different reference there (opposed to 'in the air'). Most of the terminology of this passage, however, we may note, is not derived from Plato, nor even from Aristotle (such words as *parathalattios*, 'by the sea', *pezomakhia*, 'land warfare', and *geōlophos*, 'gently rolling country').]

The doctrine of the community of wives of *Republic* 5 (cf. 457c–d) is here minimally alluded to, by way of denying it of this sort of constitution. It is plainly not a feature of Plato's political theory that A. is concerned to stress.

5. He now sums up, in a passage that draws heavily on the *Statesman*, particularly on the passage 303d–305e, comprising the final definition of the statesman. It is here that the art of statesmanship (*politikē tekhnē*) is stated to hold in subordination to it the arts of war, generalship, and the administration of justice, in the sense that it decides when and how these arts are to be used (cf. esp. 304b, 304e). We may note that Plato includes rhetoric as one of the main subordinate arts to statesmanship, but A. ignores it here.

The statement at the outset that politics is an art both theoretical and practical is probably ultimately derived in its phraseology from Aristotle, *Nicomachean Ethics* 6. 8. 1141^{b}23 ff., where he equates *politikē* and *phronēsis*, or 'practical wisdom', and divides it into a theoretical, or 'architectonic' aspect, and a practical one, but is in substance derivable from the above-mentioned passage of the *Statesman*. Apuleius presents the same thought at *de Platone* 232 ('[Politics] . . . he [Plato] does not see as at work only on the practical level and in the administration of affairs, but in its capability for discerning the universal' (*nec solum agentem atque in ipsis administrationibus rerum spectari, sed ab ea universa discerni*)). It is notable that Arius Didymus uses very much this terminology (*ap.* Stob. 2. 145. 15–16) to describe Peripatetic ethical virtue—*hexis theōretikē kai prohairetikē kai praktikē tōn en praxesi kalōn*, 'a state concerned with the contemplation and choice and performance of what is fine in the sphere of actions' (A. also uses the term *prohairetikē*, 'such as to choose', which I have rendered here—rather loosely, perhaps—'the aim of which is'). This contrasts, it must be said, with the characterization of politics back in chapter 3. 153. 38–42, where it is definitely stated to be a part of *practical* philosophy. It might be argued, certainly, that the contradiction is more apparent than real. In the context, all A. need mean here is that politics *theorizes* about the application of various remedies in practical situations. This may, however, be to treat A. rather too charitably. It is just as likely to be a case of his following different sources in the two passages.

A.'s political theory, then, while being derived from the obvious sources of the *Republic* and the *Laws* (though suppressing some of the more bizarre proposals of the former work), can be seen to be influenced significantly also by the theorizing of the *Statesman*, while adopting, as one would expect, a certain amount of Aristotelian terminology.

CHAPTER 35

1. The contrast between the philosopher and the sophist is a fairly obvious philosophical *topos* (an example from before A. in Philo, *Post. Cain.* 150; from after him in Proclus, *in Prm.* 695. 26 ff. Cousin). It derives a good deal of its ammunition from Plato's remarks in the *Sophist*, as we shall see. Why A. chooses to round off his work with this subject, however, is not so clear, though one could make suggestions. It reads a little like a warning against accepting inferior imitations of the real thing, which in A.'s own day (assuming him to be a second-century figure) had considerable relevance, since he lived in the great days of the Second Sophistic.

The claim to have described the characteristics of the philosopher is a reference back most properly to the first three chapters of the work, where he detailed, first, the requirement of the philosophic character, and then the proper subjects of his concern, so there is an element of 'ring composition' here. The reference to 'being available for hire (*mistharnia*) by young men' is inspired by *Sophist* 231d ('the hired hunter of rich young men'), but actually employs the terminology (*mistharnountōn*) of *Republic*, 6. 493a, where sophists are also being referred to. The contrast between appearance and reality in the case of the sophist is taken from *Sophist* 233b–c (*sophoi phainontai . . . ouk ontes ge*).

The description of the sophist 'retreating into an area so dark that it is difficult to discern anything clearly' is borrowed from the later passage, *Sophist* 253e–254a: 'The sophist takes refuge in the darkness of not-being, where he is at home and has the knack of feeling his way; and it is the darkness of the place that makes him so hard to perceive'—though the actual adjective *dysdioratos*, 'difficult to discern', is not only not Platonic, but found nowhere else in surviving Greek literature.

2. This contrast between the respective subject-matter (*hylē*) of philosopher and sophist leads A. to make a contrast between being and not-being which in its turn owes much to the *Sophist*, first 257b–c

and 258e–259b (not-being is not the contrary of being, but rather 'the different'); then back to 238c–d, for the thought that absolute not-being is 'unthinkable, not to be spoken of or uttered or expressed (*adianoēton te kai arrhēton kai aphthengton kai alogon*)'—though A. manages to use none of these epithets, but rather two others, *anhyparkton* and *anennoēton*, which are not attested before the Hellenistic era—and that 'it reduces one who is refuting its claims to such straits that, as soon as he sets about doing so, he is forced to contradict himself'; and finally to the whole passage 255e–259d, a survey of the five 'greatest kinds', which shows that there is any number of true statements asserting that 'what is' in a sense 'is not', as being *different* from being.

[Some aspects of the terminology here are notable. The phrase *katho exakouetai* (189. 23) is not easy to render. This use of the passive of *exakouō*, in the sense of 'be understood', is found only in the Aristotelian commentators (Alexander Aphr., *in APr.* 166. 1 Wallies; Ammonius, *in Int.* 205. 12), as Whittaker (1990: 72 n. 571) points out. I have translated: 'to the extent that one can attribute a sense to it'; perhaps, 'in the sense in which it should be understood'? The term *synemphasis*, which I have rendered 'secondary relationship', occurs otherwise only in Athenaeus, *Deipnosophistae* 7. 325b, and Sextus Empiricus, *M.* 7. 239, where the term is identified as Stoic. A *synemphasis*, as it appears from these passages, is something which is implied in a given statement, and is to be understood along with it.

CHAPTER 36

This little concluding chapter contains nothing of doctrinal interest, but some interesting terminology.

First of all, the word *dogmatopoiia*, 'body of doctrine' seems not to be otherwise attested in the purely Hellenic tradition, though it is common enough in the Judaeo-Christian tradition, beginning with Aristobulus, as quoted by Eusebius, *Praeperatio Evangelica* 13. 12. 1. There seems no particular reason for this.

Then, the quasi-apology made by A., that 'some things have been presented in proper order (*tetagmenōs*), others somewhat randomly and out of order (*sporadēn kai ataktōs*)', seems hardly fair to himself, since he has followed a fairly coherent sequence of topics in logic, physics, and ethics; but he may mean that in some cases (such as the long passage in the middle of the work where he is really summarizing the *Timaeus*) he is following Plato in an orderly manner, whereas in others he is picking out doctrines from various works. However, this may just be a generalized sort of apology for any incoherences the reader may discern.

Finally, the protreptic remark that the present work may at least give one the capability to explore the subject more deeply on one's own is to be found in various forms at the conclusion of other similar texts, though mainly in the medical and theosophical traditions, e.g. Galen, *Scripta minora* 1. 81. 17–18 Marquardt; 2. 8. 20–3 Müller; *Corpus Hermeticum* 11. 22; Iamblichus, *de Myst.* 10. 8. 293. 14–15 Des Places.

The term *heuretikos* (189. 32), 'capable of discovering', may well embody a reference to the passage of *Republic* 5. 455b, where it is stated that the person of good natural ability (*euphyēs*) 'will be able on the basis of brief instruction to discover much for himself on the subject he is studying', since it is persons of good natural ability which A. calls for back in chapter 1 as suitable candidates for philosophical instruction.

BIBLIOGRAPHY

A. Texts and Translations of Alcinous

HERMANN, C. F. (1853) (ed.), *Alcinoou Didaskalikos tōn Platōnos dogmatōn*, in *Platonis dialogi secundum Thrasylli tetralogias dispositi*, vi, Leipzig; 2nd edn., 1884; 3rd edn., 1907: 152–89.

INVERNIZZI, G. (1976), *Il Didaskalikos di Albino e il medioplatonismo: saggio di interpretazione storico-filosofica con introduzione e commento del Didaskalikos*, 2 vols., Rome.

LOUIS, P., (1945), *Albinos, Epitome*, Les Belles Lettres edn., Paris and Rennes.

WHITTAKER, J. (1990), *Alcinoos, Enseignement des doctrines de Platon*, Les Belles Lettres edn., Paris.

B. Texts of Other Authors Commonly Quoted

APULEIUS, *Opuscules philosophiques et fragments*, ed. with trans. J. Beaujeu, Budé edn., Paris, 1973

ATTICUS, *Fragments*, ed. É. Des Places, Budé edn., Paris, 1977.

CALCIDIUS, *In Timaeum*, ed. J. H. Waszink, London and Leiden, 1962.

NUMENIUS, *Fragments*, ed. É. Des Places, Budé edn., Paris, 1973.

PHILO ALEXANDRINUS, *Opera*, ed. L. Cohn and P. Wendland, 7 vols., Berlin 1896–1915.

—— ed. with trans. F. H. Colson and G. H. Whitaker, 10 vols., with 2 supplementary vols. ed. by R. Marcus, Loeb Classical Library, Harvard and London, 1930–53.

PLUTARCH, *Moralia*, various eds., 7 vols., Teubner, Leipzig, 1959– .

—— various eds., 17 vols. Loeb Classical Library, Harvard and London, 1927–76.

POSIDONIUS, *The Fragments*, ed. L. Edelstein and I. G. Kidd, 3 vols., Cambridge, 1972–88.

Pythagorica: The Pythagorean Texts of the Hellenistic Period, ed. H. Thesleff, Abo, 1965.

SEXTUS EMPIRICUS, *Works*, ed. with trans. R. G. Bury, 4 vols., Loeb Classical Library, 1933–49.

SPEUSIPPUS of Athens: *A Critical Study with a Collection of the Related Texts and Commentary*, by L. Tarán, Leiden, 1981.

STOBAEUS, Johannes, *Anthologium*, ed. C. Wachsmuth and O. Hense, 5 vols., Berlin, 1884–1912 (repr. 1974).

XENOCRATES: *Darstellung der Lehre und Sammlung der Fragmente*, by R. Heinze, Leipzig, 1892 (repr. Olms, Hildesheim, 1965).
—— *Senocrate–Hermodoro: Frammenti*, ed. M. Isnardi Parente, Naples, 1982.

C. Secondary Works

ALLINE, H. (1915), *Histoire du texte de Platon*, Paris.
ARMSTRONG, A. H. (1960), 'The Background of the Doctrine "That the Intelligibles are not Outside the Intellect"', in *Les Sources de Plotin*, Entretiens Fondation Hardt, 5, Vandœuvres and Geneva.
—— (1970) (ed.), *The Cambridge History of Later Greek and Early Mediaeval Philosophy*, 2nd edn., Cambridge.
BALTES, M. (1972), *Timaios Lokros über die Natur des Kosmos und der Seele*, Leiden.
—— (1976–8), *Der Weltentstehung des Platonischen Timaios nach dem antiken Interpreten*, Leiden.
BARNES, J. (1975), *Aristotle's Posterior Analytics*, Oxford.
—— (1985), 'Theophrastus and Hypothetical Syllogistic', in J. Wiesner (ed.), *Aristoteles' Werk und Wirkung*, Berlin, i. 557–76.
—— (1989), 'Antiochus of Ascalon', in M. Griffin and J. Barnes (eds.), *Philosophia Togata*, Oxford.
BÄUMKER, C. (1890), *Das Problem der Materie in der griechischen Philosophie*, Münster.
BOEFT, J. DEN (1970), *Calcidius on Fate: His Doctrine and Sources*, Philosophia Antiqua, 18, Leiden.
—— (1977) *Calcidius on Demons*, Philosophia Antiqua, 33, Leiden.
CHERNISS, H. (1938), Review of Witt (1937), *American Journal of Philology*, 59: 351–6 (repr. in Cherniss, *Selected Papers*, ed. L. Tarán, Leiden, 1977).
—— (1944) *Aristotle's Criticism of Plato and the Academy*, Baltimore.
—— (1949) Review of Louis (1945), *American Journal of Philology*, 70: 76–80 (repr. in *Selected Papers*).
DEUSE, W. (1983), *Untersuchungen zur mittelplatonischen und neuplatonischen Seelenlehre*, Wiesbaden.
DILLON, J. M. (1977), *The Middle Platonists: 80 BC to AD 220*, London and Ithaca, NY.
—— (1983) '*Metriopatheia* and *Apatheia*: Some Reflections on a Controversy in Later Greek Ethics', in J. Anton and A. Preus (eds.), *Essays in Ancient Greek Philosophy*, ii, Albany, NY.
—— (1984), 'Speusippus in Iamblichus', *Phronesis*, 29: 325–32.
—— (1989), 'Tampering with the Timaeus', *American Journal of Philology*, 110: 66–70.

DILLON, J. M. (1991) *The Golden Chain: Studies in the Development of Platonism and Christianity*, Aldershot.

DODDS, E. R. (1928), 'The *Parmenides* of Plato and the Origin of the Neoplatonic "One" ', *Classical Quarterly*, 22: 129–42.

DONINI, P.-L. (1974), *Tre studi sull'Aristotelismo, nel II secolo a.C.*, Turin.

—— (1982), *Le scuole, l'anima, l'impero: la filosofia antica da Antioco a Plotino*, Turin.

—— (1988), 'La Connaissance de dieu et la hiérarchie divine chez Albinos', in R. van den Broek, T. Baarda, and J. Mansfeld (eds.), *Knowledge of God in the Graeco-Roman World*, Leiden.

DÖRRIE, H. (1954), 'Zum Ursprung der neuplatonischen Hypostasenlehre', *Hermes*, 82: 331–42.

—— (1957), 'Kontroversen um die Seelenwanderung im kaiserzeitlichen Platonismus', *Hermes*, 85: 414–35.

—— (1960), 'Die Frage nach dem Transcendenten im Mittelplatonismus', in *Les Sources de Plotin*, Entretiens Fondation Hardt, 5, Vandœuvres and Geneva, 191–241.

—— (1970) Article 'Albinos', in *RE* Suppl. 12: 14–22.

—— (1976), *Platonica Minora*, Munich.

—— (1987–), *Der Platonismus in der Antike*, 3 vols., Stuttgart.

FESTUGIÈRE, A.-J. (1953), *La Révélation d'Hermès Trismégiste*, iii. *Les Doctrines de l'âme*, Paris.

FREDE, M. (1956), 'Stoic vs. Aristotelian Syllogistic', *Archiv für Geschichte der Philosophie*, 56.

—— (1987), *Essays in Ancient Philosophy*, Minneapolis.

FREUDENTHAL, J. (1879), 'Der Platoniker Albinos und der falsche Alkinoos', *Hellenistische Studien*, 3, Berlin.

GIUSTA, M. (1960–1), '*Albinou Epitome* o *Alcinoou Didaskalikos*', in *Atti dell' Accademia delle Scienze di Torino, Classe di scienze morali, storiche e filologiche*, 95: 167–94.

—— (1967), *I dossografi di etica*, ii, Turin, 535–8.

—— (1976), *L'opuscolo pseudogalenico 'hoti hoi poiotētes asōmatoi'*, ed., trans., and annotated, Mem. dell' Accad. di Scienze di Torino, 4: 34, Turin.

GRAESER, A. (1973), *Die logische Fragmente des Theophrast*, Berlin and New York.

HUBY, P., and NEAL, G. (1989), *The Criterion of Truth*, Liverpool.

ISNARDI PARENTE, M. (1964), 'Platone e la prima Accademia di fronte al problema delle idee degli "artifacta"', *Rivista critica di storia della filosofia*, 19: 123–58.

JOLY, R. (1956), *Le Thème philosophique des genres de vie dans l'antiquité classique*, Brussels.

KIDD, I. G., and EDELSTEIN, L. (1972–88), *Posidonius: The Fragments*, Cambridge.

KLEVE, K. (1972), 'Albinus on God and the One', *Symbolae Osloenses*, 47: 66–9.

LILLA, S. (1971), *Clement of Alexandria: A Study in Christian Platonism and Gnosticism*, Oxford.

LOENEN, J. H. (1956–7), 'Albinus' Metaphysics: An Attempt at Rehabilitation', *Mnemosyne*, 4: 9, pp. 296–319; 4: 10, pp. 35–56.

LONG, A. A. (1989), 'Ptolemy on the Criterion: An Epistemology for the Practising Scientist', in Huby and Neal (1989), 151–78.

—— and SEDLEY, D. N. (eds.) (1987), *The Hellenistic Philosophers*, Cambridge.

ŁUKASIEWICZ, J. (1951), *Aristotle's Syllogistic* (Eng. trans.), Oxford.

MANSFELD, J. (1972), 'Three Notes on Albinus', *Theta-Pi*, 1: 61–80, repr. in *Studies in Later Greek Philosophy and Gnosticism*, London, 1989.

MERKI, H. (1952), *Homoiosis Theoi: Von der Platonischen Angleichung an Gott zur Gottähnlichkeit bei Gregor von Nyssa*, Freiburg.

MERLAN, P. (1968), *From Platonism to Neoplatonism*, 3rd edn., The Hague.

—— (1970), 'Greek Philosophy from Plato to Plotinus', in Armstrong (1970).

MORAUX, P. (1973), *Der Aristotelismus bei den Griechen, von Andronikos bis Alexander von Aphrodisias*, i, Berlin.

—— (1984), *Der Aristotelismus bei den Griechen*, ii: *Der Aristotelismus in I. und II. Jh. n. Chr.*, Berlin.

ORTH, E. (1947), 'Les œuvres d'Albinos le platonicien', *Acta Classica*, 16: 113–14.

PRANTL, C. (1855–70, repr. 1955), *Geschichte der Logik in Abendlande*, Leipzig.

RICH, A. N. M. (1954), 'The Platonic Ideas as Thoughts of God', *Mnemosyne*, 4: 7, pp. 123–33.

RIST, J. M. (1962), 'The Neoplatonic One and Plato's *Parmenides*', *TAPA* 93: 389–401.

—— (1964), 'Albinus as a Representative of Eclectic Platonism', in *Eros and Psyche*, Toronto.

RUNIA, D. T. (1986), 'A Note on Albinus/Alcinous *Didaskalikos XIV*', *Mnemosyne*, 4: 39, pp. 131–8.

SHARPLES, R. W. (1983), *Alexander of Aphrodisias on Fate*, London.

—— (1989), 'The Criterion of Truth in Philo Judaeus, Alcinous and Alexander of Aphrodisias', in Huby and Neal (1989), 231–56.

SINKO, T. (1905), *De Apulei et Albini doctrinae Platonicae adumbratione*, Cracow.

SOURY, G. (1942), *La Démonologie de Plutarque*, Paris.

SPANIER, A. (1920), 'Der Logos Didaskalikos des Platonikers Albinus', Diss., Freiburg.

STRACHE, H. (1909), *De Arii Didymi in morali philosophia auctoribus*, Berlin.

TARÁN, L. (1975), *Academica: Plato, Philip of Opus, and the Pseudo-Platonic Epinomis*, Memoirs of the American Philosophical Society, 107, Philadelphia.

TARRANT, H. A. S., 'Alcinous, Albinus, Nigrinus', *Antichthon*, 19 (1985), 87–95.

TAYLOR, A. E. (1928), *A Commentary on Plato's Timaeus*, Oxford.

THEILER, W. (1930), *Die Vorbereitung des Neuplatonismus*, Berlin.

—— (1945), 'Tacitus und die antike Schicksalslehre', in *Phyllobolia für Peter von der Mühll*, Basle, 35–90.

—— (1966), *Forschungen zum Neuplatonismus*, Berlin.

WESTERINK, L. G. (1977), *The Greek Commentaries on Plato's Phaedo*, ii. *Damascius*, Amsterdam.

WHITTAKER, J. (1974), '*Parisinus graecus* 1962 and the Writings of Albinus', *Phoenix*, 28, pt. 1, pp. 320–54; pt. 2, 450–6 (repr. in *Studies in Platonism and Patristic Thought*, London, 1984).

—— (1987), 'Platonic Philosophy in the Early Empire', in *Aufstieg und Niedergang der römischen Welt* pt. 2, 36: 2, Berlin and New York, 81–102.

—— (1989), 'The Value of the Indirect Tradition in the Establishment of Greek Philosophical Texts, or the Art of Misquotation', in *Problems of Editing Greek and Latin Texts*, ed. J. N. Grant, New York, 63–95.

WINDEN, J. C. M. VAN (1965), *Calcidius on Matter: His Doctrine and Sources*, Philosophia Antiqua, 9, Leiden.

WITT, R. E. (1937), *Albinus and the History of Middle Platonism*, Cambridge, repr. (1971), Amsterdam.

WLOSOK, A. (1960), *Laktanz und die philosophische Gnosis*, Abhandl. der Heidelberger Akad. der Wiss., philosophisch-historische Klasse, Heidelberg.

WOLFSON, H. (1952), 'Albinus and Plotinus on the Divine Attributes', *Harvard Theological Review*, 45: 115–30.

INDEX LOCORUM

INDEX NOMINUM

SUBJECT INDEX